cakes

cakes

APPLE

First published in the UK in 2009 by
Apple Press
7 Greenland Street
London NW1 0ND
United Kingdom
www.apple-press.com

ISBN 978 1 84543 341 3

This book was conceived, edited and designed by McRae Books
Via del Salviatino, 1
50016 Fiesole
Florence Italy
info@mcraebooks.com
www.mcraebooks.com
Publishers Anne McRae, Marco Nardi

Project Director Anne McRae
Art Director Marco Nardi
Photography Alan Benson
Text Rachel Lane, Carla Bardi, Ting Morris
Editing Anne McRae
Food Styling Claire Pietersen
Layouts Aurora Granata
Prepress Filippo Delle Monache

NOTE TO OUR READERS
Eating eggs or egg whites that are not completely cooked poses the possibility of salmonella food poisoning. The risk is greater for pregnant women, the elderly, the very young, and persons with impaired immune systems. If you are concerned about salmonella, you can use reconstituted powdered egg whites or pasteurized eggs.

Printed in China

CONTENTS

INTRODUCTION

Cakes are a celebration in themselves. They are perfect for any occasion, from casual family brunches or coffee with friends, to elegant receptions with many guests. In this stunningly illustrated cookbook you will find more than 200 recipes from cake-making traditions around the world. All the recipes have short introductions with hints and tips for successful baking as well as the folklore and history associated with many of the more famous cakes.

Developed by an international team of food writers, the recipes are a mixture of time-tested classics and modern cakes, developed for contemporary budgets, taste buds, and schedules. Here you will find recipes for many of the great European cakes, including Blackforest Cake, Dobos Torte, Saint Honoré Gateau, Galette de Rois, Sacher Torte, and Kugelhof. But you will also find some old favorites, such as Key Lime Cheesecake, Devil's Food Cake, and Dundee Cake, alongside a host of modern recipes, such as Chocolate Beet Cake, Pina Colada Cheesecake, and Bull's-Eye Cupcakes.

◁ Devil's Food Cake (see page 112)

Home cooks will particularly appreciate the feature panels that give instructions for special techniques. Want to know how to make the perfect French sponge cake? How to work with chocolate successfully? The authors answer these and many other common baking questions, letting you in on their personal tips and tricks to ensure that every cake turns out perfectly every time.

A slice of luscious, home-baked cake is a great way to begin the day, end a meal, or celebrate a meaningful moment with friends and family. Here you will the inspiration for more than 200 scrumptious cakes for every occasion. Enjoy!

RECIPES FOR PEOPLE WITH SPECIAL HEALTH NEEDS

For those people who often have to skip cake because of dietary restrictions, this book features a selection of delicious recipes for them as well. Included are recipes for those with an allergy to dairy or eggs, for people who are dealing with gluten intolerance, and for anyone who is required to follow a sugar-free diet. You can locate these recipes by looking for one of the little icons shown above.

When you prepare food for anyone with food allergies and intolerances, be aware that traces of gluten, egg, and dairy can be found where you least expect them (for example, in chocolate and vanilla extract), so read labels carefully. In many countries, food manufacturers are required by law to list every ingredient used in their products. But to be perfectly sure, look online or inquire at health food stores for the names of reliable brands of gluten-, egg-, or dairy-free products.

Saint-Honoré Gateau (see page 261) ▷

CUPCAKES

Cupcakes are miniature cakes that are usually baked in paper liners. In the United Kingdom they are also known as fairy cakes, presumably because they are tiny, delicate, and pretty—just like the fairies who were thought to feast on them! Cupcakes have been around for many years, but they are enjoying a revival at the moment. They used to be baked in fluted tin or ceramic molds, but the modern alternative of colored paper liners makes them even more attractive.

◄ Smartie Cupcakes (see page 32)

Coconut and Pineapple Cupcakes

These pretty cupcakes are delicious with tea or coffee and make a wonderful family dessert. If liked, substitute the lime juice and zest in the frosting with the same amount of freshly squeezed lemon juice and zest.

Makes: 12 · Prep: 20 min. · Cooking: 25–30 min. · Level: 1

CUPCAKES

1	cup (150 g) all-purpose (plain) flour
3/4	cup (125 g) coconut milk powder
1	teaspoon baking powder
1	cup (200 g) sugar
1/2	cup (125 g) butter, softened
1	teaspoon vanilla extract (essence)
4	large eggs
1	(14-ounce/400-g) can crushed pineapple, drained

LIME BUTTER FROSTING

1/2	cup (125 g) butter, softened
1 1/2	teaspoons finely grated lime zest
1 1/2	cups (225 g) confectioners' (icing) sugar
1	tablespoon freshly squeezed lime juice
1/4	cup (30 g) shredded (dessicated) coconut, lightly toasted

1. Preheat the oven to 325°F (170°C/gas 3). Line a standard 12-cup muffin tin with paper liners.

2. To prepare the cupcakes, combine the flour, coconut milk powder, and baking powder in a medium bowl. Beat the sugar, butter, and vanilla in a medium bowl with an electric mixer on medium-high speed until pale and creamy. Add the eggs one at a time, beating until just blended after each addition. With mixer on low speed, add the mixed dry ingredients. Stir the pineapple in by hand.

3. Spoon the batter into the prepared cups, filling each one three-quarters full. Bake for 25–30 minutes, until golden brown and firm to the touch. Transfer the muffin tin to a wire rack. Let cool completely before removing the cupcakes.

4. To prepare the frosting, beat the butter and lime zest in a small bowl until creamy. Gradually add the confectioners' sugar and lime juice, beating until combined. Spread the frosting on the cupcakes and sprinkle with the coconut.

Blueberry and Yogurt Cupcakes

These cupcakes are a healthy option for breakfast or brunch. Blueberries are rich in vitamin C and packed with dietary fiber.

Makes: 12 · Prep: 15 min. · Cooking: 20–25 min. · Level: 1

CUPCAKES

1 1/4	cups (180 g) all-purpose (plain) flour
1	teaspoon baking powder
1/8	teaspoon salt
1/2	cup (125 g) butter, softened
1/2	cup (100 g) sugar
1	teaspoon finely grated lemon zest
2	large eggs
1/3	cup (90 ml) plain yogurt
1	cup (150 g) fresh or frozen (thawed) blueberries

TOPPING

1/3	cup (90 ml) plain yogurt
1	tablespoon honey
	Fresh blueberries, to decorate

1. Preheat the oven to 350°F (180°C/gas 4). Line a standard 12-cup muffin tin with paper liners.

2. To prepare the cupcakes, combine the flour, baking powder, and salt in a small bowl. Beat the butter, sugar, and lemon zest in a medium bowl with an electric mixer on medium-high speed until pale and creamy. Add the eggs one at a time, beating until just blended after each addition. With mixer on low speed, add the mixed dry ingredients and yogurt. Stir the blueberries in by hand.

3. Spoon the batter into the prepared cups, filling each one three-quarters full. Bake for 20–25 minutes, until golden brown and firm to the touch. Transfer the muffin tin to a wire rack. Let cool completely before removing the cupcakes.

4. To prepare the topping, mix the yogurt and honey in a small bowl. Top each cupcake with a dollop of sweetened yogurt and a few fresh blueberries.

Coconut and Pineapple Cupcakes ▷

Chocolate Brownie Cupcakes

These double chocolate cupcakes have a rich brownie-like texture. Serve them with little cups of espresso coffee.

Serves: 12 • Prep: 20 min. • Cooking: 20–25 min. • Level: 1

CUPCAKES

10	ounces (300 g) dark chocolate, coarsely chopped
1¼	cups (300 g) butter, softened
5	large eggs
½	cup (100 g) firmly packed light brown sugar
1	teaspoon vanilla extract (essence)
¾	cup (125 g) all-purpose (plain) flour
1	teaspoon baking powder
⅛	teaspoon salt
½	cup (90 g) white chocolate chips
½	cup (80 g) hazelnuts, coarsely chopped

CHOCOLATE GANACHE

6	ounces (180 g) dark chocolate, coarsely chopped
⅓	cup (90 ml) light (single) cream
3	ounces (90 g) white chocolate, shaved, to decorate

1. Preheat the oven to 350°F (180°C/gas 4). Line a standard 12-cup muffin tin with paper liners.

2. To prepare the cupcakes, melt the dark chocolate and butter in a double boiler over barely simmering water.

3. Beat the eggs, brown sugar, and vanilla in a medium bowl with an electric mixer on medium-high speed until creamy. With mixer on low speed, beat in the flour, baking powder, and salt. Fold in the melted chocolate. Stir the white chocolate and hazelnuts in by hand.

4. Spoon the batter into the prepared cups, filling each one three-quarters full. Bake for 20–25 minutes, until risen and firm to the touch. Transfer the muffin tin to a wire rack. Let cool completely before removing the cupcakes.

5. To prepare the ganache, melt the dark chocolate and cream in a double boiler over barely simmering water. Remove from the heat and leave to cool and thicken.

6. Spread over the cupcakes. Top with the white chocolate shavings.

Chocolate Berry Cupcakes

These cupcakes are quick and easy to make. Decorate them with a mixture of fresh red and black berries for a striking effect.

Serves: 12 • Prep: 20 min. • Cooking: 20–25 min. • Level: 1

CUPCAKES

3	ounces (90 g) dark chocolate, coarsely chopped
¼	cup (60 g) butter, softened
1½	cups (225 g) all-purpose (plain) flour
¾	cup (150 g) firmly packed light brown sugar
2	tablespoons unsweetened cocoa powder
1½	teaspoons baking powder
1	teaspoon baking soda (bicarbonate of soda)
⅛	teaspoon salt
1	cup (250 ml) milk
1	cup (150 g) fresh mixed berries, chopped + extra, to decorate

CHOCOLATE FROSTING

3	ounces (90 g) dark chocolate, coarsely chopped
1	tablespoon butter
⅓	cup (90 ml) heavy (double) cream
2	tablespoons confectioners' (icing) sugar

1. Preheat the oven to 350°F (180°C/gas 4). Line a standard 12-cup muffin tin with paper liners.

2. To prepare the cupcakes, melt the chocolate and butter in a double boiler over barely simmering water. Let cool.

3. Combine the flour, brown sugar, cocoa, baking powder, baking soda, and salt in a medium bowl. Pour the melted chocolate and milk into the mixed dry ingredients and beat until just combined. Stir the berries in by hand.

4. Spoon the batter into the prepared cups, filling each one three-quarters full. Bake for 20–25 minutes, until risen and firm to the touch. Transfer the muffin tin to a wire rack. Let cool completely.

5. To prepare the frosting, melt the chocolate, butter, and cream in a double boiler over barely simmering water. Add the confectioners' sugar, stirring until smooth. Set aside to cool and thicken.

6. Spread over the cupcakes and top with extra berries.

Chocolate Brownie Cupcakes ▷

Espresso Swirl Cupcakes

If serving these cupcakes for breakfast, you may prefer not to frost them. In that case serve them while still warm. Later in the day, the frosted cupcakes are perfect with a reviving cup of coffee.

Makes: 12 • Prep: 20 min. • Cooking: 25–30 min. • Level: 1

CUPCAKES

1	cup (200 g) sugar
2	large eggs
1	teaspoon vanilla extract (essence)
1½	cups (225 g) all-purpose (plain) flour
1½	teaspoons baking powder
⅛	teaspoon salt
1	cup (250 ml) light (single) cream
1½	tablespoons unsweetened cocoa powder dissolved in 2 tablespoons espresso coffee

COFFEE BUTTER FROSTING

½	cup (125 g) butter, softened
½	tablespoon coffee liqueur
1½	cups (225 g) confectioners' (icing) sugar
1½	teaspoons freeze-dried coffee granules, dissolved in ½ teaspoon boiling water

1. Preheat the oven to 325°F (170°C/gas 3). Line a standard 12-cup muffin tin with paper liners.

2. To prepare the cupcakes, beat the sugar, eggs, and vanilla in a medium bowl with an electric mixer on medium-high speed until pale and thick. With mixer on low speed, gradually beat in the flour, baking powder, salt, and cream. Divide the mixture evenly between two bowls. Blend the coffee mixture into one of the bowls to create an espresso batter.

3. Spoon the batters alternately into the prepared cups, filling each one three-quarters full. Create a swirl pattern through the batter using a skewer. Bake for 20–25 minutes, until golden brown and firm to the touch. Transfer the muffin tin to a wire rack. Let cool completely before removing the cupcakes.

4. To prepare the frosting, beat the butter and coffee liqueur in a small bowl until creamy. Gradually beat in the confectioners' sugar.

5. Spread the frosting roughly over the cupcakes. Drizzle the dissolved coffee mixture over the top in a spiral pattern.

Frappé Cupcakes

With coffee, nuts, and chocolate, these cupcakes are prefect for a special brunch or coffee morning.

Makes: 12 • Prep: 15 min. • Cooking: 25–30 min. • Level: 1

CUPCAKES

1	cup (150 g) all-purpose (plain) flour
⅓	cup (30 g) ground hazelnuts
1	teaspoon baking powder
⅛	teaspoon salt
½	cup (125 g) butter, softened
½	cup (100 g) firmly packed light brown sugar
3	teaspoons freeze-dried coffee granules, dissolved in 1 tablespoon boiling water
2	large eggs
½	cup (125 ml) light (single) cream

TOPPING

½	cup (125 ml) crème fraîche
	Chocolate-coated coffee beans, to decorate

1. Preheat the oven to 325°F (170°C/gas 3). Line a standard 12-cup muffin tin with paper liners.

2. To prepare the cupcakes, combine the flour, hazelnuts, baking powder, and salt in a small bowl. Beat the butter, brown sugar, and coffee mixture in a medium bowl with an electric mixer on medium-high speed until creamy. Add the eggs one at a time, beating until just blended after each addition. With mixer on low speed, add the mixed dry ingredients, alternating with the cream.

3. Spoon the batter into the prepared cups, filling each one three-quarters full. Bake for 25–30 minutes, until golden brown and firm to the touch. Transfer the muffin tin to a wire rack. Let cool completely before removing the cupcakes.

4. Top each cupcake with a dollop of crème fraîche and finish with 2–3 chocolate-coated coffee beans.

Espresso Swirl Cupcakes ▷

Jeweled Cupcakes

Place the candied fruit and nuts for the topping lightly on the tops of the uncooked cupcake batter. They should not sink in but stay at least half visible to "glitter" like jewels.

Makes: 12 • Prep: 25 min. + 15 min. to plump • Cooking: 25–30 min. • Level: 1

CUPCAKES
- ⅓ cup (60 g) green and red candied (glacé) cherries, coarsely chopped
- ⅓ cup (60 g) raisins
- ⅓ cup (60 g) dates, pitted and coarsely chopped
- ¼ cup (40 g) Brazil nuts, coarsely chopped
- ¼ cup (40 g) blanched almonds, coarsely chopped
- 3 tablespoons candied (glacé) orange peel, coarsely chopped
- 3 tablespoons brandy
- 1 cup (150 g) all-purpose (plain) flour
- 1 teaspoon baking powder
- 1 teaspoon ground cinnamon
- ½ cup (125 g) butter, softened
- ¾ cup (150 g) firmly packed light brown sugar
- 2 large eggs, lightly beaten

FRUIT TOPPING
- ½ cup (90 g) green and red candied (glacé) cherries
- ⅓ cup (50 g) Brazil nuts
- ⅓ cup (50 g) whole blanched almonds
- ¼ cup (45 g) candied orange peel, chopped
- ¼ cup (80 g) apricot preserves (jam), warmed

1. Preheat the oven to 325°F (170°C/gas 3). Line a standard 12-cup muffin tin with paper liners.

2. To prepare the cupcakes, combine the cherries, raisins, and dates in a small bowl. Add the brandy and let plump for 15 minutes. Stir in the Brazil nuts, almonds, and orange peel. Combine the flour, baking powder, and cinnamon in a small bowl.

3. Beat the butter and brown sugar in a medium bowl with an electric mixer on medium-high speed until creamy. Add the eggs, beating until just blended. With mixer on low speed, add the mixed dry ingredients. Stir the fruit and nuts in by hand. Spoon the batter into the prepared cups, filling each one three-quarters full.

4. To prepare the topping, combine the fruit and nuts in a small bowl. Spread over the cupcakes. Bake for 20–25 minutes, until golden brown and firm to the touch. Brush the tops with the preserves.

◁ **Jeweled Cupcakes**

English Rose Cupcakes

Prepare these cupcakes for your mother on Mother's Day. Or make them for a friend who is getting married or celebrating a birthday or anniversary. If liked, dress them up in pretty decorated paper. Cut the paper into strips with scalloped scissors. When cool, wrap the cupcakes with the paper, scalloped edge up, and secure with tape.

Makes: 12 • Prep: 25 min. • Cooking: 25–30 min. • Level: 1

CUPCAKES
- 3 ounces (90 g) white chocolate, coarsely chopped
- ⅓ cup (90 ml) light (single) cream
- 1 cup (150 g) all-purpose (plain) flour
- ½ cup (50 g) ground pistachios
- 1 teaspoon baking powder
- ⅛ teaspoon salt
- ⅓ cup (90 g) butter, softened
- 1 cup (200 g) sugar
- 2 large eggs
- 2 tablespoons rose water
- 12 pink sugar roses, to decorate

ROSE FROSTING
- ½ cup (125 g) butter, softened
- ½ tablespoon rose water
- 1½ cups (225 g) confectioners' (icing) sugar

1. Preheat the oven to 325°F (170°C/gas 3). Line a standard 12-cup muffin tin with paper liners.

2. To prepare the cupcakes, melt the chocolate and cream in a double boiler over barely simmering water. Combine the flour, pistachios, baking powder, and salt in a small bowl.

3. Beat the butter, sugar, and vanilla in a medium bowl with an electric mixer on medium-high speed until pale and creamy. Add the eggs one at a time, beating until just blended after each addition. With mixer on low speed, add the mixed dry ingredients, melted chocolate, and rose water.

4. Spoon the batter into the prepared cups, filling each one three-quarters full. Bake for 25–30 minutes, until golden brown and firm to the touch. Let cool completely.

5. To prepare the frosting, beat the butter and rose water in a small bowl until light and fluffy. Gradually add the confectioners' sugar. Place the frosting in a pastry bag fitted with a star nozzle. Pipe a large rosette of frosting on each cupcake and top with a sugar rose.

Bulls-Eye Cupcakes

The topping on these cupcakes mimics the concentric circles on a target and the bulls-eye is the red circle in the middle. Hitting the bulls-eye with a dart or arrow means scoring a direct hit and winning. You can serve these cupcakes to a friend or family member who has just scored a bulls-eye by passing all their exams or winning a sporting competition.

Makes: 12 • Prep: 35 min. • Cooking: 25–30 min. • Level: 2

CUPCAKES

½	cup (125 g) butter, softened
1	cup (200 g) sugar
1	teaspoon vanilla extract (essence)
2	large eggs
1⅓	cups (200 g) all-purpose (plain) flour
1½	teaspoons baking powder
⅛	teaspoon salt
½	cup (125 ml) milk
12	candied (glacé) cherries

TO DECORATE

2	cups (300 g) confectioners' (icing) sugar
2½	tablespoons water
⅛	teaspoon red food coloring
1	tube black frosting (icing)

1. Preheat the oven to 325°F (170°C/gas 3). Line a standard 12-cup muffin tin with paper liners.

2. To prepare the cupcakes, beat the butter, sugar, and vanilla in a medium bowl with an electric mixer on medium-high speed until pale and creamy. Add the eggs one at a time, beating until just blended after each addition. With mixer on low speed, add the flour, baking powder, salt, and milk.

3. Spoon half of the batter into the prepared cups. Place a cherry in the center of each one and cover with the remaining batter. Bake for 20–25 minutes, until golden brown and firm to the touch. Transfer the muffin tin to a wire rack. Let cool completely.

4. To decorate, combine the confectioners' sugar and water in a small bowl, stirring until smooth. Transfer one quarter of the mixture to a small bowl and add a few drops of red food coloring.

5. Spread the white frosting over the cupcakes. Add a tip to the black tube frosting and pipe three circles on top of each cupcake. Spoon the red frosting into a paper envelope and cut the corner off using scissors. Fill in the central circles with red frosting.

Alphabet Cupcakes

These cupcakes are great for children who are just learning to write. They will enjoy helping to decorate the cupcakes.

Makes: 12 • Prep: 40 min. • Cooking: 20–25 min. • Level: 2

CUPCAKES

1	cup (150 g) all-purpose (plain) flour
¼	cup (30 g) shredded (desiccated) coconut
1	teaspoon baking powder
⅛	teaspoon salt
⅓	cup (90 g) butter, softened
½	cup (100 g) sugar
1	teaspoon finely grated lemon zest
2	large eggs
¼	cup (60 ml) fresh or canned passion fruit pulp, strained

TO DECORATE

1½	cups (225 g) confectioners' (icing) sugar
2	tablespoons water
⅛	teaspoon red food coloring
⅛	teaspoon blue food coloring
⅛	teaspoon yellow food coloring
1	tube black frosting (icing)

1. Preheat the oven to 350°F (180°C/gas 4). Line a standard 12-cup muffin tin with paper liners.

2. To prepare the cupcakes, combine the flour, coconut, baking powder, and salt in a small bowl. Beat the butter, sugar, and lemon zest in a medium bowl with an electric mixer on medium-high speed until pale and creamy. Add the eggs one at a time, beating until just blended after each addition. With mixer on low speed, add the mixed dry ingredients and passion fruit pulp.

3. Spoon the batter into the prepared cups, filling each one three-quarters full. Bake for 20–25 minutes, until golden brown and firm to the touch. Transfer the muffin tin to a wire rack. Let cool completely before removing the cupcakes.

4. To decorate, combine the confectioners' sugar and water in a small bowl, stirring until smooth. Divide the frosting evenly among three small bowls. Dye each bowl a different color. Spread the frostings over the cupcakes, creating four of each color. Add a tip to the black tube frosting and pipe capital letters on top of the cupcakes.

Bulls-Eye Cupcakes ▷

Leopard Cupcakes

Children will love these animal-themed cupcakes.

Makes: 12 • Prep: 30 min. • Cooking: 20–25 min. • Level: 2

CUPCAKES

1½	cups (225 g) all-purpose (plain) flour
1½	teaspoons baking powder
3	tablespoons unsweetened cocoa powder
½	cup (125 g) butter, softened
¾	cup (150 g) firmly packed light brown sugar
1	teaspoon vanilla extract (essence)
2	large eggs
½	cup (125 ml) milk
½	cup (90 g) milk chocolate chips

BUTTER FROSTING

½	cup (125 g) butter, softened
½	teaspoon vanilla extract (essence)
1½	cups (225 g) confectioners' (icing) sugar
1	tablespoon unsweetened cocoa powder

1. Preheat the oven to 325°F (170°C/gas 3). Line a standard 12-cup muffin tin with paper liners.

2. To prepare the cupcakes, combine the flour, baking powder, and cocoa in a small bowl. Beat the butter, brown sugar, and vanilla in a medium bowl with an electric mixer on medium-high speed until pale and creamy. Add the eggs one at a time, beating until just blended after each addition. With mixer on low speed, add the mixed dry ingredients and milk. Stir the chocolate chips in by hand.

3. Spoon the batter into the prepared cups, filling each one three-quarters full. Bake for 20–25 minutes, until golden brown and firm to the touch. Leave to cool completely.

4. To prepare the frosting, beat the butter and vanilla in a small bowl using an electric mixer, until creamy. Gradually add the confectioners' sugar, beating on low speed until combined. Place one third of the frosting in a small bowl and stir in the cocoa.

5. Spread the plain frosting over the cupcakes. Spoon the melted chocolate into an envelope and cut the tip off one corner using scissors. Pipe shapes to resemble leopard spots on each cupcake and fill in with the chocolate frosting.

Black Cat Cupcakes

You can change the decoration of these cupcakes to suit the occasion or the person you are making them for. Any small confectionary shape can be placed on top.

Makes: 12 • Prep: 20 min. • Cooking: 20–25 min. • Level: 1

CUPCAKES

¾	cup (125 g) all-purpose (plain) flour
3	tablespoons unsweetened cocoa powder
1	teaspoon baking powder
⅛	teaspoon salt
½	cup (125 g) butter, softened
¾	cup (150 g) firmly packed dark brown sugar
½	teaspoon vanilla extract (essence)
2	large eggs
3	tablespoons milk

TO DECORATE

1½	cups (225 g) confectioners' (icing) sugar
2	tablespoons water
⅛	teaspoon yellow food coloring
12	confectionery black cats

1. Preheat the oven to 325°F (170°C/gas 3). Line a standard 12-cup muffin tin with paper liners.

2. To prepare the cupcakes, combine the flour, cocoa, baking powder, and salt in a small bowl. Beat the butter, brown sugar, and vanilla in a medium bowl with an electric mixer on medium-high speed until creamy. Add the eggs one at a time, beating until just blended after each addition. With mixer on low speed, add the mixed dry ingredients, alternating with the milk.

3. Spoon the batter into the prepared cups, filling each one three-quarters full. Bake for 20–25 minutes, until golden brown and firm to the touch. Transfer the muffin tin to a wire rack. Let cool completely before removing the cupcakes.

4. To decorate, combine the confectioners' sugar and water in a small bowl, stirring until smooth. Add yellow food coloring to create a bright yellow frosting. Spread the frosting over the cupcakes and place the black cats on top.

Leopard Cupcakes ▷

Caramello Cupcakes

Dulce de leche is a Spanish milk-based sauce. It is made by slowly heating sweetened milk to produce a sauce that is very like caramel.

Makes: 12 • Prep: 25 min. • Cooking: 125–30 min. • Level: 1

CUPCAKES

3	ounces (90 g) dark chocolate, coarsely chopped
1/3	cup (90 ml) light (single) cream
1	cup (150 g) all-purpose (plain) flour
2	tablespoons unsweetened cocoa powder
1	teaspoon baking powder
1/8	teaspoon salt
1	cup (200 g) firmly packed brown sugar
1/3	cup (90 g) butter, softened
1	teaspoon vanilla extract (essence)
2	large eggs

TO DECORATE

4	ounces (120 g) dark chocolate, coarsely chopped
1	cup (250 g) dulce de leche

1. Preheat the oven to 325°F (170°C/gas 3). Line a standard 12-cup muffin tin with paper liners.

2. To prepare the cupcakes, melt the chocolate and cream in a double boiler over barely simmering water. Set aside.

3. Combine the flour, cocoa, baking powder, and salt in a small bowl. Beat the brown sugar, butter, and vanilla in a medium bowl with an electric mixer on medium-high speed until creamy. Add the eggs one at a time, beating until just blended after each addition. With mixer on low speed, add the mixed dry ingredients and melted chocolate.

4. Spoon the batter into the prepared cups, filling each one three-quarters full. Bake for 25–30 minutes, until risen and firm to the touch. Leave to cool completely.

4. To decorate, melt the chocolate in a double boiler over barely simmering water, stirring until smooth. Let cool.

5. Cut a teaspoon sized hole out of the top of each cupcake. Fill with dulce de leche and spread the remaining sauce over the top of the cakes. Top with a layer of cooled melted chocolate.

◁ **Caramello Cupcakes**

White Chocolate and Pear Cupcakes

Serve these cupcakes after dinner with a glass of pear liqueur or brandy. If making them for children, you can replace the pear liqueur with pear juice.

Makes: 12 • Prep: 25 min. • Cooking: 20–25 min. • Level: 1

CUPCAKES

1 1/3	cups (200 g) all-purpose (plain) flour
1	teaspoon baking powder
1/8	teaspoon salt
1/3	cup (90 g) butter
1	cup (200 g) sugar
1	large egg
2	tablespoons pear liqueur
1	teaspoon vanilla extract (essence)
2/3	cup (150 ml) milk
1/2	cup (60 g) finely chopped toasted hazelnuts

CREAM CHEESE FROSTING

4	ounces (125 g) white chocolate
1/4	cup (60 g) butter, softened
3	ounces (90 g) cream cheese, softened
1	tablespoon finely grated lemon zest
1	tablespoon pear liqueur
1 1/2	cups (225 g) confectioners' (icing) sugar
24	toasted hazelnuts and 6 strawberries, sliced, to decorate

1. Preheat the oven to 350°F (180°C/gas 4). Line a standard 12-cup muffin tin with paper liners.

2. To prepare the cupcakes, mix the flour, baking powder, and salt in a medium bowl. Beat the butter and sugar in a medium bowl with an electric mixer on high speed until pale and creamy. Add the egg and beat until just combined. With the mixer at low speed, gradually beat in the dry ingredients, pear liqueur, vanilla, and milk. Stir in the hazelnuts by hand.

3. Spoon the batter into the prepared cups, filling each one three-quarters full. Bake for 20–25 minutes, until golden brown and firm to the touch. Transfer the muffin tin to a wire rack. Let cool completely.

4. To prepare the frosting, melt the chocolate in a double boiler over barely simmering water. Beat the chocolate, butter, cream cheese, lemon zest, liqueur, and confectioners' sugar in a bowl until smooth. Spread on the cupcakes. Top with the hazelnuts and strawberries.

Florentine Cupcakes

The topping on these cupcakes is inspired by the famous Florentine cookies. These wafer-thin Italian cookies are made from a mixture of sugar, butter, cream, nuts, and candied (glacé) fruit. They are usually finished with a thin coat of dark or white chocolate.

Makes: 12 • Prep: 45 min. • Cooking: 25–30 min. • Level: 2

CUPCAKES
- 3 ounces (90 g) dark chocolate, coarsely chopped
- ⅓ cup (90 ml) light (single) cream
- ⅔ cup (100 g) all-purpose (plain) flour
- ½ cup (50 g) ground almonds
- 2 tablespoons unsweetened cocoa powder
- 1 teaspoon baking powder
- ⅓ cup (90 g) butter, softened
- 1 cup (200 g) firmly packed brown sugar
- 2 large eggs

CHOCOLATE GANACHE
- 4 ounces (120 g) dark chocolate, coarsely chopped
- ¼ cup (60 ml) light (single) cream

TOPPING
- 2 ounces (60 g) dark chocolate, coarsely chopped
- ¾ cup (120 g) slivered almonds
- ⅔ cup (120 g) candied (glacé) cherries, coarsely chopped
- ¼ cup (45 g) candied (glacé) ginger, coarsely chopped
- 2 tablespoons candied (glacé) orange peel

1. Preheat the oven to 325°F (170°C/gas 3). Line a standard 12-cup muffin tin with paper liners.

2. To prepare the cupcakes, melt the chocolate and cream in a double boiler over barely simmering water. Combine the flour, almonds, cocoa, and baking powder in a small bowl. Beat the butter and brown sugar in a medium bowl with an electric mixer on medium-high speed until creamy. Add the eggs one at a time, beating until just blended after each addition. With mixer on low speed, add the mixed dry ingredients and melted chocolate.

3. Spoon the batter into the prepared cups, filling each one three-quarters full. Bake for 25–30 minutes, until risen and firm to the touch. Leave to cool completely.

4. To prepare the ganache, melt the chocolate and cream in a double boiler over barely simmering water. Let cool. Spread on the cupcakes.

5. To prepare the topping, melt the chocolate in a double boiler over barely simmering water. Let cool. Combine the almonds, cherries, ginger, and orange peel in a small bowl. Cover the tops of the cupcakes with this mixture then drizzle with melted chocolate.

MELTING CHOCOLATE STEP-BY-STEP

Chocolate needs to be melted very slowly to prevent it from turning coarse and grainy. Chop coarsely before you begin, then place the chocolate in the top pan of a double boiler over barely simmering water. If you don't have a double boiler, use a heatproof bowl or saucepan over a larger saucepan of barely simmering water. Dark chocolate will turn grainy if heated above 120°F (49°C) and white chocolate at (115°F/45°C), so keep the water in the bottom pan just below simmering point.

1 Chop the chocolate coarsely with a large knife.

2 Place in a double boiler (or a heatproof bowl over a saucepan) over barely simmering water and stir gently.

3 When the chocolate is glossy and smooth remove from the heat and let cool a little.

Florentine Cupcakes ▷

Chocolate Macadamia Cupcakes

These cupcakes are quick and easy to prepare. If making them for people with allergies to egg, make sure the chocolate does not contain any traces of egg by reading the label carefully.

Makes: 18 • Prep: 20 min. • Cooking: 25–30 min. • Level: 1

CUPCAKES

2	cups (300 g) all-purpose (plain) flour
4	tablespoons unsweetened cocoa powder
1	teaspoon ground cinnamon
1/4	teaspoon ground cloves
1/8	teaspoon salt
1	cup (250 g) butter
1	cup (200 g) firmly packed light brown sugar
1/2	teaspoon baking soda (bicarbonate of soda)
1/2	tablespoon warm water
1	cup (250 ml) milk
1/2	cup (90 g) macadamia nuts, coarsely chopped
1/2	cup (90 g) milk chocolate chips

TOPPING

3/4	cup (125 g) confectioners' (icing) sugar
1 1/2	tablespoons unsweetened cocoa powder
1 1/2	tablespoons water
1/2	teaspoon vanilla extract (essence)
1/3	cup (50 g) macadamia nuts, coarsely chopped and lightly toasted

1. Preheat the oven to 325°F (170°C/gas 3). Line two standard 12-cup muffin tins with 18 paper liners.

2. To prepare the cupcakes, combine the flour, cocoa, cinnamon, cloves, and salt in a medium bowl. Beat the butter and brown sugar in a medium bowl with an electric mixer on medium-high speed until creamy. Dissolve the baking soda in the water and add to the butter mixture. With mixer on low speed, add the mixed dry ingredients and milk. Stir the macadamia nuts and chocolate chips in by hand.

3. Spoon the batter into the prepared cups, filling each one three-quarters full. Bake for 25–30 minutes, until risen and firm to the touch. Transfer the muffin tins to a wire rack. Let cool completely before removing the cupcakes.

4. To prepare the topping, combine the confectioners' sugar, cocoa, water, and vanilla in a small bowl, stirring until smooth. Spread the frosting over the cupcakes and top with macadamia nuts.

Apricot and Ginger Cupcakes

When preparing food for those with gluten intolerance always make sure that gluten is not hidden in the baking powder, vanilla extract, or other ingredients. Read labels carefully.

Makes: 12 • Prep: 20 min. • Cooking: 20–25 min. • Level: 1

2/3	cup (100 g) rye flour
1/3	cup (50 g) rice flour
3	tablespoons potato flour
1/2	teaspoon baking powder
1/4	teaspoon baking soda (bicarbonate of soda)
1/8	teaspoon salt
1/2	cup (125 g) dairy-free spread
1/4	cup (50 g) sugar
1	teaspoon vanilla extract (essence)
3	large eggs
1/2	cup (90 g) dried apricots, coarsely chopped
2	tablespoons candied (glacé) cherries
1	tablespoon candied (glacé) ginger, chopped, + extra, to decorate
3	tablespoons orange marmalade, warmed, to glaze

1. Preheat the oven to 350°F (180°C/gas 4). Line a standard 12-cup muffin tin with paper liners.

2. To prepare the cupcakes, sift the three flours, baking powder, baking soda, and salt into a medium bowl. Beat the dairy-free spread, sugar, and vanilla in a medium bowl with an electric mixer on medium-high speed until creamy. Add the eggs one at a time, beating until just blended after each addition. With mixer on low speed, add the mixed dry ingredients. Stir the apricots, cherries, and ginger in by hand.

3. Spoon the batter into the prepared cups, filling each one three-quarters full. Bake for 20–25 minutes, until golden brown and firm to the touch. Transfer the muffin tin to a wire rack. Glaze with orange marmalade. Top with candied ginger. Let cool completely before removing the cupcakes.

Birthday Cupcakes

You can prepare a small paper piping bag to decorate these cupcakes: Cut a piece of parchment paper into an 8 x 12 x 14-inch (20 x 30 x 35-cm) triangle. Curl the paper into a cone-shape, forming the cone's point mid way along the long side. Tighten the cone and tuck the top flap inside the cone, securing with tape.

Makes: 12 · Prep: 45 min. · Cooking: 25–30 min. · Level: 3

CUPCAKES
2	cups (250 g) pecans, finely ground
1¼	cups (250 g) sugar
¼	cup (30 g) unsweetened cocoa powder
1	teaspoon baking powder
1	teaspoon ground cinnamon
⅛	teaspoon salt
4	large eggs
½	cup (125 ml) melted butter
1	teaspoon vanilla extract (essence)
1	teaspoon finely grated orange zest

CHOCOLATE GANACHE
4	ounces (120 g) dark chocolate, coarsely chopped
¼	cup (60 ml) light (single) cream

TO DECORATE
1½	cups (225 g) confectioners' (icing) sugar
2	tablespoons water
	Numbered candles

1. Preheat the oven to 325°F (170°C/gas 3). Line a standard 12-cup muffin tin with paper liners.

2. To prepare the cupcakes, combine the ground pecans, sugar, cocoa, baking powder, cinnamon, and salt in a medium bowl. Beat the eggs, butter, vanilla, and orange zest in a small bowl. Pour the egg mixture into the mixed dry ingredients and stir well.

3. Spoon the batter into the prepared cups, filling each one three-quarters full. Bake for 25–30 minutes, until golden brown and firm to the touch. Transfer the muffin tin to a wire rack. Let cool completely.

4. To prepare the ganache, melt the chocolate and cream in a double boiler over barely simmering water, stirring until smooth. Let cool then spread on the cupcakes.

5. To decorate, combine the confectioners' sugar and water in a small bowl. Spoon into the piping bag (see note above) and cut the tip off using scissors or a sharp knife. Pipe a border around the cupcakes and arrange the candles on one cupcake. Pipe the birthday age on the remaining cupcakes.

Chocolate Berry Cream Cupcakes

Chocolate goes beautifully with berry fruit, as these cupcakes will confirm. With no egg or sugar, these are a healthy choice for children with food allergies. Blue agave is a natural sweetener extracted from the core of the blue agave plant. It is available at many natural food stores and from online suppliers.

Makes: 16 · Prep: 20 min. · Cooking: 15–20 min. · Level: 1

CUPCAKES
2	cups (300 g) all-purpose (plain) flour
⅓	cup (50 g) unsweetened cocoa powder
2	teaspoons baking powder
1	teaspoon baking soda (bicarbonate of soda)
⅛	teaspoon salt
½	cup (125 g) butter, melted
1	cup (250 ml) blue agave
1	cup (250 ml) milk
1½	teaspoons vanilla extract (essence)

FILLING
½	cup (125 ml) heavy (double) cream
1	teaspoon blue agave
½	teaspoon vanilla extract (essence)
¼	teaspoon ground cinnamon
½	cup (60 g) fresh raspberries
½	cup (60 g) fresh strawberries, chopped
½	cup (60 g) fresh blueberries
	Unsweetened cocoa powder, to dust

1. Preheat the oven to 350°F (180°C/gas 4). Line two standard 12-cup muffin tins with 16 paper liners.

2. To prepare the cupcakes, combine the flour, cocoa, baking powder, baking soda, and salt in a medium bowl. Beat the butter, blue agave, milk, and vanilla in a medium bowl. Pour the blue agave mixture into the mixed dry ingredients and stir until combined. Do not over mix.

3. Spoon the batter into the prepared cups, filling each one three-quarters full. Bake for 15–20 minutes, until risen and firm to the touch. Transfer the muffin tins to a wire rack. Let cool completely before removing the cupcakes.

4. To prepare the filling, whip the cream, blue agave, vanilla, and cinnamon in a small bowl using an electric mixer on medium speed until soft peaks form. Stir in the berries. Cut a small circle about ½ inch (1 cm) deep from the top of each cupcake. Spoon the berry cream inside. Sit the cupcake lids on top and dust with cocoa.

Smartie Cupcakes

These colorful cupcakes are perfect for a children's birthday party or to liven up a buffet or party spread. See the photograph on page 12.

Makes: 12 · Prep: 30 min. · Cooking: 20–25 min. · Level: 1

CUPCAKES

1	cup (150 g) all-purpose (plain) flour
4	tablespoons unsweetened cocoa powder
1	teaspoon baking powder
1/4	teaspoon baking soda (bicarbonate of soda)
1/2	cup (100 g) firmly packed brown sugar
1/3	cup (90 g) butter, softened
1	teaspoon vanilla extract (essence)
1	large egg
1/4	cup (60 ml) milk

COLORED FROSTING

1 1/2	cups (225 g) confectioners' (icing) sugar
2	tablespoons water
1/8	teaspoon yellow food coloring
1/8	teaspoon red food coloring
1/8	teaspoon blue food coloring
1/8	teaspoon green food coloring
	Candy-coated chocolate buttons, to decorate

1. Preheat the oven to 325°F (170°C/gas 3). Line a standard 12-cup muffin tin with paper liners.

2. To prepare the cupcakes, combine the flour, cocoa, baking powder, and baking soda in a small bowl. Beat the brown sugar, butter, and vanilla in a medium bowl with an electric mixer on medium-high speed until creamy. Add the egg, beating until just combined. With mixer on low, beat in the mixed dry ingredients and milk.

3. Spoon the batter into the prepared cups, filling each one three-quarters full. Bake for 20-25 minutes, until golden brown and firm to the touch. Leave to cool completely.

4. To prepare the frosting, combine the confectioners' sugar and water in a small bowl, stirring until smooth. Divide the frosting evenly among four small bowls. Add a few drops of food coloring to each bowl to make bright yellow, red, blue, and green frostings. Spread the frostings over the cupcakes, making four of each color. Decorate with candy-coated buttons.

Raspberry and Yogurt Cupcakes

These pretty cupcakes are perfect with tea or coffee for an afternoon snack. Replace the raspberries with sliced fresh strawberries, if preferred.

Makes: 12 · Prep: 20 min. · Cooking: 20–25 min. · Level: 1

1 1/4	cups (180 g) all-purpose (plain) flour
1	teaspoon baking powder
1/8	teaspoon salt
1/2	cup (125 g) butter, softened
1/2	cup (100 g) sugar
1	teaspoon finely grated lemon zest
2	large eggs
1/3	cup (90 ml) plain yogurt
1/2	cup (125 g) fresh raspberries, mashed with a fork

TOPPING

1/2	cup (125 ml) plain yogurt
1	tablespoon honey
	Fresh raspberries

1. Preheat the oven to 325°F (170°C/gas 3). Line a standard 12-cup muffin tin with paper liners.

2. To prepare the cupcakes, combine the flour, baking powder, and salt in a small bowl. Beat the butter, sugar, and lemon zest in a medium bowl with an electric mixer on medium-high speed until pale and creamy. Add the eggs one at a time, beating until just blended after each addition. With mixer on low speed, add the mixed dry ingredients and yogurt. Stir the mashed raspberries in by hand.

3. Spoon the batter into the prepared cups, filling each one three-quarters full. Bake for 20–25 minutes, until golden brown and firm to the touch. Transfer the muffin tin to a wire rack. Let cool completely before removing the cupcakes.

4. To prepare the topping, combine the yogurt and honey in a small bowl. Top each cupcake with a dollop of sweetened yogurt and 2–3 fresh raspberries.

Raspberry and Yogurt Cupcakes ▷

Neenish Cupcakes

These cupcakes are named after Neenish tarts, which have a sharply divided two-toned frosting.

Makes: 12 • Prep: 20 min. • Cooking: 20–25 min. • Level: 1

CUPCAKES
1⅓ cups (200 g) all-purpose (plain) flour
⅓   cup (30 g) ground almonds
1½ teaspoons baking powder
1   teaspoon ground cinnamon
⅛   teaspoon salt
1   cup (200 g) sugar
2   large eggs, lightly beaten
1   teaspoon vanilla extract (essence)
1   cup (250 ml) light (single) cream
½   cup (160 g) raspberry preserves (jam)

FROSTING
1½ cups (225 g) confectioners' (icing) sugar
2   tablespoons milk
1   tablespoon unsweetened cocoa powder

1. Preheat the oven to 325°F (170°C/gas 3). Line a standard 12-cup muffin tin with paper liners.

2. To prepare the cupcakes, combine the flour, almonds, baking powder, cinnamon, and salt in a small bowl. Beat the sugar, eggs, and vanilla in a medium bowl with an electric mixer on medium-high speed until pale and creamy. With mixer on low speed, add the mixed dry ingredients and cream.

3. Spoon the batter into the prepared cups, filling each one three-quarters full. Bake for 20–25 minutes, until golden brown and firm to the touch. Transfer the muffin tin to a wire rack. Let cool completely before removing the cupcakes.

4. Spread a teaspoon of raspberry preserves on each cupcake.

5. To prepare the frosting, combine the confectioners' sugar and milk in a small bowl. Divide evenly between two small bowls and add the cocoa to one.

6. Spread the white frosting over half of each cupcake and chocolate over the other half, making a definite line down the center.

Happy New Year Cupcakes

These cakes are both tasty and fun to serve. Children will especially enjoy the sparklers.

Makes: 12 • Prep: 30 min. • Cooking: 20–25 min. • Level: 2

CUPCAKES
1⅓ cups (200 g) all-purpose (plain) flour
⅓   cup (30 g) ground almonds
1½ teaspoons baking powder
½   teaspoon ground cinnamon
⅛   teaspoon salt
1   cup (200 g) sugar
2   large eggs
1   teaspoon finely grated orange zest
1   teaspoon vanilla extract (essence)
1   cup (250 ml) light (single) cream
12 milk chocolate squares
    Small cachous, to decorate
12 sparklers, to decorate

ORANGE GANACHE
4   ounces (120 g) dark chocolate, coarsely chopped
¼   cup (60 ml) light (single) cream
2   teaspoons finely grated orange zest

1. Preheat the oven to 350°F (180°C/gas 4). Line a standard 12-cup muffin tin with paper liners.

2. To prepare the cupcakes, combine the flour, almonds, baking powder, cinnamon, and salt in a small bowl. Beat the sugar, eggs, orange zest, and vanilla in a medium bowl with an electric mixer on medium-high speed until pale and creamy. With mixer on low speed, gradually add the mixed dry ingredients and cream.

3. Spoon half the batter into the prepared cups. Place a chocolate square in the center of each one and spoon in the remaining batter, filling each one three-quarters full. Bake for 20–25 minutes, until golden brown and firm to the touch. Let cool completely.

4. To prepare the ganache, melt the chocolate and cream in a double boiler over barely simmering water. Remove from the heat, stir in the orange zest, and let cool. Spread over the cupcakes and sprinkle with cachous. Cut the sparklers down to a shorter size and insert into the cupcakes. Light when ready to serve.

Neenish Cupcakes ▷

Lemon and Poppy Seed Cupcakes

These lemon flavored cupcakes are great with a cup of tea.

Makes: 12 • Prep: 25 min. • Cooking: 25–30 min. • Level: 1

CUPCAKES

1⅓	cups (200 g) all-purpose (plain) flour
⅓	cup (30 g) ground almonds
¼	cup (30 g) poppy seeds
1½	teaspoons baking powder
⅛	teaspoon salt
½	cup (125 g) butter, softened
¾	cup (150 g) sugar
2	teaspoons finely grated lemon zest
2	large eggs
2	tablespoons milk
2	tablespoons freshly squeezed lemon juice

LEMON CREAM CHEESE FROSTING

½	cup (125 g) butter, softened
1	pound (500 g) cream cheese
1⅓	cups (200 g) confectioners' (icing) sugar
2	teaspoons peeled, finely grated fresh ginger
1	teaspoon finely grated lemon zest

1. Preheat the oven to 325°F (170°C/gas 3). Line a standard 12-cup muffin tin with paper liners.

2. To prepare the cupcakes, combine the flour, ground almonds, poppy seeds, baking powder, and salt in a small bowl. Beat the butter, sugar, and lemon zest in a medium bowl with an electric mixer on medium-high speed until pale and creamy. Add the eggs one at a time, beating until just blended after each addition. With mixer on low speed, add the mixed dry ingredients, milk, and lemon juice.

3. Spoon the batter into the prepared cups, filling each one three-quarters full. Bake for 25–30 minutes, until golden brown and firm to the touch. Transfer the muffin tin to a wire rack. Let cool completely before removing the cupcakes.

4. To prepare the frosting, beat the butter in a medium bowl with an electric mixer on medium-high speed until smooth. Add the cream cheese and beat until smooth. Beat in the confectioners' sugar, ginger, and lemon. Spread the frosting over the cupcakes.

Carrot and Walnut Cupcakes

These are healthy cupcakes, perfect for breakfast. If you want to make them dairy-free, just leave off the frosting.

Makes: 12 • Prep: 15 min. • Cooking: 20–25 min. • Level: 1

CUPCAKES

1⅓	cups (200 g) all-purpose (plain) flour
1½	teaspoons baking powder
½	teaspoon ground cinnamon
½	teaspoon ground nutmeg
⅛	teaspoon salt
⅔	cup (150 ml) sunflower oil
½	cup (100 g) firmly packed light brown sugar
2	large eggs, lightly beaten
2	medium carrots (150 g), grated
⅓	cup (50 g) walnuts, coarsely chopped

FROSTING

½	cup (125 ml) mascarpone cheese
1	tablespoon honey
	Coarsely chopped walnuts, to decorate

1. Preheat the oven to 350°F (180°C/gas 4). Line a standard 12-cup muffin tin with paper liners.

2. To prepare the cupcakes, combine the flour, baking powder, cinnamon, nutmeg, and salt in a small bowl. Combine the oil, sugar, and eggs in a medium bowl. Stir in the carrots and walnuts. Mix in the dry ingredients until well combined.

3. Spoon the batter into the prepared cups, filling each one three-quarters full. Bake for 20–25 minutes, until golden brown and firm to the touch. Transfer the muffin tin to a wire rack. Let cool completely before removing the cupcakes.

4. To prepare the frosting, mix the mascarpone cheese and honey in a small bowl. Top each cupcake with a dollop of sweetened mascarpone and few chopped walnut pieces.

Lemon and Poppy Seed Cupcakes ▷

Easter Cupcakes

These cupcakes are decorated with Flake chocolate bars. If liked, substitute with curls of milk chocolate. Make the curls by melting the chocolate and pouring it onto a cold glass or marble surface. Let set, then use a knife to scrape off the curls.

Makes: 12 • Prep: 30 min. • Cooking: 20–25 min. • Level: 2

CUPCAKES

1½	cups (225 g) all-purpose (plain) flour
3	tablespoons unsweetened cocoa powder
1½	teaspoons baking powder
⅛	teaspoon salt
1	cup (200 g) sugar
2	large eggs
1	teaspoon vanilla extract (essence)
1	cup (250 ml) light (single) cream
½	cup (90 g) milk chocolate chips

TO DECORATE

1	recipe Chocolate Butter Cream (see page 276)
3	small Flake chocolate bars, to decorate, crumbled
12	mini speckled Easter eggs, to decorate
1	ounce (30 g) milk chocolate, melted

1. Preheat the oven to 350°F (180°C/gas 4). Line a standard 12-cup muffin tin with paper liners.

2. To prepare the cupcakes, combine the flour, cocoa, baking powder, and salt in a small bowl. Beat the sugar, eggs, and vanilla in a medium bowl with an electric mixer on medium-high speed until pale and creamy. With mixer on low speed, add the mixed dry ingredients and cream. Stir in the chocolate chips by hand.

3. Spoon the batter into the prepared cups, filling each one three-quarters full. Bake for 20–25 minutes, until golden brown and firm to the touch. Transfer the muffin tin to a wire rack. Let cool completely before removing the cupcakes.

4. To decorate, spread the butter cream on the cupcakes. Break the chocolate bars into pieces and use to create little "nests" on top of each cupcake. Place speckled eggs in each nest, securing with melted chocolate.

Halloween Cupcakes

These cupcakes are decorated with a Jack-o'-Lantern motif (the-hollowed out pumpkin face made at Halloween.) Prepare them for friends and family at Halloween.

Makes: 12 • Prep: 30 min. • Cooking: 25–30 min. • Level: 2

CUPCAKES

¾	cup (125 g) all-purpose (plain) flour
1	teaspoon baking powder
1	teaspoon allspice or pumpkin pie spice
⅛	teaspoon salt
½	cup (125 ml) sunflower oil
½	cup (100 g) firmly packed light brown sugar
2	large eggs
1	teaspoon finely grated orange zest
½	cup (120 g) grated butternut pumpkin

TO DECORATE

1½	cups (225 g) confectioners' (icing) sugar
2½	tablespoons water
⅛	teaspoon orange food coloring
1	tube black frosting (icing)

1. Preheat the oven to 325°F (170°C/gas 3). Line a standard 12-cup muffin tin with paper liners.

2. To prepare the cupcakes, combine the flour, baking powder, spice, and salt in a small bowl. Combine the oil, sugar, eggs, and zest in a medium bowl. Stir in the pumpkin and dry ingredients.

3. Spoon the batter into the prepared cups, filling each one three-quarters full. Bake for 25–30 minutes, until golden brown and firm to the touch. Transfer the muffin tin to a wire rack. Let cool completely before removing the cupcakes.

4. To decorate, combine the confectioners' sugar and water in a small bowl, stirring until smooth. Add orange food coloring to create a bright orange frosting and spread over the cup cakes. Fit the tube of black frosting with a tip and pipe a Jack-o'-Lantern design on the cupcakes.

◁ **Easter Cupcakes**

BREAKFAST AND BRUNCH CAKES

What better way to begin the day than with a freshly baked cake? In this chapter we have included some healthy choices, based on yogurt, fruit, nuts, cereals, and whole-wheat. In some cases you can prepare the batter the night before and just pop the cake in the oven when you get up. We have also included some bread-like yeast cakes, including plain and filled Brioche (see page 74), Apple Breakfast Cake (see page 65), and Swedish Breakfast Cake (see page 72).

◁ Rhubarb and Orange Cake (see page 50)

Blueberry Streusel Cake

Streusal is a German word meaning scattered or sprinkled. In baking, it refers to a crumbly topping usually made of butter, flour, and spices, which is sprinkled over cakes or breads before going into the oven. It adds a lovely crunchy top layer to the baked goods.

Serves: 8–10 · Prep: 20 min. · Cooking: 1 hr. 15 min. · Level: 1

CAKE
- 3/4 cup (180 g) butter, softened
- 3/4 cup (150 g) sugar
- 1 teaspoon finely grated lemon zest
- 2 large eggs
- 2 cups (300 g) all-purpose (plain) flour
- 2 teaspoons baking powder
- 3/4 cup (180 ml) milk
- 2 cups (300 g) fresh blueberries

STREUSEL TOPPING
- 1/4 cup (60 g) butter, chopped
- 1/3 cup (50 g) all-purpose (plain) flour
- 1/3 cup (70 g) firmly packed brown sugar
- 1 teaspoon ground cinnamon
- 1 cup (125 g) pecan halves

1. Preheat the oven to 350°F (180°C/gas 4). Lightly grease a 9-inch (23 cm) round springform cake pan and line the base with parchment paper.

2. To prepare the cake, beat the butter, sugar, and lemon zest in a medium bowl with an electric mixer on medium-high speed until pale and creamy. Add the eggs one at a time, beating until just blended after each addition. With mixer on low speed, add the flour, baking powder, and salt, alternating with the milk. Spoon the batter into the prepared pan and sprinkle with the blueberries.

3. To prepare the topping, place the butter, flour, brown sugar, and cinnamon in a small bowl. Rub in the butter until the mixture resembles coarse bread crumbs. Stir in the pecans and sprinkle the topping over the blueberries.

4. Bake for 1 hour, then cover with aluminum foil and bake for 15 more minutes, or until a skewer comes out clean when tested. Leave to cool in the pan for 10 minutes, then turn out onto a wire rack. Serve warm or at room temperature.

Cinnamon Spice Breakfast Cake

This is a serious breakfast cake—not too sweet, with a pleasing biscuit-like texture and spicy sugar topping. Serve while still warm or at room temperature.

Serves: 8–10 · Prep: 15 min. · Cooking: 30–40 min. · Level: 1

CAKE
- 2 cups (300 g) all-purpose (plain) flour
- 1/3 cup (75 g) firmly packed brown sugar
- 1 tablespoon baking powder
- 1/2 teaspoon salt
- 1/4 cup (60 g) cold butter, cut up
- 1/2 cup (125 ml) milk
- 1 large egg, lightly beaten
- 1/2 cup (60 g) raisins

TOPPING
- 1/4 cup (50 g) sugar
- 1 teaspoon ground cinnamon
- 1 teaspoon ground pumpkin pie spice or allspice
- 1 teaspoon ground ginger
- 3 tablespoons butter, melted

1. Preheat the oven to 375°F (170°C/gas 3). Lightly grease and flour a 9-inch (23-cm) square baking pan.

2. To prepare the cake, stir the flour, brown sugar, baking powder, and salt in a large bowl. Use a pastry blender to cut in the butter until the mixture resembles fine crumbs. Stir in the milk and egg, then the raisins. The batter will be sticky and thick, like a cookie dough. Spread the batter in the prepared pan.

3. To prepare the topping, mix the sugar, cinnamon, pumpkin pie spice, and ginger in a small bowl. Sprinkle over the batter. Drizzle with the butter.

4. Bake for 30–40 minutes, or until a toothpick inserted into the center comes out clean. Cool the cake in the pan on a rack.

Blueberry Streusel Cake ▷

Apple and Cranberry Crumble Cake

With apples and cranberries, this breakfast or brunch cake is not only delicious but also a healthy choice.

Serves: 8–10 · Prep: 20 min. · Cooking: 50–60 min. · Level: 1

CAKE

½	cup (125 g) butter, softened
1	cup (200 g) sugar
2	large eggs
1	cup (150 g) all-purpose (plain) flour
1	teaspoon baking powder
1	teaspoon ground cinnamon
½	teaspoon ground nutmeg
2	medium tart apples, such as Granny Smith, peeled, cored, and diced
1	cup (150 g) fresh cranberries

CRUMBLE TOPPING

¼	cup (50 g) firmly packed brown sugar
¼	cup (30 g) all-purpose (plain) flour
¼	cup (30 g) shredded (desiccated) coconut
3	tablespoons butter, chopped

1. Preheat the oven to 350°F (180°C/gas 4). Lightly grease a 9-inch (23 cm) springform cake pan and line the base with parchment paper.

2. To prepare the cake, beat the butter and sugar in a medium bowl with an electric mixer on medium-high speed until pale and creamy. Add the eggs one at a time, beating until just blended after each addition. Combine the flour, baking powder, cinnamon, and nutmeg in a medium bowl. With mixer on low speed, gradually beat in the mixed dry ingredients. Stir the apple and cranberries in by hand. Spoon the batter into the prepared pan and set aside.

3. To prepare the topping, place the brown sugar, flour, coconut, and butter in a small bowl. Rub in the butter until the mixture resembles coarse bread crumbs. Sprinkle the topping over the batter.

4. Bake for 50–60 minutes, until golden brown and firm to the touch. Leave to cool in the pan for 10 minutes, then turn out onto a wire rack. Serve warm or at room temperature.

Cinnamon Crumble Apple Cake

Another delicious apple and spice cake. For a special Sunday brunch, serve warm with a spoonful of crème fraîche or yogurt on each portion.

Serves: 8–10 · Prep: 30 min. · Cooking: 40–50 min. · Level: 1

CAKE

3	medium tart apples, such as Granny Smith, peeled, and thinly sliced
¼	cup (60 ml) freshly squeezed lemon juice
2	tablespoons brown sugar
¾	cup (180 g) butter, softened
¾	cup (150 g) sugar
2	large eggs
2¼	cups (230 g) all-purpose (plain) flour
2	teaspoons baking powder
¼	teaspoon salt
¾	cup (180 ml) milk

CINNAMON CRUMBLE

1	cup (150 g) all-purpose (plain) flour
½	cup (100 g) firmly packed brown sugar
1	tablespoon ground cinnamon
⅓	cup (90 g) cold butter
1	cup (120 g) walnuts, coarsely chopped

1. Preheat the oven to 350°F (180°C/gas 4). Lightly grease a 9-inch (23-cm) square baking pan.

2. To prepare the cake, bring the apples, lemon juice, and brown sugar to a boil in a medium saucepan. Cover, reduce the heat, and simmer until tender, about 10 minutes. Drain well and let cool.

3. Beat the butter and sugar in a large bowl with an electric mixer at medium speed until pale and creamy. Add the egg one at a time, beating until just blended after each addition. With mixer on low, gradually beat in the flour, baking powder, and salt, alternating with the milk. Spoon two-thirds of the batter into the prepared pan. Spoon the apples over the top. Spread the remaining batter on top.

4. To prepare the crumble, mix the flour, brown sugar, and cinnamon in a large bowl. Use a pastry blender to cut in the butter until the mixture resembles coarse crumbs. Stir in the walnuts. Sprinkle over the cake. Bake for 40–50 minutes, or until a toothpick inserted into the center comes out clean. Cool the cake in the pan on a rack. Serve warm or at room temperature.

Apple and Cranberry Crumble Cake ▷

Pecan Crunch Yogurt Cake

This is an excellent cake with a lovely flavor and texture and a pretty swirl of crunch throughout.

Serves: 8–10 · Prep: 25 min. · Cooking: 55–65 min. · Level: 1

TOPPING

1	cup (150 g) pecans, coarsely chopped
½	cup (100 g) sugar
½	cup (75 g) all-purpose (plain) flour
¼	cup (60 g) butter, melted
2	teaspoons ground cinnamon
1	teaspoon vanilla extract (essence)

CAKE

2	cups (300 g) all-purpose (plain) flour
2	teaspoons baking powder
¼	teaspoon salt
½	cup (125 g) butter, softened
1	cup (200 g) sugar
2	teaspoons vanilla extract (essence)
2	large eggs
1	cup (250 ml) plain yogurt

1. Preheat the oven to 350°F (180°C/gas 4). Lightly grease and flour a 9-inch (23-cm) square baking pan.

2. To prepare the topping, stir the pecans, sugar, flour, butter, cinnamon, and vanilla in a medium bowl.

3. To prepare the cake, mix the flour, baking powder, and salt in a medium bowl. Beat the butter, sugar, and vanilla in a large bowl with an electric mixer at medium speed until pale and creamy. Add the eggs one at a time, beating until just blended after each addition. With mixer at low speed, beat in the dry ingredients, alternating with the yogurt.

4. Spoon half the batter into the prepared pan. Sprinkle with half the topping. Spoon the remaining batter over the top and sprinkle with the remaining topping.

5. Bake for 55–65 minutes, or until springy to the touch and a toothpick inserted into the center comes out clean. Cool the cake in the pan on a rack. Serve warm or at room temperature.

Banana Crunch Cake

Banana cakes have a rich, moist crumb which contrasts deliciously with the crumbly topping on this cake.

Serves: 8–10 · Prep: 25–30 min. · Cooking: 25–30 min. · Level: 1

TOPPING

½	cup (75 g) all-purpose (plain) flour
½	cup (100 g) firmly packed brown sugar
1	teaspoon cinnamon
½	teaspoon ground nutmeg
¼	cup (60 g) cold butter
½	cup (60 g) almonds, coarsely chopped

CAKE

2	cups (300 g) all-purpose (plain) flour
1	teaspoon baking soda (bicarbonate of soda)
½	teaspoon baking powder
¼	teaspoon salt
½	cup (125 g) butter, softened
¾	cup (150 g) sugar
1	tablespoon finely grated orange zest
1	teaspoon vanilla extract (essence)
2	large eggs
2	large, very ripe bananas, peeled and mashed
2	tablespoons sour cream
½	cup (90 g) raisins

1. Preheat the oven to 350°F (180°C/gas 4). Lightly grease and flour a 9-inch (23-cm) tube pan.

2. To prepare the topping, stir the flour, brown sugar, cinnamon, and nutmeg in a medium bowl. Use a pastry blender to cut in the butter until the mixture resembles fine crumbs. Stir in the almonds.

3. To prepare the cake, stir the flour, baking soda, baking powder, and salt in a large bowl. Beat the butter, sugar, orange zest, and vanilla in a large bowl with an electric mixer at medium speed until pale and creamy. Add the eggs one at a time, beating until just blended after each addition. With mixer on low speed, beat in the bananas, sour cream, dry ingredients, and raisins.

4. Spoon the batter into the prepared pan. Sprinkle with the topping. Bake for 25–30 minutes, or until golden brown and a toothpick inserted into the center comes out clean. Cool the cake in the pan on a rack. Serve warm or at room temperature.

Lemon Yogurt Cake

Tart and invigorating, lemon and yogurt are a great flavor combination for breakfast and brunch cakes.

Serves: 8–10 · Prep: 20 min. · Cooking: 35–45 min. · Level: 1

CAKE

2	cups (300 g) all-purpose (plain) flour
2	teaspoons baking powder
¼	teaspoon salt
½	cup (125 g) butter, softened
1	cup (200 g) sugar
1	tablespoon finely grated lemon zest
3	large eggs, separated
1	cup (250 ml) lemon-flavored yogurt

LEMON FROSTING

2	cups (300 g) confectioners' (icing) sugar
3	tablespoons butter, melted
2	tablespoons freshly squeezed lemon juice
2	tablespoons candied (glacé) lemon peel, coarsely chopped

1. Preheat the oven to 325°F (170°C/gas 3). Lightly grease a 9-inch (23-cm) round cake pan. Line with parchment paper.

2. To prepare the cake, mix the flour, baking powder, and salt in a medium bowl. Beat the butter, sugar, and lemon zest in a large bowl with an electric mixer at medium speed until pale and creamy. Add the egg yolks one at a time, beating until just blended after each addition. With mixer on low speed, gradually beat in the dry ingredients, alternating with the yogurt.

3. With mixer at high speed, beat the egg whites in a medium bowl until stiff peaks form. Use a large rubber spatula to fold them into the batter.

4. Spoon the batter into the prepared pan. Bake for 35–45 minutes, or until the cake shrinks from sides of the pan and a toothpick inserted into the center comes out clean. Cool the cake in the pan for 5 minutes. Turn out onto a rack. Carefully remove the paper and let cool completely.

5. To prepare the frosting, mix the confectioners' sugar and butter in a medium bowl. Beat in the lemon juice. Spread the top and sides of the cake with the frosting. Decorate with the candied lemon peel.

Gingerbread With Lime Frosting

The lime frosting adds a new dimension to this classic cake. If preferred, omit the frosting and serve the slices lightly spread with butter.

Serves: 6–8 · Prep: 30 min. · Cooking: 45–55 min. · Level: 1

LOAF

½	cup (120 ml) molasses
¼	cup (60 g) butter
1	cup (150 g) all-purpose (plain) flour
¾	cup (150 g) sugar
1	teaspoon baking powder
½	teaspoon baking soda (bicarbonate of soda)
1	teaspoon ground ginger
1	teaspoon ground cinnamon
¼	teaspoon ground cloves
¼	teaspoon ground mace
¼	teaspoon salt
½	cup (125 ml) milk
1	large egg, lightly beaten

LIME FROSTING

½	cup (125 g) butter, softened
1	tablespoon finely grated lime zest
2	cups (300 g) confectioners' (icing) sugar
2	tablespoons freshly squeezed lime juice

1. Preheat the oven to 350°F (180°C/gas 4). Lightly grease a 9 x 5-inch (23 x 13-cm) loaf pan. Line with parchment paper.

2. To prepare the loaf, stir the butter and molasses in a small saucepan over low heat until the butter has melted. Keep warm. Stir the flour, sugar, baking powder, baking soda, ginger, cinnamon, cloves, mace, and salt in a large bowl. With an electric mixer at low speed, gradually beat in the milk and egg. Stir the hot butter mixture into the batter by hand.

3. Spoon the batter into the prepared pan. Bake for 45–55 minutes, or until a toothpick inserted into the center comes out clean. Cool the loaf in the pan for 15 minutes. Turn out onto a rack. Carefully remove the paper and let cool completely.

4. To prepare the frosting, beat the butter and lime zest in a medium bowl until creamy. Gradually beat in the confectioners' sugar and lime juice. Spread the frosting over the top and sides of the loaf.

Pear, Walnut, and Ginger Cake

Serves: 8–10 · Prep: 15 min. · Cooking: 40–45 min. · Level: 1

2	cups (300 g) all-purpose (plain) flour
1	teaspoon baking powder
1	teaspoon ground ginger
1/4	teaspoon salt
1/2	cup (125 g) butter, softened
1/2	cup (100 g) firmly packed brown sugar
3	tablespoons light corn (golden) syrup
2	large eggs
1/2	cup (125 ml) milk
1	teaspoon baking soda (bicarbonate of soda)
1/4	cup (30 g) candied (glacé) ginger, finely chopped
1/3	cup (50 g) walnuts, coarsely chopped
3	medium pears, peeled, cored and sliced
3	tablespoons maple syrup

1. Preheat the oven to 350°F (180°C/gas 4). Lightly grease a 9-inch (23 cm) square cake pan and line the base with parchment paper.

2. To prepare the cake, combine the flour, baking powder, ginger, and salt in a small bowl. Beat the butter, sugar, and corn syrup in a medium bowl with an electric mixer on medium-high speed until creamy. Add the eggs one at a time, beating until just blended after each addition.

3. Combine the milk and baking soda in a small bowl. With mixer on low speed, beat the mixed dry ingredients and milk into the batter. Stir the ginger and walnuts in by hand. Spoon the batter into the prepared pan and press the pear slices decoratively on top.

4. Bake for 40–45 minutes, until golden brown and firm to the touch. Leave to cool in the pan for 10 minutes, then turn out onto a wire rack. Brush with maple syrup. Serve warm or at room temperature.

Walnut Crunch Cake

Serves: 8–10 · Prep: 20 min. · Cooking: 50–60 min. · Level: 1

TOPPING

3/4	cup (150 g) firmly packed brown sugar
1/3	cup (50 g) all-purpose (plain) flour
1/4	cup (60 g) cold butter, cut up
3/4	cup (90 g) walnuts, coarsely chopped

CAKE

2	cups (300 g) all-purpose (plain) flour
2	teaspoons baking powder
1	teaspoon nutmeg
1/4	teaspoon salt
1/2	cup (125 g) butter, softened
3/4	cup firmly (150 g) packed brown sugar
1	teaspoon vanilla extract (essence)
4	large eggs
3/4	cup (180 ml) milk

1. Preheat the oven to 350°F (180°C/gas 4). Lightly grease and flour a 9-inch (23-cm) Bundt pan.

2. To prepare the topping, stir the brown sugar and flour in a medium bowl. Use a pastry blender to cut in the butter until the mixture resembles fine crumbs. Stir in the walnuts.

3. To prepare the cake, stir the flour, baking powder, nutmeg, and salt in a medium bowl. Beat the butter, brown sugar, and vanilla in a large bowl with an electric mixer at medium speed until creamy. Add the eggs one at a time, beating until just blended after each addition. With mixer on low speed, gradually beat in the dry ingredients, alternating with the milk.

4. Spoon half the batter into the prepared pan. Sprinkle with half the crunch mixture. Spoon the remaining batter over the top and sprinkle with the remaining crunch mixture.

5. Bake for 50–60 minutes, or until golden brown. Cool the cake in the pan on a rack for 15 minutes. Carefully turn out, turn topping-side up, and serve warm.

Pear, Walnut, and Ginger Cake ▷

Rhubarb and Orange Cake

Rhubarb is rich in dietary fiber and vitamins C and K. Its slightly acerbic, earthy flavor is perfect with a wake-up cup of coffee or tea in the mornings.

Serves: 8–10 · Prep: 30 min. · Cooking: 45–50 min. · Level: 1

2	cups (300 g) all-purpose (plain) flour
2	teaspoons baking powder
½	cup (125 g) butter, softened
1	cup (200 g) sugar
2	teaspoons finely grated orange zest
1	teaspoon vanilla extract (essence)
2	large eggs
½	cup (125 ml) milk
½	teaspoon baking soda (bicarbonate of soda)
2	cups (300 g) rhubarb, thinly sliced
	Confectioners' (icing) sugar, to dust

1. Preheat the oven to 325°F (170°C/gas 3). Lightly grease a 9-inch (23 cm) round springform cake pan and line the base with parchment paper.

2. Combine the flour and baking powder in a medium bowl. Beat the butter, sugar, orange zest, and vanilla in a medium bowl with an electric mixer on medium-high speed until pale and creamy. Add the eggs one at a time, beating until just blended after each addition.

3. Combine the milk and baking soda in a small bowl. With mixer on low speed, beat the milk and mixed dry ingredients into the batter. Spoon the batter into the prepared pan and sprinkle the rhubarb over the top.

4. Bake for 45–50 minutes, until golden brown and firm to the touch. Leave to cool in the pan for 10 minutes, then turn out onto a wire rack and let cool.

5. Dust with confectioners' sugar. Serve warm or at room temperature.

Quick Mix Breakfast Cake

You can whip up this nutritious cake in just a few minutes. Bake while the family gets ready for the day, then serve it piping hot with coffee.

Serves: 10–12 · Prep: 15 min. · Cooking: 55–65 min. · Level: 1

CAKE

2	cups (300 g) all-purpose (plain) flour
2	cups (400 g) sugar
1	tablespoon baking powder
¼	teaspoon salt
½	cup (125 g) butter, melted
1	large ripe banana, mashed
1	cup (250 ml) plain yogurt
2	large eggs, separated
2	teaspoons vanilla extract (essence)
½	teaspoon almond extract (essence)

NUT FILLING

½	cup (100 g) sugar
1	tablespoon ground cinnamon
1	cup (100 g) mixed nuts, chopped

1. Preheat the oven to 350°F (180°C/gas 4). Lightly grease and flour a 10-inch (25-cm) tube pan.

2. To prepare the cake, stir the flour, 1½ cups (300 g) of sugar, baking powder, and salt in a large bowl. With an electric mixer at medium speed, beat in the butter, banana, yogurt, egg yolks, vanilla, and almond.

3. With mixer at medium speed, beat the egg whites in a large bowl until frothy. With mixer at high speed, gradually add the remaining sugar, beating until stiff, glossy peaks form. Use a large rubber spatula to fold the beaten whites into the batter. Spoon half the batter into the prepared pan.

4. To prepare the filling, mix the sugar, cinnamon, and nuts in a bowl. Sprinkle half the filling mixture over the batter in the pan. Spoon the remaining batter over the top and sprinkle with the remaining filling.

5. Bake for 55–65 minutes, or until a toothpick inserted into the center comes out clean. Cool the cake in the pan for 15 minutes. Carefully turn out, topping-side up, and serve warm.

Rhubarb and Orange Cake ▷

Apricot and Almond Cake

In their dried form, apricots are one of the best natural sources of vitamin A and beta-carotene available. Almonds are a good source of protein and fiber. Together they make this cake a very healthy choice.

Serves: 8 · Prep: 15 min. · Cooking: 50–60 min. · Level: 1

CAKE

- 1½ ounces (50 g) slightly stale bread crumbs
- 1 cup (200 g) sugar
- 1 cup (100 g) ground almonds
- 1½ teaspoons baking powder
- 1 teaspoon ground cinnamon
- ¾ cup (180 ml) vegetable oil
- ⅔ cup (120 g) dried apricots, finely chopped and soaked in boiling water
- 4 large eggs, lightly beaten
- 1 teaspoon finely grated orange zest

APRICOT AND CINNAMON GLAZE

- ½ cup (90 g) dried apricots
- 1 orange, zest finely grated and juiced
- 1 large cinnamon stick, broken in half
- 2 tablespoons honey

1. Lightly grease an 8-inch (20 cm) springform cake pan and line the base with parchment paper.

2. To prepare the cake, combine the bread crumbs, sugar, ground almonds, baking powder, and cinnamon in a medium bowl. Add the oil, drained apricots, eggs, and orange zest and stir to combine. Pour into the prepared pan.

3. Put in a cold oven and set the temperature to 375°F (190°C/gas 5). Bake for 40–50 minutes until golden brown and a skewer comes out clean when tested. Leave to cool in the pan for 10 minutes, then turn out onto a wire rack and let cool completely.

4. To prepare the glaze, place the apricots, orange juice and zest, cinnamon stick, and honey in a small saucepan over medium heat and bring to a boil. Decrease the temperature and gently simmer until the liquid is syrupy. 5–10 minutes.

5, Pierce holes in the cake with a skewer and pour the hot syrup over the top. Leave the apricots and cinnamon on top to decorate.

◁ **Apricot and Almond Cake**

Almond Torte

Serve this cake with a raspberry coulis. To prepare the coulis, purée 1 pound (500 g) of fresh raspberries with ½ cup (100 g) of sugar and 2 tablespoons of freshly squeezed lemon juice.

Serves: 8–10 · Prep: 25 min. · Cooking: 45–55 min. · Level: 1

- 1⅓ cups (200 g) all-purpose (plain) flour
- 1½ teaspoons baking powder
- ¼ teaspoon salt
- ½ cup (125 g) butter, softened
- ¾ cup (150 g) sugar
- 1 package (7 oz/200 g) almond paste, softened
- 4 large eggs
- ½ teaspoon almond extract (essence)
- 1 cup (250 ml) heavy (double) cream
- 2 tablespoons confectioners' (icing) sugar

1. Preheat the oven to 350°F (180°C/gas 4). Lightly grease a 9-inch (23-cm) round cake pan. Line with parchment paper.

2. Mix the flour, baking powder, and salt in a large bowl. Beat the butter, sugar, and almond paste in a large bowl with an electric mixer at medium speed until creamy. Add the eggs one at a time, beating until just blended after each addition. With mixer at low speed, gradually beat in the dry ingredients and almond extract.

3. Spoon the batter into the prepared pan. Bake for 45–55 minutes, or until a toothpick inserted into the center comes out clean. Cool the cake in the pan for 15 minutes. Turn out onto a rack. Carefully remove the paper and let cool completely.

4. With mixer at high speed, beat the cream and confectioners' sugar in a medium bowl until thickened. Spoon the cream over the top of the cake.

Oat, Apple, and Pecan Cake

This breakfast cake combines the nutritional value of oats, apples, and nuts with the delicious sweetness of its cinnamon glaze.

Serves: 8–10 · Prep: 20 min. · Cooking: 50–60 min. · Level: 1

1½	cups (375 ml) water
1	cup (125 g) quick-cooking oats
1²⁄₃	cups (250 g) all-purpose (plain) flour
1	teaspoon baking powder
1	teaspoon baking soda (bicarbonate of soda)
1	teaspoon ground cinnamon
⅓	cup (80 g) butter, softened
⅔	cup (140 g) sugar
2	large eggs
2	medium tart cooking apples, such as Granny Smith, peeled, cored, and grated
¾	cup (90 g) pecans, coarsely chopped

CINNAMON FROSTING

1¼	cups (180 g) confectioners' (icing) sugar
1½	teaspoons ground cinnamon
2	tablespoons milk
	Pecan halves, to decorate

1. Preheat the oven to 350 F (180 C/gas 4). Lightly grease a 9-inch (23 cm) round springform cake pan and line with parchment paper.

2. To prepare the cake, place the water and oats in a small saucepan over medium heat and bring to the boil. Remove from the heat and set aside to cool.

3. Combine the flour, baking powder, baking soda, and cinnamon in a medium bowl. Beat the butter and sugar in a medium bowl with an electric mixer until pale and creamy. Add the eggs one at a time, beating until just blended after each addition. With mixer on low, gradually beat in the mixed dry ingredients. Stir the apple and pecans in by hand. Spoon the batter into the prepared pan.

4. Bake for 30-40 minutes, until golden brown and a skewer comes out clean when tested. Leave to cool in the pan for 10 minutes, then turn out onto a wire rack and let cool completely.

5. To prepare the frosting, mix the confectioners' sugar and cinnamon in a small bowl. Add the milk and stir until smooth. Spread over the cake and decorate with pecan halves.

Dutch Apple Breakfast Cake

Apple sauce is a purée made from cooked apples. It is widely available in cans or bottles in supermarkets. For a special touch, make homemade apple sauce by stewing cooking apples (such as Gravensteins or Granny Smiths) with a small amount of sugar and lemon juice until smooth. Chop in a food processor or mash with a fork.

Serves: 10–12 · Prep: 25 min. · Cooking: 50–60 min. · Level: 1

TOPPING

⅔	cup (100 g) all-purpose (plain) flour
½	cup (100 g) firmly packed brown sugar
2	teaspoons ground cinnamon
1	teaspoon ground nutmeg
⅓	cup (90 g) cold butter, cut up
½	cup (60 g) walnuts, coarsely chopped

CAKE

3	cups (450 g) all-purpose (plain) flour
2	teaspoons baking powder
1	teaspoon baking soda (bicarbonate of soda)
½	teaspoon salt
½	cup (125 g) butter, softened
1	cup (200 g) sugar
2	teaspoons vanilla extract (essence)
3	large eggs
1	cup (250 ml) sour cream
½	cup (60 g) raisins
2½	cups (500 g) apple sauce

1. Preheat the oven to 350 F (180 C/gas 4). Lightly grease and flour a 13 x 9-inch (33 x 23-cm) baking pan.

2. To prepare the topping, stir the flour, brown sugar, cinnamon, and nutmeg in a medium bowl. Use a pastry blender to cut in the butter until the mixture resembles fine crumbs. Stir in the walnuts.

3. To prepare the cake, combine the flour, baking powder, baking soda, and salt in a large bowl. Beat the butter, sugar, and vanilla in a large bowl with an electric mixer at medium speed until creamy. Add the eggs one at a time, until just blended after each addition. With mixer at low speed, gradually beat in the dry ingredients, alternating with the sour cream and raisins.

4. Spoon the batter into the prepared pan. Top with the apple sauce and sprinkle with the topping. Bake for 50-60 minutes, or until golden brown, and a toothpick inserted into the center comes out clean. Cool the cake completely in the pan. Serve warm.

Oat, Apple, and Pecan Cake ▷

Orange Spiced Loaf

This spicy loaf can be prepared and baked in the mornings in less than an hour. Your family and friends will be delighted to eat a slice with their morning tea or coffee.

Serves: 6–8 · Prep: 20 min. · Cooking: 35–45 min. · Level: 1

1¼ cups (180 g) all-purpose (plain) flours flour
½ cup (75 g) finely ground hazelnuts
2 teaspoons ground cardamom
1½ teaspoons baking powder
1 teaspoon ground cinnamon
1 teaspoon ground nutmeg
½ teaspoon ground cloves
½ teaspoon ground ginger
½ teaspoon baking soda (bicarbonate of soda)
½ cup (125 g) butter, softened
⅔ cup (140 g) firmly packed brown sugar
2 teaspoons finely grated orange zest
2 large eggs, lightly beaten
½ cup (125 g) sour cream
¼ cup (60 ml) milk
⅓ cup (100 g) orange marmalade

1. Preheat the oven to 325°F (170°C/gas 3). Lightly grease a 9 x 5-inch (23 x 13-cm) loaf pan and line the base with parchment paper.

2. Combine the flour, ground hazelnuts, cardamom, baking powder, cinnamon, nutmeg, cloves, ginger, and baking soda in a medium bowl. Beat the butter, sugar, and orange zest in a medium bowl with an electric mixer on medium-high speed until pale and creamy. Add the eggs one at a time, beating until just combined after each addition. With mixer on low, beat in the mixed dry ingredients.

3. Spoon the batter into the prepared pan. Bake for 1 hour, until golden brown and a skewer comes out clean when tested. Leave to cool in the pan for 10 minutes, then turn out onto a wire rack and let cool completely.

4. Warm the marmalade in a small saucepan over low heat and brush on top of the cake.

Cinnamon Banana Loaf

Here is another quick loaf that can be made in the mornings. You don't need to wait until this loaf is completely cold before frosting—the frosting will melt into the warm cake creating a wonderful flavor and texture all of its own.

Serves: 6–8 · Prep: 15 min. · Cooking: 35–45 min. · Level: 1

LOAF
1½ cups (225 g) all-purpose flour
¾ cup (150 g) sugar
1½ teaspoons baking powder
1 teaspoon ground cinnamon
¼ teaspoon salt
2 large very ripe bananas, peeled and sliced
2 large eggs, at room temperature
⅔ cup (180 g) butter, melted

VANILLA FROSTING
2 cups (300 g) confectioners' (icing) sugar
2 tablespoons butter, cut up
1 teaspoon vanilla extract (essence)
2–3 tablespoons boiling water

1. Preheat the oven to 350°F (180°C/gas 4). Lightly grease and flour an 8½ x 4½-inch (22 x 10-cm) loaf pan.

2. To prepare the loaf, combine the flour, sugar, baking powder, cinnamon, and salt in a large bowl. Process the bananas and eggs in a food processor until frothy. Stir the banana mixture and butter into the flour mixture until just blended.

3. Spoon the batter into the prepared pan. Bake for 35–45 minutes, or until a toothpick inserted into the center comes out clean. Cool the loaf in the pan for 10 minutes. Turn out onto a rack to cool.

4. To prepare the frosting, combine the confectioner's sugar, butter, and vanilla extract in a small bowl. Add enough water to obtain a smooth frosting and stir until smooth. Drizzle over the loaf.

◁ **Orange Spiced Loaf**

Rise and Shine Breakfast Cake

Use very ripe, peeled fresh peaches during the summer when they are in season. During the rest of the year use well-drained canned peaches.

Serves: 8-10 · Prep: 25 min. · Cooking: 55-60 min. · Level: 1

CAKE

- 1 cup (150 g) whole-wheat (wholemeal) flour
- 1 cup (150 g) all-purpose (plain) flour
- 1 teaspoon baking powder
- ½ teaspoon baking soda (bicarbonate of soda)
- 1 teaspoon ground cinnamon
- 1 teaspoon ground ginger
- ¼ teaspoon salt
- ½ cup (125 g) butter, softened
- ¾ cup (150 g) firmly packed brown sugar
- 1 tablespoon finely grated orange zest
- 2 large eggs
- 1 cup (250 g) plain yogurt
- 1 tablespoon freshly squeezed orange juice
- 2 cups chopped fresh peaches, nectarines, or apricots

TOPPING

- ⅓ cup (50 g) all-purpose (plain) flour
- ¼ cup (50 g) firmly packed brown sugar
- 2 tablespoons butter, melted
- 1 tablespoon wheat germ
- 1 tablespoon grated orange zest
- 1 teaspoon ground cinnamon
- 1 teaspoon ground ginger

1. Preheat the oven to 350°F (180°C/gas 4). Lightly grease and flour a 10-inch (25-cm) tube pan.

2. To prepare the cake, combine both flours, baking powder, baking soda, cinnamon, ginger, and salt in a large bowl. Beat the butter, brown sugar, and orange zest in a large bowl with an electric mixer at medium speed until creamy. Add the eggs one at a time, beating until just blended after each addition. With mixer on low, beat in the dry ingredients, yogurt, and orange juice. Stir in the fruit. Spoon the batter into the prepared pan.

3. To prepare the topping, stir all the ingredients in a medium bowl until crumbly. Sprinkle over the batter. Bake for 55-60 minutes, or until a toothpick inserted into the center comes out clean. Cool the cake in the pan on a rack. Serve warm.

Frosted Chocolate Banana Cake

This is a fairly rich cake for the early morning. It's a great way to treat a chocoholic family member or friend on their birthday!

Serves: 8-10: · Prep: 30 min. · Cooking: 35-40 min. · Level: 1

CAKE

- 2 cups (300 g) all-purpose (plain) flour
- ½ cup (75 g) unsweetened cocoa powder
- 1½ teaspoons baking powder
- ½ teaspoon baking soda (bicarbonate of soda)
- ¼ teaspoon salt
- 1 cup (200 g) sugar
- 2 large eggs
- ¾ cup (180 ml) hot water
- 1 cup (250 g) mashed very ripe bananas (about 3 large bananas)
- 1½ teaspoons vanilla extract (essence)

CREAM CHEESE FROSTING

- 3 ounces (90 g) cream cheese, softened
- ¼ cup (60 g) butter, softened
- 1 teaspoon vanilla extract (essence)
- 2 cups (300 g) confectioners' (icing) sugar
- ¼ cup (30 g) unsweetened cocoa powder

1. Preheat the oven to 350°F (180°C/gas 4). Lightly grease a 9-inch (23-cm) square baking pan. Line with parchment paper.

2. Mix the flour, cocoa, baking powder, baking soda, and salt in a large bowl. Stir in the sugar. Beat in the eggs, water, banana, and vanilla. Spoon the batter into the prepared pan.

3. Bake for 35-40 minutes, or until a toothpick inserted into the center comes out clean. Cool the cake in the pan for 10 minutes. Turn out onto a rack. Carefully remove the paper and let cool completely.

4. To prepare the frosting, beat the cream cheese, butter, and vanilla in a large bowl with an electric mixer at medium speed until creamy. With mixer at low speed, beat in the confectioners' sugar and cocoa until smooth. Spread the cake with the frosting.

Rise and Shine Breakfast Cake ▷

Banana and Pistachio Cake

The rosewater and cinnamon in the frosting add a slightly exotic flavor to this delicious cake.

Serves: 8–10 · Prep: 25 min. · Cooking: 55–65 min. · Level: 1

CAKE

2	cups (300 g) all-purpose (plain) flour
2	teaspoons baking powder
1	teaspoon ground cinnamon
½	teaspoon baking soda (bicarbonate of soda)
¾	cup (150 g) firmly packed brown sugar
2	large ripe bananas, mashed
2	large eggs, lightly beaten
⅓	cup (80 ml) vegetable oil
½	cup (125 g) sour cream
1	cup (150 g) pistachios, coarsely chopped

ROSEWATER FROSTING

1¼	cups (180 g) confectioners' (icing) sugar
1	tablespoon rosewater
1½	tablespoons water
½	teaspoon ground cinnamon, to dust

1. Preheat the oven to 350 F (180 C/gas 4). Lightly grease an 8-inch (20 cm) square cake pan and line the base and sides with parchment paper.

2. To prepare the cake, combine the flour, baking powder, cinnamon, and baking soda in a medium bowl. Add the brown sugar and stir to combine. Combine the banana, eggs, oil, and sour cream in a small bowl. Add to the dry ingredients with the pistachios and stir until just combined. Spoon the batter into the prepared pan.

3. Bake for 30–35 minutes, until golden brown and a skewer comes out clean when tested. Leave to cool in the pan for 10 minutes, then turn out onto and wire rack and let cool completely.

4. To prepare the frosting, sift the confectioners' sugar into a small bowl, add the rosewater and water and stir until smooth. Spread the frosting over the cake.

Moist Yogurt Coffee Cake

An excellent cake with a beautiful flavor and texture, and a pretty swirl of crunch throughout.

Serves: 8–10 · Prep: 25 min. · Cooking: 55–65 min. · Level: 1

TOPPING

1	cup (120 g) pecans, coarsely chopped
½	cup (100 g) sugar
½	cup (75 g) all-purpose (plain) flour
¼	cup (60 g) butter, melted
2	teaspoons ground cinnamon
1	teaspoon vanilla extract (essence)

CAKE

2	cups (300 g) all-purpose (plain) flour
2	teaspoons baking powder
¼	teaspoon salt
½	cup (125 g) butter, softened
1	cup (200 g) sugar
2	teaspoons vanilla extract (essence)
2	large eggs
1	cup (250 ml) plain yogurt

1. Preheat the oven to 350°F (180°C/gas 4). Lightly grease and flour a 9-inch (23-cm) square baking pan.

2. To prepare the topping, stir the pecans, sugar, flour, butter, cinnamon, and vanilla in a medium bowl.

3. To prepare the cake, combine the flour, baking powder, and salt in a medium bowl. Beat the butter, sugar, and vanilla in a large bowl with an electric mixer on medium speed until creamy. Add the eggs one at a time, until just blended after each addition. With mixer on low speed, beat in the dry ingredients, alternating with the yogurt.

4. Spoon half the batter into the prepared pan. Sprinkle with half the topping. Spoon the remaining batter over the top and sprinkle with the remaining topping.

5. Bake for 55–65 minutes, or until springy to the touch and a toothpick inserted into the center comes out clean. Cool the cake in the pan on a rack. Serve warm or at room temperature.

◄ **Banana and Pistachio Cake**

Banana and Passion Fruit Cake

The tropical flavors of banana and passion fruit make this cake a special treat for brunch or breakfast any day of the week!

Serves: 8–10 · Prep: 30 min. · Cooking: 35–40 min. · Level: 1

CAKE
- ½ cup (125 g) butter, softened
- 1 cup (200 g) sugar
- 3 large eggs, lightly beaten
- 1 cup (150 g) all-purpose (plain) flour
- 1 teaspoon baking powder
- ½ cup (125 g) sour cream
- 2 large bananas, mashed
- ¼ cup (30 g) shredded (desiccated) coconut

PASSION FRUIT FROSTING
- 3 large passion fruit, halved and pulp scooped out
- 1 cup (150 g) confectioners' (icing) sugar
- ½ cup (125 g) butter, softened

1. Preheat the oven to 325°F (170°C/gas 3). Lightly grease a 9-inch (23 cm) springform cake pan and line with parchment paper.

2. To prepare the cake, beat the butter and sugar in a medium bowl with an electric mixer on medium-high speed until pale and creamy. Add the eggs one at a time, beating until just blended after each addition. Combine the flour and baking powder in a small bowl. With mixer on low speed, gradually beat in the flour and sour cream. Stir the banana and coconut in by hand. Spoon the batter into the prepared pan.

3. Bake for 40–50 minutes, until golden brown and firm to the touch. Leave to cool in the pan for 10 minutes, then turn out onto a wire rack and let cool completely.

4. To prepare the frosting, combine the confectioners' sugar and butter in a medium bowl and beat until smooth and creamy. Strain the passion fruit pulp through a fine mesh sieve into the bowl (reserving some of the seeds) and stir to combine. Spread over the cooled cake and scatter a few of the reserved seeds on top.

Frosted Orange Cake

This cake is gluten-free and perfect for Sunday brunch.

Serves: 10–12 · Prep 1 hr. · Cooking: 35–40 min. · Level: 2

CAKE
- 1 cup (150 g) brown rice flour
- ½ cup (75 g) white rice flour
- ½ cup (75 g) tapioca starch (flour)
- ½ cup (75 g) potato starch
- ½ teaspoon salt
- 1 tablespoon baking powder
- 1 teaspoon xanthan gum
- 1 cup (250 ml) milk
- 1 cup (250 ml) canola oil
- 1 teaspoon vanilla extract (essence)
- 1 tablespoon finely grated orange zest
- 2 cups (400 g) sugar
- 4 large eggs
- ½ cup (150 g) orange marmalade

ORANGE FROSTING:
- ⅓ cup (90 g) butter, softened
- 2 cups (300 g) confectioners' (icing) sugar
- 2 tablespoons freshly squeezed orange juice
- 2 teaspoons finely grated orange zest

1. Preheat the oven to 375°F (190°C/gas 5). Oil two 9-inch (23-cm) round cake pans. Line with parchment paper. Oil the paper.

2. To prepare the cake, combine both rice flours, tapioca starch, potato starch, salt, baking powder, and xanthan gum in a large bowl. Stir the milk, canola oil, vanilla, and zest in another bowl. Beat the sugar and eggs in a large bowl with an electric mixer at medium speed until combined. With mixer on low, add the flour and milk mixtures. Spoon into the prepared cake pans.

3. Bake for 35–40 minutes, until a skewer inserted into the center comes out clean. Cool on racks 10 minutes. Peel off the paper let cool.

4. To prepare the frosting, beat the butter with the confectioners' sugar, orange juice, and zest until creamy and smooth. Spread one cake with the marmalade. Top with the remaining cake. Frost the top and sides of the cake with the frosting.

Banana and Passion Fruit Cake ▷

Apple Breakfast Cake

If liked, prepare the dough for this hearty breakfast cake the night before. Leave it in a bowl under a clean kitchen towel in a warm place and bake first thing in the morning.

Serves: 10–12 · Prep: 1 hr. + 2 hr. to rise · Cooking: 25–30 min. · Level: 2

CAKE

1	(¼-ounce/7-g) package active dry yeast or ½ ounce (15 g) compressed fresh yeast
⅓	cup (90 ml) honey
1	cup (250 ml) lukewarm water
3	cups (450 g) whole-wheat (wholemeal) flour
¼	teaspoon salt
¾	cup (90 g) raisins
½	cup pecans, coarsely chopped
1½	teaspoons ground cinnamon

TOPPING

½	cup (75 g) whole-wheat (wholemeal) flour
½	teaspoon ground cinnamon
¼	cup (60 ml) honey
¼	cup (50 g) firmly packed dark brown sugar
2	tablespoons coarsely chopped pecans
2	large apples, cored, peeled, and thinly sliced

1. Set out a 13 x 9-inch (33 x 23-cm) baking pan. Stir the yeast, honey, and water in a small bowl. Set aside until foamy, about 10 minutes. Combine 1½· cups (225 g) of flour and the salt in a large bowl. Stir in the yeast mixture. Cover with a clean kitchen towel and let rise in a warm place for 30 minutes.

2. Soak the raisins in enough warm water to cover for 10 minutes. Drain well and pat dry with paper towels.

3. Stir the batter and add the raisins, pecans, and cinnamon. Gradually stir in the remaining flour. Knead until smooth. Shape into a ball and place in a clean bowl. Cover with a kitchen towel and let rise in a warm place until doubled in bulk, about 1 hour. Punch down the dough. Place in the pan, spreading it out.

4. To prepare the topping, stir the flour, cinnamon, honey, brown sugar, and pecans in a medium bowl. Arrange the apple slices on top of the dough. Sprinkle with the pecan mixture. Cover and let rise in a warm place for 30 minutes.

5. Preheat the oven to 350°F (180°C/gas 4). Bake for 25–30 minutes, or until golden brown. Serve warm.

PREPARING YEAST STEP-BY-STEP

Yeast cakes fall somewhere between cake and bread and are great in the mornings. For best results use either active dry yeast or very fresh compressed yeast. Yeast doughs are not hard to prepare; they just require a little time and practise.

1 Put the fresh or active dry yeast in a small bowl. Add the sugar and a little warm water fromm the recipe. Stir until the yeast has dissolved. Set aside until foamy, about 10 minutes.

2 Place the flour and salt in a bowl. Pour in the yeast mixture, remaining water, and any other ingredients in the recipe. Use a wooden spoon to stir until the flour has been absorbed.

3 The dough will be a rough and shaggy ball in the bowl. Sprinkle a work surface with flour.

4 Place the dough on the work surface. Curl your fingers around it and press to form a compact ball. Knead gently for 8–10 minutes. When ready, the dough will be smooth and elastic, show definite air bubbles beneath the surface, and will spring back if you flatten it with your palm.

5 Place in an oiled bowl, cover with a cloth and let rise. To test if ready, poke your finger gently into the dough; if the impression remains, it is ready.

Babkas with Streusel Topping

A babka, or bobka, is a sweet spongy yeast cake from Russia and eastern Europe. Traditionally, it was baked and served on Easter Sunday.

Serves: 10–12 · Prep: 35 min. + 2 hr. to rise · Cooking: 30–40 min. · Level: 3

CAKE

- 2 (¼-ounce/7-g) packages active dry yeast or 1 ounce (30 g) compressed fresh yeast
- ½ cup (125 ml) lukewarm water
- ⅓ cup (120 g) sugar
- ⅔ cup (180 ml) lukewarm milk
- ½ teaspoon salt
- 1 teaspoon vanilla extract (essence)
- ⅓ cup (90 g) butter, softened
- About 4 cups (600 g) all-purpose (plain) flour
- 3 large eggs

CHOCOLATE FILLING

- ⅓ cup (50 g) unsweetened cocoa powder
- ¾ cup (150 g) sugar
- 1 cup (120 g) walnuts, coarsely chopped

STREUSEL TOPPING

- ¾ cup (150 g) firmly packed brown sugar
- ½ cup (75 g) all-purpose (plain) flour
- 1 teaspoon ground cinnamon
- ½ teaspoon ground nutmeg
- ¼ cup (60 g) butter, softened

1. Preheat the oven to 350°F (180°C/gas 4). Lightly grease and flour two 5 x 9-inch (23 x 13-cm) loaf pans.

2. To prepare the cake, stir the yeast, water, and 1 teaspoon of sugar in a large bowl. Set aside until foamy, about 10 minutes. Stir in the remaining sugar, milk, salt, vanilla, and ¼ cup (60 g) of butter. Using and electric mixer with a dough hook on low speed, gradually add 2 cups (300 g) of flour, beating until smooth, about 5 minutes.

3. Separate one egg, reserving the white for the glaze. With mixer at medium speed, beat in the egg yolk and remaining eggs, one at a time, until just blended after each addition. Stir in enough of the remaining flour to make a smooth dough.

4. Transfer to a lightly floured surface and knead until smooth, adding the remaining flour if the dough is too sticky. Shape into a ball and place in a bowl. Cover with plastic wrap (cling film) and let rise in a warm place until doubled in bulk, about 1 hour.

5. To prepare the filling, stir the cocoa and sugar in a small bowl.

6. Punch the dough down. Divide it in half. Roll out each half into a 10 x 20-inch (25 x 50-cm) rectangle.

7. Melt the remaining ¼ cup (60 g) of butter and brush over the dough, leaving a ½-inch (1-cm) border around the edges. Sprinkle half of the filling and walnuts over the batter. Starting with the long side, roll each rectangle up tightly, squashing the ends to seal.

8. Fit into the prepared pans and set aside in a warm place until doubled in bulk, about 1 hour.

9. To prepare the topping, stir the brown sugar, flour, cinnamon, and nutmeg in a small bowl. Use a pastry blender to cut in the butter. Beat the reserved egg white and brush over the batter in the pans. Sprinkle with the topping.

10. Bake for 30–40 minutes, or until risen and golden brown. Cool the loaves on racks. Serve warm.

Triple Twist

This Triple Twist is somewhere between a bread and a cake. It has a lovely texture and flavor.

Serves: 12–15 · Prep: 35 min. + 3 hr. 30 min. to rise and cool · Cooking: 40–50 min. large twist; 35 min. small loaves · Level: 2

DOUGH

2	(¼-ounce/7-g) packages active dry yeast or 1 ounce (30 g) compressed fresh yeast
⅔	cup (150 ml) lukewarm milk
3	cups (500 g) all-purpose (plain) flour
⅓	cup (70 g) superfine (caster) sugar
½	teaspoon salt
⅔	cup (150 g) crème fraîche
⅓	cup (90 g) butter
1	teaspoon vanilla extract (essence)

FLAVORINGS

½	cup (100 g) raisins
¼	cup (50 g) currants or dried banana, chopped
2	tablespoons rum
3	ounces (90 g) marzipan, softened
⅔	cup (100 g) almonds, toasted and chopped
1½	ounces (40 g) dried apricots, diced
⅓	cup (40 g) pecans, toasted and chopped
2	tablespoons brown sugar
1	small egg, beaten

1. To prepare the dough, mix the yeast with the milk in a small bowl. Set aside until foamy, about 10 minute. Combine the flour, sugar, and salt in a large bowl. Add the yeast mixture, crème fraîche, butter, and vanilla. Mix with a plastic spatula, gradually working in the flour.

2. Transfer to a lightly floured work surface and knead until smooth and elastic, about 10 minutes, or beat with a dough hook until smooth and elastic, 5 minutes. Form into a ball, place in an oiled bowl, and cover. Leave to rise until doubled in bulk, about 2 hours.

3. To prepare the flavorings, soak the fruit in the rum. Cut the marzipan into small pieces and mix with the almonds. Combine the apricots, pecans, and sugar.

4. Dust the risen dough with flour, punch down, and knead briefly on a floured surface. Cut into 3 equal pieces. Flatten the dough with your hand and knead one of the flavorings into each one, dusting with a little more flour.

5. When the flavorings have been incorporated, form each piece of dough into a ball. Flour your hands and roll each one into 3 strips of even length. Braid (plait) into a loaf. (You can make 2 small loaves, in which case divide the balls into 6 strips and braid.)

6. Line a baking sheet with parchment paper and place the loaf on it. Cover with a towel and leave until doubled in bulk, 30–60 minutes.

7. Preheat the oven to 375°F (190°C/gas 5). Brush the loaf (or loaves) with egg and bake for 40–50 minutes, until golden brown. (Bake small loaves for 30–35 minutes.). Cool for 30 minutes on a rack before serving.

◁ Triple Twist

Pear Breakfast Cake

Prepare this cake in the fall when pears have just ripened on the trees and are full of flavor and nutrients

Serves: 8–10 · Prep: 1 hr. + 2 hr. to rise · Cooking: 25–30 min. · Level: 2

CAKE

2	(¼-ounce/7-g) packages active dry yeast or 1 ounce (30 g) compressed fresh yeast
⅓	cup (90 ml) honey
1	cup (250 ml) lukewarm water
3	cups (450 g) whole-wheat (wholemeal) flour
¼	teaspoon salt
¾	cup (100 g) raisins (soaked in warm water for 10 minutes, drained)
½	cup (60 g) walnuts, coarsely chopped
1½	teaspoons ground cinnamon

TOPPING

½	cup (75 g) whole-wheat (wholemeal) flour
½	teaspoon ground cinnamon
¼	cup (60 g) honey
¼	cup (50 g) firmly packed dark brown sugar
2	tablespoons walnuts, coarsely chopped
2	large pears, peeled, cored, and thinly sliced

1. Set out a 13 x 9-inch (33 x 23-cm) baking pan.

2. To prepare the cake, stir the yeast, honey, and water in a small bowl. Set aside until foamy, about 10 minutes. Combine 1½ cups (225 g) of flour and salt in a large bowl. Stir in the yeast mixture. Cover with a kitchen towel and let rise in a warm place for 30 minutes.

3. Stir the raisins, walnuts, and cinnamon into the batter. Gradually stir in the remaining flour until smooth. Transfer to a lightly floured work surface and knead until smooth and elastic, about 10 minutes, or beat with a dough hook until smooth and elastic, 5 minutes. Shape into a ball and place in a clean bowl. Cover with a kitchen towel and let rise in a warm place until doubled in bulk, about 1 hour. Place in the pan, spreading it out. Cover and let rise for 15 minutes more.

4. To prepare the topping, stir the flour, cinnamon, honey, brown sugar, and walnuts in a medium bowl. Arrange the pear slices on top of the dough. Sprinkle with the topping mixture. Cover and let rise in a warm place for 30 minutes.

5. Preheat the oven to 350°F (180°C/gas 4). Bake for 25–30 minutes, or until golden brown. Serve warm.

Trentino Cake

This cake comes from the Trentino region, in northeastern Italy. It take a little while to make but is well worth the effort.

Serves: 10–12 · Prep: 1 hr. + 4 hr. to rise · Cooking: 60–70 min. · Level: 3

2	(¼-ounce/7-g) packages active dry yeast or 1 ounce (30 g) compressed fresh yeast
1	cup (250 ml) lukewarm milk
4	cups (600 g) all-purpose (plain) flour
½	cup (125 g) butter, softened
3	large egg yolks + 1 large egg, lightly beaten
1	cup (200 g) superfine (caster) sugar
¼	teaspoon salt
1	cup (180 g) golden raisins (sultanas)
1½	cups (250 g) candied (glacé) lemon peel
1	teaspoon coriander seeds, crushed
⅔	cup (120 g) pine nuts
½	cup (125 ml) dark rum
2	tablespoons finely grated orange zest
1	cup (120 g) mixed nuts, finely chopped

1. Lightly grease a deep 10-inch (26-cm) round cake pan.

2. To prepare the cake, stir the yeast and milk in a small bowl. Set aside until foamy, about 10 minutes. Place 1½ cups (200 g) of flour in a large bowl. Mix in the yeast mixture. Cover and let rest until doubled in bulk, about 1 hour. Stir 1¼ cups (175 g) of flour into the batter. Knead until smooth and elastic, about 10 minutes. Cover and let rise until doubled in bulk, about 1 hour.

3. Beat the butter, the egg yolks, and sugar with an electric mixer at medium speed until creamy. Add to the dough with the remaining flour and salt and knead on a lightly floured work surface for 5 minutes. Shape into a ball. Cover and let rise for 1 hour, or until doubled in bulk.

4. Mix the golden raisins, lemon peel, coriander seeds, pine nuts, rum, and orange zest in a large bowl. Cover and soak for 15 minutes. Knead the fruit mixture into the dough until well blended. Shape into a long rope and join the two ends to form a ring. Transfer to the prepared pan, cover with a kitchen towel, and let rise for 1 hour.

5. Preheat the oven to 375°F (190°C/gas 5). Brush with the beaten egg and sprinkle with the nuts. Bake for 60–70 minutes, or until golden. Cool completely in the pan.

Sweet Poppy Loaf

Serve this tasty loaf spread with butter while still warm.

Serves: 8–10 · Prep: 30 min. + 2 hr. 30 min. to rise · Cooking: 35–45 min. Level: 2

1	(¼-ounce/7-g) package active dry yeast or ½ ounce (15 g) compressed fresh yeast
¾	cup (180 ml) lukewarm milk
3²⁄₃	cups (550 g) all-purpose (plain) flour
½	cup (100 g) sugar
½	teaspoon salt
3	large egg yolks + 1 large egg
¼	cup (60 ml) vegetable oil
1	teaspoon anise extract (essence)
1	cup (180 g) raisins
1	cup (250 ml) anisette
½	cup (90 g) poppy seeds

1. Lightly grease and flour a large baking sheet. Stir the yeast and milk in a small bowl. Set aside until foamy, about 10 minutes.

2. Place the flour, sugar, and salt in a large bowl and make a well in the center. Stir in the yeast mixture, egg yolks, oil, and anise extract. Transfer to a lightly floured work surface and knead by hand until smooth and elastic, about 10 minutes, or beat with a dough hook until smooth and elastic, 5 minutes. Cover with a clean kitchen towel and let rise in a warm place until doubled in bulk, about 1 hour.

3. Soak the raisins in the anisette for 15 minutes. Punch the dough down and roll out on a lightly floured work surface to about ¼-inch (5-mm) thick. Drain the raisins. Do not squeeze out all the liqueur; it will add to the flavor of the bread. Sprinkle the raisins over the dough and roll it up. Beat the remaining egg and brush it over the surface of the rolled dough. Sprinkle with the poppy seeds. Place the roll on the baking sheet. Cover with a clean kitchen towel and set aside in a warm place to rise for about 90 minutes.

4. Preheat the oven to 350°F (180°C/gas 4). Bake for 35–45 minutes, or until golden brown. Cool the loaf on a rack. Serve warm or at room temperature.

Candied Fruit and Pine Nut Buns

Serve these buns warm at breakfast with plenty of butter to spread.

Serves: 12 · Prep: 30 min. + 4 hr. to rise · Cooking: 12–15 min. · Level: 2

1	(¼-ounce/7-g) package active dry yeast or ½ ounce (15 g) compressed fresh yeast
¾	cup (180 ml) lukewarm water
¼	cup (50 g) sugar
2	cups (300 g) all-purpose (plain) flour
¼	teaspoon salt
2	tablespoons vegetable oil
½	cup (90 g) golden raisins (sultanas), plumped in warm water for 15 minutes, well drained
3	tablespoons pine nuts
2	tablespoons chopped mixed candied (glacé) orange and lemon peel

1. Oil a large baking sheet. Stir the yeast, ¼ cup (60 ml) of water, and 1 teaspoon of sugar in a small bowl. Set aside until foamy, about 10 minutes.

2. Place 1²⁄₃ cups (250 g) of flour and the salt in a large bowl and make a well in the center. Stir in the yeast mixture, remaining ½ cup (125 ml) of water, remaining sugar, and oil. Cover with a clean kitchen towel and let rise in a warm place until doubled in bulk, about 2 hours.

3. Transfer the dough to a lightly floured work surface. Knead in the remaining ⅓ cup (50 g) of flour, raisins, pine nuts, and candied fruit. Knead thoroughly until smooth and elastic.

4. Roll the dough into a fat sausage and cut into 12 even pieces. Shape each one into a smooth ball. Arrange the dough balls, well spaced, on the prepared baking sheet. Cover with a kitchen towel and let rise in a warm place until doubled in bulk, about 2 hours.

5. Preheat the oven to 375°F (190°C/gas 5). Bake for 12–15 minutes, or until golden. Transfer to racks to cool. Serve warm or at room temperature.

Swedish Breakfast Cake

Despite its name, this cake belongs to an Austrian and German tradition.
Serve warm for a special family breakfast or brunch.

Serves: 6–8 · Prep: 25 min. · Cooking: 25 min. · Level 1

2	tablespoons fine dry bread crumbs
1	(¼-ounce/7-g) package active dry yeast or ½ ounce (15 g) compressed fresh yeast
½	cup (125 ml) lukewarm milk
½	cup (100 g) sugar
1²⁄₃	cups (250 g) all-purpose (plain) flour
½	teaspoon vanilla extract (essence)
¼	teaspoon salt
4	large egg yolks + 1 large egg, lightly beaten
½	cup (125 g) butter, melted
1	cup (180 g) golden raisins (sultanas)

1. Lightly grease a 10-inch (26-cm) springform pan. Sprinkle with the bread crumbs.

2. To prepare the cake, stir the yeast, milk, and 1 teaspoon sugar in a small bowl. Set aside until foamy, about 10 minutes.

3. Combine the flour, 1 tablespoon sugar, vanilla, and salt in a large bowl. Add the egg yolks. Stir in the yeast mixture until a smooth dough is formed. Transfer to a lightly floured work surface and knead by hand until smooth and elastic, about 10 minutes, or beat with a dough hook until smooth and elastic, about 5 minutes.

4. Break off a piece of dough slightly larger than an egg and knead for a few seconds. Knead the remaining dough for a few seconds. Shape each piece of dough into a ball and place in two separate bowls. Cover with a clean kitchen towel and let rise in a warm place until doubled in bulk, about 30 minutes.

5. Roll out the smaller ball of dough on a lightly floured work surface to ⅛ inch (3 mm) thick. Fit the dough into the prepared pan.

6. Roll out the larger ball of dough into a 16 x 7-inch (40 x 18-cm) rectangle. Brush with the melted butter and sprinkle with the remaining sugar and raisins. From a long side, roll up the dough jelly-roll fashion. Cut into 1½-inch (4-cm) thick slices.

7. Arrange the slices evenly on the dough base. Cover with a kitchen towel and let rest in a warm place until the slices have expanded to fill the pan, about 1 hour.

8. Preheat the oven to 350°F (180°C gas 4). Brush the dough with the beaten egg.

9. Bake for 30–35 minutes, or until golden brown. Cool the cake in the pan for 10 minutes. Loosen and remove the pan sides and bottom and let cool completely.

Swedish Breakfast Cake ▷

Basic Brioche

Brioche is a buttery French bread with a soft, cake-like texture. It is baked in a deep, round fluted mold. The traditional Parisian brioche is made by placing a small ball of dough on top of a large one.

Serves: 8–10 · Prep: 30 min. + 2 hr. to rise · Cooking: 15–20 min. · Level: 2

2	(¼-ounce/7-g) packages active dry yeast or 1 ounce (30 g) compressed fresh yeast
2	tablespoons lukewarm water
2	large eggs
1½	cups (225 g) bread flour
½	teaspoon salt
1	tablespoon superfine (caster) sugar
¼	cup (60 g) butter, melted

1. Butter a 2-quart (2-liter) brioche mold.

2. Stir the yeast and water in a small bowl. Set aside until foamy, about 10 minutes.

3. Combine the flour and salt in a large bowl. Stir in the sugar. Use your fingers to rub in the butter. Knead until a smooth dough is formed. Cover with a clean kitchen towel and let rise in a warm place until doubled in bulk, about 1 hour.

4. Break off a small ball of dough. Set aside. Punch down the larger piece of dough, transfer to the prepared pan, and let rise until doubled in bulk, about 40 minutes.

5. Make a hole in the center of the dough and press in the small ball of dough. Cover with a kitchen towel and let rise in a warm place until the dough has risen just above the top of the mold, about 30 minutes.

6. Preheat the oven to 400°F (200°C/gas 6). Bake for 15–20 minutes, or until well risen and golden brown. Cool the brioche in the pan for 15 minutes. Turn out onto a rack to cool completely.

Filled Strawberry Brioche

This rich filled brioche is perfect for brunch and it also makes a great dessert. If liked, replace the strawberries with the same quantity of raspberries or fill with one recipe of Chantilly Cream (see page 275) instead of Bavarian Cream.

Serves: 8–10 · Prep: 45 min. · Cooking: 40–50 min. · Level: 2

1	recipe Basic Brioche (see recipe, left)
1	large egg, lightly beaten
3	cups (450 g) fresh strawberries, hulled
⅓	cup (50 g) confectioners' (icing) sugar
2	tablespoons fresh lemon juice
½	cup (125 ml) amaretto
1	recipe Bavarian Cream (seepage 275)

1. Prepare the brioche and Bavarian Cream

2. Set aside 6 perfect strawberries for decoration and slice the remainder. Mix the strawberries, confectioners' sugar, lemon juice, and amaretto in a large bowl.

3. Fold the strawberries and their juice into the Bavarian Cream. Cut the top off the brioche and hollow out the inside. (These can be toasted and served separately.) Fill with the cream. Decorate with the reserved strawberries and replace the top.

Filled Strawberry Brioche ▷

TEA AND COFFEE CAKES

In this chapter we have selected 40 scrumptious cakes that can be served with a reviving cup of coffee or tea throughout the day. Many are also suitable for family desserts and celebrations. To get you started, we have included a feature panel with step-by-step instructions for making basic butter cake. They will be useful for most of the recipes in this chapter, so we suggest you look at them first.

◁ Caramel Layer Cake (see page 104)

Basic Butter Cake

A basic butter cake has a moist, sweet crumb and is very versatile. You can flavor the batter with extracts and aromas, slice the cooked cake and fill it with cream, preserves, or fruit, glaze or frost it, or simply enjoy a plain slice with a cup of tea of coffee. They are not hard to make; here is our favorite, never-fail recipe.

Serves: 10–12 · Prep: 15 min. · Cooking: 45–55 min. · Level: 1

3	cups (450 g) all-purpose (plain) flour
1	tablespoon baking powder
½	teaspoon salt
1	cup (250 g) butter, softened
2	cups (400 g) sugar
2	teaspoons vanilla extract (essence)
4	large eggs, separated
1	cup (250 ml) milk

1. Preheat the oven to 350°F (180°C/gas 4). Line two 8- or 9-inch (20- or 23-cm) round cake pans with parchment paper. Butter the paper.

2. Combine the flour, baking powder, and salt in a large bowl. Beat the butter, sugar, and vanilla in a large bowl with an electric mixer at medium speed until creamy. Add the egg yolks one at a time, beating until just blended after each addition. With mixer at low speed, gradually beat in the mixed dry ingredients, alternating with the milk.

3. In another bowl, using a clean beater, beat the egg whites until stiff but not dry. Use a large rubber spatula to fold the into the batter. Spoon the batter into the prepared pans.

4. Bake for 45–55 minutes, or until a toothpick inserted into the center comes out clean. Cool the cake in the pan for 10 minutes. Turn out onto a rack. Carefully remove the waxed paper and let cool completely.

BASIC BUTTER CAKE STEP-BY-STEP

A well-made butter cake has a moist, fine-grained crumb and an even texture. Success depends on incorporating enough air bubbles into the batter. Begin by creaming the butter and sugar together in a large bowl. Make sure that the butter is not cold; it should be softened, not straight from the refrigerator. The eggs and milk (or other liquid) should also be at room temperature. Sometimes the eggs are added whole, other times the white are beaten separately and folded in at the end. Folding is not stirring; you should lift the batter gently upward and fold it over the whites so that the mixture does not deflate. Repeat until just combined.

1 Beat the softened butter and sugar in a large bowl with a mixer on medium speed until pale and creamy. Add the eggs (or egg yolks) one at a time, beating until just combined. If the batter begins to curdle as you add the eggs, add them more slowly and beat a little faster until smooth.

2 After the eggs are in, begin gradually adding the flour and dry ingredients, alternately with the milk or other liquid. Make sure that the liquid is at room temperature. Adding these ingredients alternately helps prevent the batter from curdling and keeps it light and creamy.

3 If adding the whites separately, beat them in a large bowl until stiff peaks form. Use a large rubber spatula. Add a little of the whites at first and gently run the spatula under the batter, folding it over the top. Add the rest in 1–2 batches, folding carefully so as not to burst the air bubbles.

Frosted Peanut Butter Loaf

Slice this rich, peanut-flavored loaf thinly to serve. If liked, change the frosting to an orange flavor by replacing the lemon juice and zest with the same quantity of freshly squeezed orange juice and zest.

Serves: 8–10 · Prep: 35 min. · Cooking: 35–45 min. · Level: 2

LOAF

1	cup (250 g) unsalted butter
1½	cups (300 g) sugar
½	cup (125 g) smooth peanut butter
5	large eggs
2	cups (300 g) all-purpose (plain) flour
1	teaspoon baking soda

LEMON FROSTING

2	cups (300 g) confectioners' (icing) sugar
3	tablespoons butter
1	tablespoon freshly squeezed lemon juice
2	teaspoons finely grated lemon zest
1–2	tablespoons boiling water

1. Preheat the oven to 350°F (180°C/gas 4). Lightly grease and flour a 9 x 5-inch (23 x 13-cm) loaf pan.

2. To prepare the loaf, beat the butter, sugar, and peanut butter in a large bowl with an electric mixer on medium-high speed until pale and creamy. Add the eggs one at a time, beating until just blended after each addition. Gradually beat in the flour and baking soda.

3. Spoon the batter into the prepared pan, spreading evenly. Bake until golden brown and a toothpick inserted into the center comes out clean. Cool in the pan for 15 minutes. Turn out onto the rach and let cool completely.

4. To prepare the frosting, mix the confectioners' sugar, butter, lemon juice, and zest in the medium bowl. Stir in enough of the boiling water to obtain a smooth, thick frosting. Spread over the loaf.

Chocolate Chip Loaf

If liked, substitute the dark chocolate chips with the same quantity of white chocolate chips. You may also like to try replacing the orange juice in the frosting with the same amount of Grand Marnier.

Serves: 8–10 · Prep: 20 min. · Cooking: 45–55 min. · Level: 1

LOAF

1½	cups (225 g) all-purpose (plain) flour
1	teaspoon baking powder
½	teaspoon baking soda (bicarbonate of soda)
¼	teaspoon salt
⅓	cup (90 g) butter, softened
¾	cup (150 g) sugar
1	teaspoon vanilla extract (essence)
1	large egg
1	cup (250 ml) sour cream
¾	cup (120 g) dark chocolate chips

ORANGE FROSTING

2	cups (300 g) confectioners' (icing) sugar
3	tablespoons butter, melted
1	tablespoon finely grated orange zest
2	tablespoons freshly squeezed orange juice

1. Preheat the oven to 350°F (180°C/gas 4). Lightly grease a 9 x 5-inch (23 x 13-cm) loaf pan. Line with aluminum foil, letting the edges overhang. Butter the foil.

2. To prepare the loaf, combine the flour, baking powder, baking soda, and salt in a medium bowl. Beat the butter, sugar, and vanilla in a large bowl with an electric mixer on medium speed until pale and creamy. Add the egg, beating until just blended. With mixer on low, beat in the dry ingredients, alternating with the sour cream. Stir in the chocolate chips by. Spoon the batter into the prepared pan.

3. Bake for 45–55 minutes, or until springy to the touch and a toothpick inserted into the center comes out clean. Cool the loaf in the pan for 5 minutes. Using the foil as a lifter, remove from the pan. Carefully remove the foil and let cool completely on a rack.

4. To prepare the frosting. mix the confectioners' sugar, butter, and orange zest in a medium bowl. Add enough orange juice to make a thick, spreadable frosting. Spread over the top of the loaf.

Frosted Peanut Butter Loaf ▷

Basic Pound Cake

Pound cake is named for the fact that traditionally it was made with a pound each of butter, sugar, eggs, and flour, with spices or nuts and seeds added for flavor. Originally baking powder was not used and the leavening was provided by the eggs. Nowadays we use baking powder and sometimes baking soda for reliable, easy leavening.

Serves: 10–12 · Prep: 15 min. · Cooking: 50–60 min. · Level: 1

- 3 cups (450 g) all-purpose (plain) flour
- 1 teaspoon baking powder
- ½ teaspoon baking soda (bicarbonate of soda)
- ½ teaspoon salt
- 1 cup (250 g) butter, softened
- 2 cups (400 g) sugar
- 2 teaspoons vanilla extract (essence)
- 1 teaspoon almond extract (essence)
- 5 large eggs
- 1 cup (250 ml) milk

1. Preheat the oven to 350°F (180°C/gas 4). Lightly grease and flour a 10-inch (25-cm) tube pan.

2. Combine the flour, baking powder, baking soda, and salt in a large bowl. Beat the butter, sugar, and vanilla and almond extracts in a large bowl with an electric mixer at medium speed until pale and creamy. Add the eggs one at a time, beating until just blended after each addition. With mixer at low speed, gradually beat in the dry ingredients, alternating with the milk. Spoon the batter into the prepared pan.

3. Bake for 50–60 minutes, or until a toothpick inserted into the center comes out clean. Run a knife around the edges of the pan to loosen the cake. Cool the cake in the pan for 15 minutes. Turn out onto a rack and let cool completely.

◁ **Pineapple Pound Cake**

Pineapple Pound Cake

This is a big cake with a strong pineapple flavor. The sweet potatoes add moisture to the crumb and an intriguing touch to both the texture and taste.

Serves: 14–16 · Prep: 25 min. · Cooking: 70–80 min. · Level: 1

CAKE
- 3 cups (450 g) all-purpose (plain) flour
- 2 teaspoons baking powder
- 1 teaspoon cinnamon
- 1 teaspoon ground ginger
- 1 teaspoon ground nutmeg
- ½ teaspoon baking soda (bicarbonate of soda)
- ½ teaspoon salt
- 1 cup (250 g) butter, softened
- 2 cups (400 g) sugar
- 2 teaspoons pineapple extract (essence)
- 1 teaspoon vanilla extract (essence)
- 4 large eggs
- 2 cups (400 g) cooked, mashed sweet potatoes

GLAZE
- 2 cups (300 g) confectioners' (icing) sugar
- ¼ cup (60 g) butter, melted
- 2 teaspoons pineapple extract (essence)
- 2 tablespoons hot water

1. Preheat the oven to 350°F (180°C/gas 4). Lightly grease and flour a 10-inch (23-cm) Bundt pan.

2. To prepare the cake, combine the flour, baking powder, cinnamon, ginger, nutmeg, baking soda, and salt in a large bowl. Beat the butter, sugar, pineapple extract, and vanilla in a large bowl with an electric mixer at medium speed until creamy. Add the eggs one at a time, beating until just blended after each addition. With mixer at low speed, gradually beat in the sweet potatoes and dry ingredients. Spoon the batter into the prepared pan.

3. Bake for 70–80 minutes, or until a toothpick inserted into the center comes out clean. Run a knife around the edges of the pan to loosen the cake. Cool the cake in the pan for 15 minutes. Turn out onto a rack and let cool completely.

4. To prepare the glaze, beat the confectioners' sugar, butter, and pineapple extract in a medium bowl until smooth. Beat in enough of the water to make a soft glaze. Drizzle over the cake.

Honey and Spice Pound Cake

Vary the spices in the filling to suit your tastes. Try adding a little nutmeg, cardamom, or mace.

Serves: 10–12 · Prep: 25 min. · Cooking: 70–80 min. · Level: 1

CAKE
- 2 cups (300 g) all-purpose (plain) flour
- 1 teaspoon baking powder
- ½ teaspoon baking soda (bicarbonate of soda)
- ½ teaspoon salt
- 1 cup (250 g) butter, softened
- 1 cup (200 g) sugar
- ⅓ cup (90 ml) honey
- 2 teaspoons vanilla extract (essence)
- 3 large eggs
- ¾ cup (180 ml) sour cream
- ⅓ cup (50 g) confectioners' (icing) sugar, to dust

FILLING
- 1 cup (200 g) sugar
- 2 teaspoons ground cinnamon
- 1 teaspoon ground ginger

1. Preheat the oven to 325°F (160°C/gas 3). Lightly grease and flour a 10-inch (25-cm) Bundt pan.

2. To prepare the cake, combine the flour, baking powder, baking soda, and salt in a medium bowl. Beat the butter, sugar, honey, and vanilla in a large bowl with an electric mixer at medium speed until pale and creamy. Add the eggs one at a time, beating until just blended after each addition. With mixer at low speed, gradually beat in the dry ingredients, alternating with the sour cream. Spoon half the batter into the prepared pan.

3. To prepare the filling, mix the sugar, cinnamon, and ginger in a small bowl. Sprinkle over the batter in the pan. Spoon the remaining batter over the top.

4. Bake for 70–80 minutes, or until golden brown and a toothpick inserted into the center comes out clean. Run a knife around the edges of the pan to loosen the cake. Cool the cake in the pan for 15 minutes. Turn out onto a rack and let cool completely. Dust with the confectioners' sugar just before serving.

Almond Pound Cake

This pound cake—and the other ones on these pages—can be also be baked in tube or loaf pans. This is a large cake, so if changing pans, be sure to choose one that will hold all the batter with plenty of room to rise.

Serves: 12–14 · Prep: 20 min. · Cooking: 75–85 min. · Level: 1

- 2 cups (300 g) all-purpose (plain) flour
- 1 cup (125 g) finely ground almonds
- 1 teaspoon baking powder
- ¼ teaspoon salt
- 1½ cups (375 g) butter, softened
- 3 cups (600 g) sugar
- 2 teaspoons almond extract (essence)
- 1 teaspoon vanilla extract (essence)
- 6 large eggs
- 1 cup (250 ml) milk
- ¾ cup (75 g) slivered almonds or almond pieces

1. Preheat the oven to 350°F (180°C/gas 4). Lightly grease and flour a 10-inch (25-cm) Bundt pan.

2. Combine the flour, ground almonds, baking powder, and salt in a large bowl. Beat the butter, sugar, and almond and vanilla extracts in a large bowl with an electric mixer at medium speed until pale and creamy. Add the eggs one at a time, beating until just blended after each addition. With mixer at low speed, gradually beat in the dry ingredients, alternating with the milk. Spoon the batter into the prepared pan. Sprinkle with the almonds.

3. Bake for 75–85 minutes, or until a toothpick inserted into the center comes out clean. Run a knife around the edges of the pan to loosen the cake. Cool the cake in the pan for 15 minutes. Turn out onto a rack and let cool completely.

Chocolate Chip Pound Cake

We have used dark chocolate chips; you can substitute with milk or white chocolate chips, if preferred.

Serves: 14–16 · Prep: 25 min. · Cooking: 75–85 min. · Level: 1

2½	cups (375 g) all-purpose (plain) flour
1	teaspoon baking powder
½	teaspoon salt
1½	cups (375 g) butter, softened
2¼	cups (450 g) sugar
2	teaspoons vanilla extract (essence)
5	large eggs
¾	cup (180 ml) buttermilk
1	cup (180 g) dark chocolate chips

1. Preheat the oven to 350°F (180°C/gas 4). Lightly grease and flour a 10-inch (25-cm) tube pan.

2. To prepare the cake, combine the flour, baking powder, and salt in a large bowl. Beat the butter, sugar, and vanilla in a large bowl with an electric mixer at medium speed until pale and creamy. Add the eggs one at a time, beating until just blended after each addition. With mixer at low speed, gradually beat in the dry ingredients, alternating with the buttermilk. Stir in the chocolate chips by hand. Spoon the batter into the prepared pan.

3. Bake for 75–85 minutes, or until a toothpick inserted into the center comes out clean. Run a knife around the edges of the pan to loosen the cake. Cool the cake in the pan for 15 minutes. Turn out onto a rack and let cool completely.

Pound Cake with Raspberry Sauce

This is a lovely light pound cake. Serve plain with coffee or tea, or with the raspberry sauce on special occasions. Remember that the raspberry sauce needs to chill in the refrigerator for at least an hour before serving.

Serves: 12–14 · Prep: 30 min. + 1 hr. to chill · Cooking: 80–90 min. · Level: 1

CAKE

3⅓	cups (500 g) all-purpose (plain) flour
1	teaspoon ground nutmeg
½	teaspoon baking soda (bicarbonate of soda)
½	teaspoon salt
2	cups (500 g) butter, softened
3	cups (600 g) sugar
2	teaspoons vanilla extract (essence)
1	teaspoon almond extract (essence)
6	large eggs
½	cup (125 ml) milk

RASPBERRY SAUCE

3	cups (500 g) fresh raspberries, lightly mashed with a fork
¼	cup (50 g) sugar
1	tablespoon crème de cassis or orange liqueur

1. Preheat the oven to 325°F (160°C/gas 3). Lightly grease and flour a 10-inch (25-cm) tube pan.

2. To prepare the cake, combine the flour, nutmeg, baking soda, and salt in a large bowl. Beat the butter, sugar, vanilla and almond extracts in a large bowl with an electric mixer at medium speed until pale and creamy. Add the eggs one at a time, beating until just blended after each addition. With mixer at low speed, gradually beat in the dry ingredients, alternating with the milk. Spoon the batter into the prepared pan.

3. Bake for 80–90 minutes, or until a toothpick inserted into the center comes out clean. Run a knife around the edges of the pan to loosen the cake. Cool the cake in the pan for 15 minutes. Turn out onto a rack to cool completely.

4. Raspberry Sauce: Place the mashed raspberries, sugar, and liqueur in a medium bowl and stir until the sugar has dissolved. Refrigerate for at least 1 hour before serving. Drizzle the sauce over the cake, or pass the sauce on the side.

Double Chocolate Pound Cake

Pound cakes are perfect for large gatherings. They look wonderful, taste great, and almost everyone likes them. This double chocolate version is ideal for a special occasion. Prepare it a day or two before the party and drizzle with the chocolate glaze on the day.

Serves: 16–18 · Prep: 25 min. · Cooking: 75–85 min. · Level: 1

CAKE

2	cups (400 g) sugar
8	ounces (250 g) white chocolate, coarsely chopped
3	cups (450 g) all-purpose (plain) flour
1	teaspoon baking powder
½	teaspoon baking soda (bicarbonate of soda)
½	teaspoon salt
1	cup (250 g) butter, softened
2	teaspoons vanilla extract (essence)
1	teaspoon almond extract (essence)
5	large eggs
1	cup (250 ml) plain yogurt

GLAZE

4	ounces (125 g) white chocolate, melted
4	ounces (125 g) dark chocolate

1. Preheat the oven to 350°F (180°C/gas 4). Lightly grease and flour a 10-inch (25-cm) Bundt pan. Sprinkle with 2 tablespoons of the sugar.

2. To prepare the cake, melt the chocolate in a double boiler over barely simmering water. Set aside to cool.

3. Mix the flour, baking powder, baking soda, and salt in a large bowl. Beat the butter, remaining sugar, and vanilla and almond extracts in a large bowl with an electric mixer at medium speed until creamy. Add the eggs one at a time, beating until just blended after each addition. With mixer at low speed, gradually beat in the dry ingredients, alternating with the yogurt. Spoon the batter into the prepared pan.

4. Bake for 75–85 minutes, or until a toothpick inserted into the center comes out clean. Run a knife around the edges of the pan to loosen the cake. Cool the cake in the pan for 15 minutes. Turn out onto the rack and let cool completely.

5. To prepare the glaze, melt the chocolates separately in double boilers over barely simmering water. Drizzle alternate spoonfuls of the melted chocolate over the cake.

Chocolate Mint Pound Cake

This cake has a lovely, deep chocolate and vanilla flavor that contrasts beautifully with the peppermint frosting.

Serves: 16–20 · Prep: 25 min. · Cooking: 1 hour 35–45 min. · Level: 1

CAKE

3½	cups (500 g) all-purpose (plain) flour
1	cup (150 g) unsweetened cocoa powder
1	teaspoon baking powder
½	teaspoon salt
1½	cups (375 g) butter, softened
3	cups (600 g) sugar
1	tablespoon vanilla extract (essence)
5	large eggs
1¼	cups (300 ml) milk

PEPPERMINT FROSTING

2	cups (300 g) confectioners' (icing) sugar
¼	cup (60 g) butter, softened
⅓	cup (50 g) unsweetened cocoa powder
1	tablespoon milk
½	teaspoon peppermint extract (essence)

1. Preheat the oven to 350°F (180°C/gas 4). Lightly grease and flour a 10-inch (25-cm) tube pan.

2. To prepare the cake, combine the flour, cocoa, baking powder, and salt in a large bowl. Beat the butter, sugar, and vanilla in a large bowl with an electric mixer at medium speed until creamy. Add the eggs one at a time, beating until just blended after each addition. With mixer at low speed, gradually beat in the dry ingredients, alternating with the milk. Spoon the batter into the prepared pan.

3. Bake for 1 hour and 30–40 minutes, or until a toothpick inserted into the center comes out clean. Run a knife around the edges of the pan to loosen the cake. Cool the cake in the pan for 15 minutes. Turn out onto a rack and let cool completely.

4. To prepare the frosting, beat the confectioners' sugar and butter in a large bowl until creamy. Beat in the cocoa, milk, and peppermint extract until smooth. Spread the top and sides of the cake with the frosting.

Double Chocolate Pound Cake ▷

Blueberry Shortcake Sandwich

You can substitute the blueberries in this cake with sliced strawberries, whole raspberries or blackberries, or other fresh, in-season fruit of your choice.

Serves: 8–10 · Prep: 25 min. · Cooking: 25–30 min. · Level: 1

CAKE

1	cup (250 g) butter, softened
1¼	cups (250 g) superfine (caster) sugar
4	large eggs
1²⁄₃	cups (250 g) all-purpose (plain) flour
2	teaspoons baking powder
1½	tablespoons milk
1	teaspoon vanilla extract (essence)
1½	cups (300 g) blueberries
8	whole strawberries
	Confectioners' sugar, to dust

VANILLA CREAM

1	cup (250 ml) heavy (double) cream
2	tablespoons confectioners' (icing) sugar
½	vanilla bean, seeds scraped out

1. Preheat the oven to 350°F (180°C/gas 4). Lightly grease two 8-inch (20-cm) round cake pans and line the bases with parchment paper.

2. To prepare the cake, beat the butter, sugar, and vanilla with an electric mixer on medium speed until pale and creamy. Add the eggs one at a time, beating until just combined. Add the flour and baking powder, alternating with the milk. Spoon half the batter into each of the prepared pans.

3. Bake for 25–30 minutes, or until golden brown, the cake springs back when lightly touched or a skewer comes out clean when tested.Cool the cakes in the pans for 10 minutes. Turn out onto a rack. Carefully remove the paper and let cool completely. Slice the top off one of the cakes to create a flat surface if necessary.

4. To prepare the vanilla cream, beat the cream, confectioners' sugar, and vanilla seeds together in a small bowl, until stiff peaks form. Spoon onto one of the cakes, spreading ¾ inch (2 cm) in from the edge. Cover with the blueberries. Place the other cake on top and dust with confectioners' sugar.

Ginger Butter Cake

This is the perfect cake for people who are fond of ginger. Apart from its wonderful taste, ginger has been used in cooking and as a home remedy for centuries. It is said to improve the appetite, relieve migraine headaches, morning sickness, and arthritis pain.

Serves: 8 · Prep: 25 min. · Cooking: 25–35 min. · Level: 1

CAKE

2	cups (300 g) all-purpose (plain) flour
2	teaspoons baking powder
2	teaspoons ground ginger
¼	teaspoon salt
¾	cup (180 g) butter, softened
¾	cup (150 g) firmly packed brown sugar
1	teaspoon vanilla extract (essence)
3	large eggs

GINGER CREAM FILLING

1	cup (250 ml) heavy (double) cream
2	tablespoons confectioners' (icing) sugar
1	teaspoon ground ginger

1. Preheat the oven to 350°F (180°C/gas 4). Lightly grease and flour two 8-inch (20-cm) round cake pans. Line with parchment paper.

2. To prepare the cake, combine the flour, baking powder, ginger, and salt in a large bowl. Beat the butter, sugar, and vanilla in a large bowl with an electric mixer at high speed until pale and creamy. With mixer at medium speed, add the eggs one at a time, beating until just blended after each addition. With mixer at low speed, gradually beat in the dry ingredients. Spoon half the batter into each of the prepared pans.

3. Bake for 25–35 minutes, or until a toothpick inserted into the center comes out clean. Cool the cakes in the pans for 10 minutes. Turn out onto a rack. Carefully remove the paper and let cool completely.

4. To prepare the filling,, beat the cream, confectioners' sugar, and ginger in a large bowl until stiff. Place one cake on a serving plate and spread with the cream. Top with the remaining cake.

Blueberry Shortcake Sandwich ▷

Linzertorte

This torte is named for the Austrian city of Linz. It is a very old recipe and the cake itself is really more like a modern tart. A layer of thick and crumbly nutty pastry is spread with raspberry (or sometimes apricot) preserves and covered with another layer of pastry in a lattice pattern.

Serves: 8 · Prep: 30 min. + 1 hr. to chill and freeze · Cooking: 25 min.· Level: 1

- ½ cup (60 g) hazelnuts
- 1 cup (150 g) blanched almonds
- 1⅓ cups (200 g) all-purpose (plain) flour
- 1 teaspoon ground cinnamon
- ½ teaspoon baking powder
- ¼ teaspoon salt
- ¾ cup (180 g) butter
- 1 cup (200 g) sugar
- 1 large egg yolk
- 1⅓ cups (350 g) raspberry preserves (jam)
  Confectioners' (icing) sugar, to dust

1. Preheat the oven to 350°F (180°C/gas 4). Line the base of a 9-inch (23-cm) springform pan with parchment paper. Lightly grease the sides.

2. Spread the hazelnuts in a baking dish and toast until golden brown, about 10 minutes. Place in a clean kitchen towel and rub off the skins. Turn off the oven. Place the hazelnuts and almonds in a food processor and chop until finely ground. Set aside.

3. Combine the flour, cinnamon, baking powder, and salt in a medium bowl. Beat the butter and sugar in a large bowl with an electric mixer on medium speed until pale and creamy. Beat in the egg yolk. With mixer on low, beat in the nut mixture and mixed dried ingredients.

4. Divide the dough in half. Press one half into the base and about ¾ inch (2 cm) up the sides of the prepared pan. Roll the remaining dough into a 12-inch (30-cm) disk on a piece of parchment paper. Place on a baking sheet. Chill the dough until firm, about 30 minutes.

5. Spread the raspberry preserves over the pastry in the pan. Use a fluted pastry wheel to cut the remaining pastry into ¾-inch (2-cm) wide strips. Place over the preserves in a lattice pattern. Place the cake in the freezer for 30 minutes.

6. Preheat the oven to 350°F (180°C/gas 4). Bake the torte until golden brown, 35–40 minutes. Place on a wire rack and let cool for 15 minutes. Loosen the pan sides and carefully remove the base. let cool completely. Dust with confectioners' sugar just before serving.

Strawberry Jam Shortcake

Shortcakes are normally prepared with fresh fruit—usually strawberries—pressed between two layers of crumbly biscuit. Our recipe uses strawberry preserves, or jam, with spectacular results!

Serves: 6–8 · Prep: 25 min. + 30 min. to chill · Cooking: 40–50 min. · Level: 1

- 2 cups (300 g) all-purpose (plain) flour
- 2 teaspoons baking powder
- ¼ teaspoon salt
- ½ cup 125 g) cold butter, cut up
- ¾ cup (150 g) sugar
- 1 large egg, lightly beaten
- 2 tablespoons freshly squeezed lemon juice
- 1 cup (300 g) strawberry preserves (jam), stirred
- 1 large egg white, lightly beaten
- ¼ cup (30 g) slivered almonds
- 1 cup (250 ml) heavy (double) cream

1. Preheat the oven to 350°F (180°C/gas 4). Lightly grease and flour a 9-inch (23-cm) springform cake pan.

2. Combine the flour, baking powder, and salt in a large bowl. Use a pastry blender to cut in the butter. Stir in the sugar, then the egg. Gradually add the lemon juice, mixing until the dough is firm. Press into a ball, wrap in plastic wrap (cling film), and refrigerate for 30 minutes.

3. Divide the dough in two, one piece twice as big as the other (keep the smaller piece chilled). Roll the larger piece out on a lightly floured surface to a 12-inch (30-cm) round. Ease the dough into the bottom and up the sides of the prepared pan. Spread with the preserves. Roll the smaller piece of dough out to a 9½-inch (24-cm) round. Place over the preserves. Seal the edges together. Brush the pastry with the beaten white and sprinkle with the almonds.

4. Bake for 40–50 minutes, or until the pastry is golden brown and flaky. Cool the cake in the pan for 10 minutes. Turn out onto a rack and turn top-side up.

5. Beat the cream until thick. Serve the shortcake warm or at room temperature with the cream.

Linzertorte ▷

Sour Cream Coffee Cake

The sour cream gives this cake a slight tang, while the molasses deepens the flavor a little.

Serves: 8–10 · Prep: 15 min. · Cooking: 50–60 min. · Level: 1

TOPPING
⅓	cup (50 g) all-purpose (plain) flour
¼	cup (50 g) firmly packed brown sugar
1	teaspoon cinnamon
½	teaspoon ground nutmeg
¼	cup (60 g) cold butter
½	cup (50 g) mixed nuts, chopped

CAKE
2	cups (300 g) all-purpose (plain) flour
1	teaspoon baking powder
1	teaspoon baking soda (bicarbonate of soda)
1	teaspoon cinnamon
¼	teaspoon salt
1	cup (250 g) butter, softened
1	cup (200 g) firmly packed brown sugar
2	tablespoons molasses
2	teaspoons vanilla extract (essence)
3	large eggs
1	cup (250 ml) sour cream

1. Preheat the oven to 325°F (160°C/gas 3). Lightly grease and flour a 13 x 9-inch (33 x 23-cm) baking pan.

2. To prepare the topping, stir the flour, brown sugar, cinnamon, and nutmeg in a medium bowl. Use a pastry blender to cut in the butter until the mixture resembles fine crumbs. Stir in the nuts.

3. To prepare the cake, combine the flour, baking powder, baking soda, cinnamon, and salt in a large bowl. Beat the butter, brown sugar, molasses, and vanilla in a large bowl with an electric mixer at medium speed until creamy. Add the eggs one at a time, beating until just blended after each addition. With mixer at low speed, gradually beat in the dry ingredients, alternating with the sour cream. Spoon the batter into the prepared pan. Sprinkle with the topping.

4. Bake for 50–60 minutes, or until a toothpick inserted into the center comes out clean. Cool the cake in the pan on a rack.

◁ **Sticky Black Ginger Cake**

Sticky Black Ginger Cake

This cakes goes beautifully with lemon tea.

Serves: 6–8 · Prep: 25 min. · Cooking: 25 min. · Level: 1

1	cup (250 g) butter
1	cup (200 g) firmly packed dark brown sugar
1	cup (250 ml) black molasses (treacle)
2⅓	cups (350 g) all-purpose (plain) flour
2	teaspoons ground ginger
1	teaspoon ground cinnamon
2	teaspoons baking soda (bicarbonate of soda)
2	large eggs, beaten
1¼	cups (300 ml) milk
¼	cup (60 g) candied (glacé) ginger, chopped

1. Preheat the oven to 300°F (150°C/gas 2). Line the base of an 8 x 12-inch (20 x 30-cm) baking pan with parchment paper.

2. Melt the butter, sugar, and molasses in a medium saucepan over medium heat. Remove from heat and let cool to room temperature.

3. Combine the flour, ground ginger, cinnamon, and baking soda in a large bowl. Make a well in the center and stir in the eggs and milk. Add the butter and sugar mixture and candied ginger and stir until well combined.

4. Spoon the batter into the prepared pan. Bake until the cake is risen and a metal skewer inserted in the middle comes out clean, about 45 minutes. Cool the cake completely in the pan on a rack.

Kugelhopf

A kugelhopf is a sweet yeast cake from southern Germany, Alsace (in France), Austria, and Switzerland. It is baked in a special fluted ring pan. There are many different versions, depending on the region.

Serves: 8–10 · Prep: 35 min. + 2–3 hr. to rise · Cooking: 50–60 min. Level: 2

2	(¼-ounce/7-g) packages active dry yeast or 1 ounce (30 g) compressed fresh yeast
1	teaspoon sugar
¾	cup (200 ml) lukewarm milk
3	cups (450 g) all-purpose (plain) flour
¾	cup (150 g) sugar
½	teaspoon salt
¾	cup (200 g) butter, melted and cooled
1	teaspoon vanilla extract (essence)
4	large eggs, beaten
½	cup (100 g) golden raisins (sultanas)
¾	cup (150 g) currants
½	cup (100 g) almonds, coarsely chopped
½	cup (50 g) mixed peel
1	tablespoon finely grated lemon zest
2	tablespoons rum or freshly squeezed lemon juice

1. Mix the yeast, sugar, and milk in a small bowl. Set aside until foamy, about 10 minutes.

2. Combine the flour, sugar, and salt in a large bowl. Pour in the yeast mixture, melted butter, and vanilla, followed by the eggs. Mix with a spatula until smooth. Alternatively, use an electric mixer fitted with a dough hook and knead for 1 minute at low speed and then at high speed for 5 minutes.

3. Add the golden raisins, currants, almonds, peel, zest, and rum or juice. Mix well for 2 minutes. Cover the bowl with a clean kitchen towel and leave in a warm place until doubled in bulk, 1–2 hours.

4. Brush the inside of a 9½-inch (24-cm) Kugelhopf mold with butter or oil. Make sure the flutes are well greased. Briefly knead the risen dough or beat for 30 seconds with the dough hook attachment. Turn the mixture into the pan and leave to rise again in a warm place until almost level with the rim of the pan, about 40 minutes.

5. Preheat the oven to 350°F (180°C/gas 4). Bake for 50–60 minutes, until golden brown and a skewer inserted into the center comes out clean. Let cool in the mold for 10 minutes before turning out onto a rack. Serve warm.

Honey and Nut Ring

This yeast cake has just a little sugar and honey to sweeten it. The orange glaze is very sweet and contrasts nicely with the bread-like interior. It goes very well with a cup of tea.

Serves: 10–12 · Prep: 35 min. + 2–3 hr. to rise · Cooking: 30 min. · Level: 2

CAKE

1	teaspoon sugar
¼	cup (60 ml) light (single) cream
1	(¼-ounce/7-g) package active dry yeast or ½ ounce (15 g) compressed fresh yeast
½	cup (125 g) butter
2	tablespoons honey
3	large eggs
2⅓	cups (350 g) all-purpose (plain) flour
¼	teaspoon salt
⅓	cup (90 ml) lukewarm milk
½	cup (60 g) almonds or hazelnuts, toasted and coarsely chopped Finely grated zest of 1 orange

GLAZE

1	cup (150 g) confectioners' (icing) sugar
3	tablespoons freshly squeezed orange juice
2	teaspoons orange zest, finely grated
2	teaspoons Cointreau

1. To prepare the cake, combine the sugar and cream in a small bowl and stir in the yeast. Set aside until foamy, about 10 minutes.

2. Beat the butter in a large bowl with an electric mixer until pale. Add the honey and beat until combined. Beat in the eggs one at a time, adding a teaspoon of flour after each addition. Gradually beat in 2 cups (300 g) of flour and the salt followed by the yeast mixture and milk. Beat until well blended, smooth, and elastic. Add the remaining flour if the dough is still sticky. Work in the nuts and zest. Cover the bowl and let rise until doubled in bulk, 1–2 hours.

3. Butter a 10-inch (25 cm) ring mold with a pastry brush. Sprinkle with the nuts. When the dough has risen, stir once to expel air. Place in the pan. Cover and let rise until almost doubled in bulk, 1–2 hours.

4. Preheat the oven to 375°F (190°C/gas 5). Bake for 30 minutes, or until golden brown and a skewer inserted into the center comes out clean. Let cool in the pan for 10 minutes. Turn out on a rack.

5. To prepare the glaze, beat all the ingredients together until smooth. Spoon over the cake and serve warm.

Kugelhopf ▷

Lamington Cake

This is one of many versions of this famous Australian cake. It is named for the Baron of Lamington, who was Governor of Queensland from 1896–1901, and whose chef apparently invented the recipe when unexpected guests arrived.

Serves: 8–10 · Prep: 25 min. · Cooking: 30–40 min. · Level: 1

CAKE

½	cup (125 g) butter, softened
¾	cup (150 g) sugar
1	teaspoon vanilla extract (essence)
2	large eggs, lightly beaten
2	cups (300 g) all-purpose (plain) flour
2	teaspoons baking powder
½	cup (125 ml) milk
⅓	cup (110 g) raspberry preserves (jam)

CHOCOLATE FROSTING

3	cups (450 g) confectioners' (icing) sugar
3	tablespoons unsweetened cocoa powder
4	tablespoons boiling water
1	teaspoon butter
½	teaspoon vanilla extract (essence)
¾	cup (90 g) shredded (desiccated) coconut

1. Preheat the oven to 350°F (180°C/gas 4). Lightly grease an 8-inch (20 cm) springform cake pan and line with parchment paper.

2. To prepare the cake, beat the butter, sugar, and vanilla in a medium bowl with an electric mixer on medium speed until pale and creamy. Add the eggs in one at a time, beating until just blended after each addition. Combine the flour and baking powder in a medium bowl. With mixer on low, gradually add the flour mixture, alternating with the milk. Spoon the batter into the prepared pan.

3. Bake for 30–35 minutes, until golden brown and a skewer comes out clean when inserted into the center. Leave to cool in the pan for 10 minutes. Turn out onto a wire rack and let cool completely.

4. Cut the cake in half crosswise. Spread raspberry jam over the bottom half of the cake and cover with the top.

5. To make the chocolate icing, mix the confectioners' sugar and cocoa in a medium bowl. Add the boiling water, butter, and vanilla, stirring until smooth. Spread the frosting over the cake and sprinkle with coconut.

Lemon Crown

This is a delicious, moist lemon ring. The sticky glaze is a real treat.

Serves: 8–10 · Prep: 25 min. · Cooking: 30–40 min. · Level: 1

CAKE

1⅔	cups (250 g) all-purpose (plain) flour
2	teaspoons baking powder
¼	teaspoon salt
¾	cup (180 g) butter, softened
1¼	cups (250 g) sugar
2	tablespoons finely grated lemon zest
3	large eggs
2	tablespoons freshly squeezed lemon juice

GLAZE

½	cup (125 g) apricot preserves (jam)
¼	cup (60 ml) freshly squeezed lemon juice
1⅔	cups (250 g) confectioners' (icing) sugar

1. Preheat the oven to 400°F (200°C/gas 6). Lightly grease and flour a 9-inch (23-cm) tube pan.

2. To prepare the cake, combine the flour, baking powder, and salt in a medium bowl. Beat the butter, sugar, and lemon zest in a large bowl with an electric mixer at medium speed until pale and creamy. Add the eggs one at a time, beating until just blended after each addition. With mixer at low speed, gradually beat in the dry ingredients and lemon juice. Spoon the batter into the prepared pan.

3. Bake for 30–40 minutes, or until a toothpick inserted into the center comes out clean. Cool the cake in the pan for 15 minutes. Turn out onto a rack and let cool completely.

4. To prepare the glaze, warm the apricot preserves in a small saucepan over low heat. Spread over the cake. Beat the confectioners' sugar and enough of the remaining lemon juice to make a thin glaze. Drizzle over the cake.

Lamington Cake ▷

Caramel Pecan Cake

This cake has a dense, rich crumb and a sweet crunchy topping.

Serves: 8–10 · Prep: 30 min. · Cooking: 30–35 min. · Level 1

CAKE

⅓	cup (90 g) butter
2	large eggs
½	cup (100 g) sugar
1	teaspoon vanilla extract (essence)
¾	cup (125 g) all-purpose (plain) flour
1	teaspoon baking powder
¼	cup (60 ml) milk

CARAMEL PECAN TOPPING

¼	cup (60 g) butter
¼	cup (50 g) sugar
2	tablespoons milk
1	tablespoon all-purpose (plain) flour
⅓	cup (50 g) pecans

1. Preheat the oven to 350°F (180°C/gas 4). Lightly grease a 9-inch (23 cm) springform cake pan and line the base with parchment paper.

2. To prepare the cake, melt the butter in a small saucepan over low heat then set aside to cool. Beat the eggs, sugar, and vanilla in a medium bowl with an electric mixer on medium speed until pale and thick. Combine the flour and baking powder into a small bowl. Fold the flour mixture, milk, and cooled butter into the egg mixture.

3. Spoon the batter into the prepared cake pan. Bake for 20 minutes, or until the cake springs back when lightly touched.

4. To prepare the topping, place the butter, sugar, milk and flour in a small saucepan over medium-low heat and bring to a boil. Boil for 5 minutes, or until thickened slightly. Stir in the pecans.

5. Spread the topping over the batter and bake for 10–15 more minutes, until the topping is golden and caramelized. Leave to cool in the pan for 10 minutes, then turn out onto a wire rack and let cool completely.

Lemon Poppy Seed Syrup Cake

This cake absorbs the flavor and sweetness of the lemon syrup and becomes dense and concentrated. If liked, serve with a little sweetened whipped cream.

Serves: 8–10 · Prep: 20 min. · Cooking: 50–60 min. · Level 1

CAKE

2	cups (300 g) all-purpose (plain) flour
½	cup (50 g) finely ground almonds
2	teaspoons baking powder
¼	teaspoon salt
⅓	cup (50 g) poppy seeds
¼	cup (60 ml) milk
¾	cup (180 g) butter, softened
1	cup (200 g) firmly packed light brown sugar
1	tablespoon finely grated lemon zest
3	large eggs
½	cup (125 ml) freshly squeezed lemon juice

LEMON SYRUP

1	cup (200 g) sugar
⅔	cup (150 ml) freshly squeezed lemon juice
⅓	cup (90 ml) water

1. Preheat the oven to 350°F (180°C/gas 4). Lightly grease and flour a 9-inch (23-cm) springform pan.

2. To prepare the cake, mix the flour, almonds, baking powder, and salt in a large bowl. Place the poppy seeds and milk in a small bowl and set aside for 15 minutes.

3. Beat the butter, sugar, and lemon zest in a large bowl with an electric mixer on medium speed until creamy. Add the eggs one at a time, beating until just blended after each addition. With mixer at low speed, beat in the dry ingredients, alternating with the lemon juice and poppy seed mixture. Spoon the batter into the prepared pan.

4. Bake for 50–60 minutes, or until a toothpick inserted into the center comes out clean. Cool the cake in the pan for 10 minutes. Turn out onto a rack.

5. To prepare the syrup, bring the sugar, lemon juice, and water to a boil in a small saucepan over low heat. Simmer for 2 minutes. Place the cake on the rack over a jelly-roll pan. Poke holes in it with a skewer. Spoon the hot syrup over the top. Scoop up any syrup from the pan and drizzle over the cake until it is all absorbed.

Caramel Pecan Cake ▷

Macaroon Ring

This cake has a crisp coconut-flavored meringue layer on top. Serve fresh, on the same day it was baked.

Serves: 8–10 · Prep: 25 min. · Cooking: 40–50 min. · Level: 1

CAKE

1½	cups (225 g) all-purpose (plain) flour	
2	teaspoons baking powder	
¼	teaspoon salt	
½	cup (125 g) butter	
½	cup (100 g) sugar	
3	large egg yolks	
1	teaspoon vanilla extract (essence)	
½	cup (125 ml) milk	
½	cup (150 g) raspberry preserves (jam)	

MACAROON TOPPING

3	large egg whites
¼	cup (50 g) sugar
½	cup (75 g) shredded (desiccated) coconut
½	teaspoon almond extract (essence)

1. Preheat the oven to 350°F (180°C/gas 4). Lightly grease and flour a 9-inch (23-cm) tube pan.

2. To prepare the cake, combine the flour, baking powder, and salt into a large bowl. Melt the butter in a saucepan over low heat. Remove from the heat. Beat in the sugar, egg yolks, and vanilla. Stir in the dry ingredients, alternating with the milk. Spoon the batter into the prepared pan. Spoon dollops of jam over the batter.

3. To prepare the topping, beat the egg whites in a large bowl with an electric mixer at medium speed until frothy. With mixer at high speed, gradually add the sugar, beating until stiff, glossy peaks form.

4. Use a large rubber spatula to fold in the coconut and almond extract. Spread the topping over the batter.

5. Bake for 40–50 minutes, or until a toothpick inserted into the center comes out clean. Cool the cake in the pan for 15 minutes. Turn out onto a rack. Turn top-side up and let cool completely.

◁ **Macaroon Ring**

Lime and Honey Syrup Cake

Serve this cake while it is still warm. It is delicious with softly whipped cream or vanilla ice cream.

Serves: 8–10 · Prep: 30 min. · Cooking: 45–55 min. · Level: 1

CAKE

2½	cups (375 g) cake flour
¾	cup (120 g) shredded (desiccated) coconut
¼	cup (30 g) almonds, finely ground
2	teaspoons baking powder
¼	teaspoon salt
1	cup (250 g) butter, softened
1	cup (200 g) sugar
1	tablespoon finely grated lime zest
3	large eggs
¾	cup (180 ml) plain yogurt
2	tablespoons freshly squeezed lime juice

HONEY AND LIME SYRUP

2	limes
½	cup (125 ml) cold water
¼	cup (60 g) honey
	Cardamom pods, smashed with flat side of a chef's knife

1. Preheat the oven to 350°F (180°C/gas 4). Lightly grease and flour a 9-inch (23-cm) Bundt pan.

2. To prepare the cake, stir the flour, coconut, almonds, baking powder, and salt in a large bowl. Beat the butter, sugar, and lime zest in a large bowl with an electric mixer at medium speed until pale and creamy. Add the eggs one at a time, beating until just blended after each addition. With mixer on low, beat in the dry ingredients, yogurt, and lime juice. Spoon the batter into the prepared pan.

3. Bake for 45–55 minutes, or until a toothpick inserted into the center comes out clean. Cool in the pan for 10 minutes. Turn out onto a rack. Place the cake on the rack in a jelly-roll pan.

4. Peel the limes and slice the zest into thin strips. Squeeze the juice from the limes and place it in a small saucepan with the zest, water, honey, and cardamom pods. Bring to a boil over low heat and simmer for 5 minutes. Scoop out the cardamom.

5. Poke holes in the cake with a skewer. Pour the syrup over the hot cake. Scoop up any syrup from the pan and drizzle over the cake until it is all absorbed.

Orange Marmalade Cake

This is an attractive cake. Serve freshly baked with a reviving cup of coffee or tea.

Serves: 8–10 · Prep: 35 min. · Cooking: 35–40 min. · Level 1

CAKE

- ⅓ cup (110 g) orange marmalade
- ½ cup (125 g) butter, softened
- ½ cup (100 g) sugar
- 1 teaspoon finely grated orange zest
- 2 large eggs
- 1 cup (150 g) all-purpose (plain) flour
- 1 teaspoon baking powder
- ½ cup (50 g) ground almonds
- ½ cup (50 g) slivered almonds

MARMALADE FROSTING

- ⅓ cup (110 g) orange marmalade
- 3 tablespoons butter
- 1 cup (150 g) confectioners' (icing) sugar
  Slices of candied (glacé) orange, to decorate

1. Preheat the oven to 350°F (180°C/gas 4). Lightly grease an 8-inch (20 cm) springform pan and line the base with parchment paper.

2. To prepare the cake, melt the marmalade in a small saucepan over low heat. Remove from the heat and set aside to cool slightly. Beat the butter, sugar, and orange zest in a large bowl with an electric mixer on medium speed until pale and creamy. Add the eggs one at a time, beating until just blended after each addition. With mixer on low, gradually beat in the flour and baking powder. Stir the marmalade, and ground and slivered almonds in by hand. Spoon the batter into the prepared pan.

3. Bake for 35–40 minutes, until golden brown and firm to the touch. Leave to cool in the pan for 10 minutes. Turn out onto a wire rack and let cool completely.

4. To prepare the frosting, melt the marmalade and butter in a small saucepan over low heat. Transfer to a small heatproof bowl and set aside to cool for 5 minutes. Stir the confectioners' sugar until smooth. Spread over the top of the cake and decorate with candied orange.

Frosted Lemon Butter Cake

Substitute the lemon extract in the cake and frosting with the same quantity of butterscotch or coffee extract for a completely different but equally delicious cake. Replace the lemon zest and juice with water or coffee, depending on the flavor you have chosen.

Serves: 8–10 · Prep: 30 min. · Cooking: 40–50 min. · Level 1

CAKE

- 2 cups (300 g) all-purpose (plain) flour
- 2 teaspoons baking powder
- ¼ teaspoon salt
- ½ cup (125 g) butter, softened
- 1 cup (200 g) sugar
- 1 tablespoon finely grated lemon zest
- 1 teaspoon lemon extract (essence)
- ½ teaspoon vanilla extract (essence)
- 3 large eggs
- 2 tablespoons milk

LEMON FROSTING

- 1½ cups (225 g) confectioners' (icing) sugar
- 2 tablespoons butter, melted
- 1 teaspoon lemon extract (essence)
- 1 tablespoon freshly squeezed lemon juice

1. Preheat the oven to 350°F (180°C/gas 4). Lightly grease and flour a 9-inch (23-cm) ring pan or savarin mold.

2. To prepare the cake, combine the flour, baking powder, and salt in a medium bowl. Beat the butter, sugar, lemon zest, lemon extract, and vanilla in a large bowl with an electric mixer on medium speed until pale and creamy. Add the eggs one at a time, beating until just blended after each addition. With mixer on low speed, gradually beat in the dry ingredients, alternating with the milk. Spoon the batter into the prepared pan.

3. Bake for 40–50 minutes, or until a toothpick inserted into the center comes out clean. Cool the cake in the pan for 10 minutes. Turn out onto a rack and let cool completely.

4. To prepare the frosting, mix the confectioners' sugar, butter, and lemon extract in a medium bowl. Beat in the lemon juice to make a spreadable frosting. Spread over the top of the cake.

Orange Marmalade Cake ▷

Date and Walnut Cake

This is a hearty cake with a delicious caramel frosting.

Serves: 10–12 · Prep: 45 min. · Cooking: 40–45 min. · Level 2

CAKE

1¼	cups (225 g) dates, pitted and coarsely chopped + extra, to decorate
1	cup (250 ml) boiling water
1	teaspoon baking soda
1½	cups (225 g) all-purpose (plain) flour
½	cup (50 g) ground almonds
1½	teaspoons baking powder
1	teaspoon pumpkin pie spice or allspice
½	cup (125 g) butter, softened
⅔	cup (140 g) firmly packed brown sugar
1	teaspoon vanilla extract (essence)
2	large eggs
½	cup (60 g) walnuts, coarsely chopped + extra halves, to decorate

CARAMEL FROSTING

2	tablespoons butter, softened
½	cup (100 g) firmly packed brown sugar
2	tablespoons milk
¾	cup (125 g) confectioners' (icing) sugar

1. Preheat the oven to 350°F (180°C/gas 4). Lightly grease a 9-inch (23 cm) springform cake pan and line the base with parchment paper.

2. To prepare the cake, place the dates, water, and baking soda in a small heatproof bowl and let stand until softened, about 20 minutes.

3. Combine the flour, almonds, baking powder, and mixed spice in a medium bowl. Beat the butter, brown sugar, and vanilla in a large bowl with an electric mixer on medium until creamy. Add the eggs one at a time, beating until just blended after each addition. With mixer on low, beat in the mixed dry ingredients, alternating with the date mixture. Stir the walnuts in by hand. Spoon the batter into the pan.

4. Bake for 40–45 minutes, until a skewer comes out clean when tested. Leave to cool in the pan for 10 minutes. Turn out onto a wire rack and let cool completely.

5. To prepare the frosting, melt the butter and sugar in a small saucepan over low heat. Add the milk and bring to a boil. Let cool. Stir in the confectioners' sugar. Spread over the top of the cake and create a decorative boarder with walnut halves and dates.

Caramel Layer Cake

This is a striking cake (see the photograph on pages 76-77) . It is ideal to serve at a coffee morning or afternoon tea.

Serves: 8–10 · Prep: 35 min. · Cooking: 35–45 min. · Level: 2

CAKE

3	cups (450 g) all-purpose (plain) flour
2	teaspoons baking powder
1	teaspoon baking soda (bicarbonate of soda)
¼	teaspoon salt
1	cup (250 g) butter, softened
1½	cups (300 g) firmly packed brown sugar
2	teaspoons caramel or butterscotch flavoring
5	large eggs, separated
1	cup (250 ml) milk
1	recipe Chantilly Cream (see page 275)

CARAMEL FROSTING

2	cups (400 g) firmly packed brown sugar
1¼	cups (300 ml) milk
5	tablespoons butter, cut up

1. Preheat the oven to 350°F (180°C/gas 4). Lightly grease two 9-inch (23-cm) springform pans.

2. To prepare the cake, combine the flour, baking powder, baking soda, and salt in a large bowl. Beat the butter, brown sugar, and caramel in a large bowl with an electric mixer on medium speed until creamy. Beat in the egg yolks one at a time. With mixer on low, beat in the dry ingredients and milk. With mixer on high, beat the egg whites in a large bowl until stiff peaks form. Fold into the batter.

3. Spoon the batter into the prepared pans. Bake for 35–45 minutes, or until golden and a toothpick inserted into the center comes out clean. Cool in the pans for 15 minutes. Turn out onto wire racks.

4. To prepare the frosting, stir the brown sugar and milk over medium heat until the sugar dissolves. Simmer until thick. Remove from the heat. Stir in the butter and let cool to warm.

5. Split the cakes horizontally. Spread a layer with half the Chantilly. Top with a second layer and spread with frosting. Top with a third layer and spread with almost all the remaining Chantilly. Top with the remaining cake. Spread the cake with the remaining frosting. Pipe the remaining Chantilly in rosettes around the edges.

Date and Walnut Cake ▷

Chocolate Chip Cake

This is a great cake to serve with coffee or tea. Children will love it as an after-school treat.

Serves: 8–10 · Prep: 35 min. · Cooking: 45–50 min. · Level: 2

CAKE

1⅓	cups (200 g) all-purpose (plain) flour
½	cup (75 g) unsweetened cocoa powder
1	teaspoon baking soda (bicarbonate of soda
½	teaspoon baking powder
¼	teaspoon salt
½	cup (125 g) butter, softened
1	cup (200 g) firmly packed light brown sugar
1	tablespoon freeze-dried instant coffee granules
1	teaspoon vanilla extract (essence)
2	large eggs
¾	cup (185 ml) milk
½	cup (90 g) dark chocolate chips

EASY CHOCOLATE FROSTING

½	cup (125 g) butter
4	ounces (125 g) dark chocolate, chopped

1. Preheat the oven to 350°F (180°C/gas 4). Line a deep 8-inch (20-cm) springform pan with parchment paper. Lightly grease the sides.

2. To prepare the cake, combine the flour, cocoa, baking soda, baking powder, and salt in a medium bowl. Beat the butter and sugar in a large bowl with an electric mixer on medium-high speed until creamy. Beat in the coffee granules and vanilla. Add the eggs one at a time, beating until just blended after each addition. With mixer on low, beat in the mixed dry ingredients, alternating with the milk and chocolate chips.

3. Spoon the batter into the prepared pan. Bake for 45–50 minutes, until risen and a toothpick inserted into the center comes out clean. Cool in the pan for 15 minutes. Turn out onto a rack and let cool.

4. To prepare the frosting, melt the butter and chocolate in a double boiler over barely simmering water. When smooth and glossy set aside to cool. Spread over the top and sides of the cake.

Chocolate Ring With Sauce

This cake has great flavor and texture. Serve it between meals with tea or coffee or add raspberries or sliced peaches and serve as a dessert.

Serves: 10–12 · Prep: 30 min. · Cooking: 40–50 min. · Level: 1

CAKE

1¼	cups (180 g) all-purpose (plain) flour
⅓	cup (50 g) unsweetened cocoa powder
1	teaspoon baking powder
1	teaspoon baking soda (bicarbonate of soda)
¼	teaspoon salt
¾	cup (150 g) sugar
⅓	cup (75 g) firmly packed dark brown sugar
¼	cup (60 g) butter, melted
1	cup (250 ml) buttermilk
½	cup (125 ml) milk
2	large eggs
1	tablespoon freeze-dried coffee granules, dissolved in 1 tablespoon milk
1	teaspoon vanilla extract (essence)

CHOCOLATE SAUCE

1	cup (180 g) dark chocolate chips
½	cup (125 ml) heavy (double) cream

1. Preheat the oven to 350°F (180°C/gas 4). Lightly grease a 9-inch (23-cm) Bundt pan. Dust with cocoa.

2. To prepare the cake, mix the flour, cocoa, baking powder, baking soda, and salt in a large bowl. Stir in both sugars. Beat the butter, buttermilk, milk, eggs, coffee mixture, and vanilla in a large bowl with an electric mixer at medium speed until well blended. With mixer at low speed, beat the butter mixture into the dry ingredients.

3. Spoon the batter into the prepared pan. Bake for 40–50 minutes, or until a toothpick inserted into the center comes out clean. Cool in the pan for 15 minutes. Turn out onto a rack and let cool completely.

4. To prepare the sauce, stir the chocolate and cream in a double boiler over barely simmering water until melted and smooth. Remove from the heat. Set aside to cool.

5. To serve, slice the cake and spoon some sauce over each portion.

Chocolate Chip Cake ▷

Mocha Cake

Mocha is a type of coffee bean from Yemen, named after the Red Sea port city of Mocha where it was traded. Mocha coffee beans are renown for their chocolaty flavor. A mocha cake is usually made with chocolate and coffee. This is a flavorful cake with a rich chocolate-coffee cream frosting.

Serves: 8–10 · Prep: 30 min · Cooking: 40–45 min. · Level 2

CAKE
1¾ cups (275 g) all-purpose (plain) flour
⅔ cup (100 g) unsweetened cocoa powder
1 teaspoon baking powder
1 teaspoon baking soda (bicarbonate of soda)
1¾ cups (350 g) firmly packed brown sugar
¾ cup (150 g) butter, softened
1 teaspoon vanilla extract (essence)
3 large eggs
1 cup (250 ml) milk
2 tablespoons very strong brewed coffee
1 tablespoon dark rum

MOCHA FROSTING
4 ounces (120 g) dark chocolate, coarsely chopped
¾ cup (180 g) butter, softened
3 teaspoons freeze dried coffee granules, dissolved in 1 tablespoon boiling water
1 teaspoon vanilla extract (essence)
2 cups (300 g) confectioners' (icing) sugar
Chocolate-coated coffee beans, to decorate

1. Preheat the oven to 350°F (180°C/gas 4). Lightly grease a 9-inch (23 cm) springform cake pan and line with parchment paper.

2. To prepare the cake, combine the flour, cocoa, baking powder and baking soda into a medium bowl. Beat the brown sugar, butter, and vanilla in a large bowl with an electric mixer on medium speed until creamy. Add the eggs one at a time, beating until just blended after each addition. Combine the milk, coffee, and rum in a small bowl. With mixer on low, gradually add the mixed dry ingredients, alternately with the milk mixture. Spoon the batter into the prepared pan.

3. Bake for 40–45 minutes, until golden brown and a skewer comes out clean when inserted into the center. Leave to cool in the pan for 10 minutes. Turn out onto a wire rack and let cool completely.

4. To prepare the frosting, melt the chocolate in a double boiler over barely simmering water, stirring occasionally until smooth. Remove from the heat and set aside to cool.

5. Beat the butter in a medium bowl with an electric mixer until pale and creamy. Add the coffee, vanilla, and melted chocolate, beating to combine. With mixer on low, beat in the confectioners' sugar until smooth and creamy.

6. Cut the cake in half horizontally to make two layers. Spread a third of the frosting on one half and sandwich the layers together. Spread the remaining frosting over the top and sides of the cake and create a decorative boarder with chocolate-coated coffee beans.

◁ Mocha Cake

Devil's Food Cake

Devil's Food Cake is a full-bodied chocolate cake, usually covered in a rich chocolate frosting. It always contains baking soda which helps to counteract the natural acidity of the chocolate and gives the cake its deep, reddish brown coloring.

Serves: 10–12 · Prep: 45 min. · Cooking: 30–40 min. · Level 2

8	ounces (240 g) dark chocolate, coarsely chopped
2¾	cups (425 g) all-purpose (plain) flour
2	teaspoons baking powder
1½	teaspoons baking soda
1	cup (250 g) butter, softened
1¾	cup (350 g) firmly packed brown sugar
1½	teaspoons vanilla extract (essence)
4	large eggs
1½	cups (375 ml) sour cream

CHOCOLATE GANACHE

12	ounces (350 g) dark chocolate, coarsely chopped
1⅓	cup (330 ml) half-and-half (single) cream

1. Preheat the oven to 350 F (180 C/gas 4). Lightly grease two 9-inch (23 cm) springform cake pans and line the bases with parchment paper.

2. Melt the chocolate in a double boiler over barely simmering water, stirring occasionally until smooth. Remove from the heat and set aside to cool.

3. Combine the flour, baking powder, and baking soda in a medium bowl. Beat the butter, sugar, and vanilla in a large bowl with an electric mixer on medium speed until creamy. Add the eggs one at a time, beating until just combined after each addition. With mixer on low speed, gradually beat in the mixed dry ingredients, alternating with the sour cream and chocolate.

4. Spoon the batter into the prepared pans. Bake for 30–40 minutes, until a skewer comes out clean when tested. Let cool in the pans for 10 minutes, then turn out onto a wire rack and let cool completely.

5. To prepare the ganache, melt the chocolate and cream in a double boiler over barely simmering water. Let cool slightly. Refrigerate, stirring occasionally until spreadable. Spread a third of the ganache over one of the cakes and sandwich the other layer on top. Spread the remaining frosting over the top and sides of the cake.

 # Frosted Chocolate Roll

This delicious roll has no flour and is perfect for people with gluten intolerance. Be sure to use good-quality chocolate and vanilla extract from reliable manufacturers of gluten-free products. Keep the cake chilled in the refrigerator and take out about 30 minutes before serving.

Serves: 10–12 · Prep: 45 min. + 30 min. to chill · Cooking: 35–40 min. · Level 3

CHOCOLATE ROLL

8	ounces (250 g) dark chocolate, coarsely chopped
8	large eggs, separated
1¼	cups (250 g) sugar
¼	teaspoon salt

CHOCOLATE CREAM FROSTING

1	pound (500 g) dark chocolate, coarsely chopped
1	cup (250 ml) heavy (double) cream
1	teaspoon vanilla extract (essence)
2	cups (300 g) confectioners' (icing) sugar

1. Preheat the oven to 350°F (180°C/gas 4). Lightly grease a 10 x 15-inch (25 x 35-cm) jelly-roll pan. Line with parchment paper.

2. To prepare the cake, melt the chocolate in a double boiler over barely simmering water. Let cool.

3. Beat the egg yolks and sugar in a large bowl with an electric mixer on high speed until pale and thick. Gradually beat in the chocolate. Beat the egg whites and salt in a large bowl until stiff peaks form. Fold them into the chocolate mixture. Spoon the batter into the prepared pan.

4. Bake for 20–25 minutes, or until springy to the touch. Cool the cake in the pan for 5 minutes.

5. To prepare the frosting, melt the chocolate, cream, and vanilla in a double boiler over barely simmering water. Sift in the confectioners' sugar and stir until combined. Strain the frosting through a sieve to remove lumps and refrigerate until cooled and thickened, about 30 minutes.

6. Carefully roll up the cake. Unroll the cake and spread with half the frosting. Reroll the cake and spread with the remaining frosting.

Devil's Food Cake ▷

Chocolate Hazelnut Cake

This cake has no flour and so is ideal for people who suffer from gluten intolerance. Check the chocolate label carefully to make sure it does not contain any traces of gluten.

Serves: 8–10 · Prep: 30 min. · Cooking: 35–40 min. · Level 1

10	ounces (300 g) dark chocolate, coarsely chopped
3/4	cup (180 g) butter, coarsely chopped
1½	teaspoons vanilla extract (essence)
6	large eggs, separated
1	cup (200 g) firmly packed dark brown sugar
1	teaspoon finely grated orange zest
1	cup (100 g) ground hazelnuts
	Confectioner's sugar, to dust

1. Preheat the oven to 325°F (170°C/gas 3). Lightly grease a 9-inch (23 cm) springform cake pan and line the base and the sides with parchment paper.

2. Melt the chocolate, butter, and vanilla in a double boiler over barely simmering water, stirring occasionally until smooth. Remove from the heat and set aside to cool.

3. Beat the egg yolks, sugar, and orange zest in a large bowl with an electric mixer on medium speed until pale and thick. Add the cooled melted chocolate and stir to combine.

4. With mixer on high speed, beat the egg whites in a separate bowl until soft peaks form. Add a third of the whites to the yolk mixture and stir to combine and then fold in the remaining whites. Fold in the ground hazelnuts. Spoon the batter into the prepared pan and cover with aluminum foil.

5. Bake for 35–40 minutes, or until a skewer comes out clean when tested. Remove the foil and leave to cool for 10 minutes. Turn out onto a wire rack and let cool completely.

6. Dust with confectioners' sugar just before serving.

Chocolate Pineapple Sheet Cake

This sheet cake is as simple and quick to prepare as it is delicious to eat.

Serves: 10–12 · Prep: 25 min. · Cooking: 35–40 min. · Level 1

1	cup (150 g) all-purpose (plain) flour
½	cup (75 g) unsweetened cocoa powder
1	teaspoon baking powder
1	teaspoon ground cinnamon
¼	teaspoon salt
3/4	cup (180 g) butter, softened
1½	cups (300 g) sugar
1	teaspoon vanilla extract (essence)
3	large eggs
1	cup (200 g) crushed canned pineapple, drained
¼	cup (60 g) walnuts, chopped
1	recipe Easy Chocolate Frosting (see page 108)

1. Preheat the oven to 350°F (180°C/gas 4). Lightly grease and flour a 13 x 9-inch (33 x 23-cm) baking pan.

2. Combine the flour, cocoa, baking powder, cinnamon, and salt in a medium bowl. Beat the butter, sugar, and vanilla in a large bowl with an electric mixer at medium speed until creamy. Add the eggs one at a time, beating until just blended after each addition. With mixer on low speed, gradually beat in the dry ingredients. Stir in the pineapple and walnuts by hand. Spoon the batter into the prepared pan.

3. Bake for 35–45 minutes, until a toothpick inserted into the center comes out clean. Cool the cake completely in the pan on a rack. Spread with the frosting.

Chocolate Hazelnut Cake ▷

FRUIT AND VEGETABLE CAKES

Fresh fruit, dried fruit, nuts, and vegetables can be used

to make some delectable cakes. In this chapter we have

included a range of dried fruit and nut cakes, such as

Dundee Cake (see page 156), as well as some delicious

upside-down cakes, including a new take on the classic

Pineapple Upside-Down cake (see page 133). Among the

vegetable cakes we have selected several carrot and

zucchini cakes, and a surprisingly good Chocolate Cake

with Beets (see page 126), among others.

◁ **Spiced Carrot Cake (see page 126)**

Pear and White Chocolate Cake

White chocolate and pears go together very nicely. Be sure to choose a high quality white chocolate that contains at least some cocoa butter.

Serves: 8–10 · Prep: 20 min. · Cooking: 45–55 min. · Level: 1

CAKE
- 4 ounces (125 g) white chocolate, coarsely chopped
- 1½ cups (225 g) all-purpose (plain) flour
- 1½ teaspoons baking powder
- ¼ teaspoon salt
- ½ cup (125 g) butter, softened
- ½ cup (100 g) sugar
- 3 large eggs, separated
- ½ cup (125 ml) milk
- 1 (15-ounce/450-g) can pears, drained and sliced (syrup reserved)

GLAZE
- 1 cup (150 g) confectioners' (icing) sugar
- 2 tablespoons butter, melted

1. Preheat the oven to 325°F (160°C/gas 3). Lightly grease and flour a 9-inch (23-cm) Bundt pan.

2. To prepare the cake, melt the chocolate in a double boiler over barely simmering water. Set aside to cool.

3. Mix the flour, baking powder, and salt in a medium bowl. Beat the butter and sugar in a large bowl with an electric mixer at medium speed until creamy. Add the egg yolks one at a time, beating until just blended after each addition. With mixer on low, beat in the chocolate, followed by the dry ingredients and milk.

3. With mixer on high, beat the egg whites in a large bowl until stiff peaks form. Use a large rubber spatula to fold them into the batter. Spoon half the batter into the prepared pan. Top with the sliced pears. Spoon the remaining batter over the pears.

4. Bake for 45–55 minutes, until a toothpick inserted into the center comes out clean. Cool the cake in the pan for 10 minutes. Turn out onto a wire rack to cool completely.

5. To prepare the glaze, beat the confectioners' sugar and butter in a medium bowl with enough of the reserved pear syrup to make a fairly thick glaze. Drizzle the glaze over the cake, letting it run down the sides.

Easy Moist Lemon Cake

You can whip this simple cake up in just a few minutes. For a slightly different flavor, replace the lemon juice and zest with the same amounts of lime juice and zest or orange juice and zest.

Serves: 8–10 · Prep: 15 min. · Cooking: 40–45 min. · Level: 1

CAKE
- 1½ cups (225 g) all-purpose (plain) flour
- ¾ cup (150 g) sugar
- 3 large eggs
- ½ cup (125 g) butter, softened
- ⅓ cup (90 ml) milk
- 1 tablespoon finely grated lemon zest
- 1½ teaspoons baking powder
- ¼ teaspoon salt

LEMON FROSTING
- 1½ cups (225 g) confectioners' (icing) sugar
- 2 tablespoons butter, melted
- 2 tablespoons freshly squeezed lemon juice
- 2 tablespoons shredded (desiccated) coconut

1. Preheat the oven to 350°F (180°C/gas 4). Lightly grease a 9-inch (23-cm) square pan.

2. To prepare the cake, beat the flour, sugar, eggs, butter, milk, lemon zest, baking powder, and salt in a large bowl with an electric mixer at low speed until well blended. Increase the mixer speed to medium and beat until pale and thick, 3–4 minutes. Spoon the batter into the prepared pan.

3. Bake for 40–45 minutes, or until a toothpick inserted into the center comes out clean. Cool the cake completely in the pan on a rack.

4. To prepare the frosting, beat the confectioners' sugar and butter in a medium bowl. Beat in enough lemon juice to make a spreadable frosting. Spread the cake with the frosting, and sprinkle with the coconut.

Easy Moist Lemon Cake ▷

Lemon and Lime Sour Cream Cake

The sour cream and lime add a pleasing touch of acerbity to this cake.

Serves: 8 · Prep: 25 min. · Cooking: 35–45 min. · Level: 1

CAKE

1¹⁄₃	cups (200 g) all-purpose (plain) flour	
1	teaspoon baking powder	
½	teaspoon baking soda (bicarbonate of soda)	
¼	teaspoon salt	
½	cup (125 g) butter, softened	
1	cup (200 g) sugar	
1	tablespoon finely grated lime zest	
2	large eggs	
⅓	cup (90 ml) sour cream	

CITRUS FROSTING

¼	cup (60 g) butter, softened	
1	tablespoon finely grated lemon zest	
2	cups (300 g) confectioners' (icing) sugar	
3–4	tablespoons freshly squeezed lime juice	

1. Preheat the oven to 325°F (170°C/gas 3). Lightly grease and flour a 9-inch (23-cm) tube pan.

2. To prepare the cake, combine the flour, baking powder, baking soda, and salt in a medium bowl. Beat the butter, sugar, and lime zest in a large bowl with an electric mixer on medium speed until creamy. Add the eggs, one at a time, until just blended after each addition. With mixer on low speed, gradually beat in the mixed dry ingredients, alternating with the sour cream. Spoon the batter into the prepared pan.

3. Bake for 35–45 minutes, or until golden and a toothpick inserted into the center comes out clean. Cool the cake in the pan for 5 minutes. Turn out onto a rack to cool completely.

4. To prepare the frosting, beat the butter and lemon zest in a medium bowl until creamy. Gradually beat in the confectioners' sugar and enough lime juice to make a spreadable frosting. Spread the top and sides of the cake with the frosting.

◁ **Lemon and Lime Sour Cream Cake**

Glazed Potato-Lemon Loaf

The potato starch gives this cake a smooth texture. Potato starch is available in natural food stores. Supermarkets often stock it in the kosher foods section.

Serves 8: · Prep: 15 min. · Cooking: 50–60 min. · Level: 1

CAKE

1	cup (150 g) all-purpose (plain) flour	
1	cup (150 g) potato starch	
½	teaspoon baking powder	
¼	teaspoon salt	
1	cup (250 g) butter, softened	
2	tablespoons finely grated lemon zest	
1¼	cups (250 g) sugar	
4	large eggs	

LEMON GLAZE

1½	cups (225 g) confectioners' (icing) sugar	
3	tablespoons freshly squeezed lemon juice	

1. Preheat the oven to 350°F (180°C/gas 4). Lightly grease a 9 x 5-inch (23 x 13-cm) loaf pan. Line with parchment paper.

2. To prepare the cake, combine the flour, potato starch, baking powder, and salt in a medium bowl. Beat the butter, sugar, and lemon zest in a large bowl with an electric mixer at medium speed until pale and creamy. Add the eggs one at a time, beating until just blended after each addition. With mixer at low speed, gradually beat in the dry ingredients. Spoon the batter into the prepared pan.

3. Bake for 50–60 minutes, or until a toothpick inserted into the center comes out clean. Cool the cake in the pan for 15 minutes. Turn out onto a rack. Carefully remove the paper.

4. To prepare the glaze, place the confectioners' sugar in a medium bowl. Beat in the lemon juice to obtain a pouring glaze. Drizzle the glaze over the cake.

Parsnip and Orange Cake

The unusual combination of parsnip and orange makes a lovely moist cake with a good rich crumb.

Serves: 8–10 · Prep: 00 min. · Cooking: 00 min. · Level: 1

1½	cups (225 g) all-purpose (plain) flour
3	teaspoons baking powder
1	teaspoon ground cinnamon
1	cup (120 g) ground almonds
⅔	cup (150 g) butter
¾	cup (150 g) sugar
1	orange, halved, seeded, and coarsely chopped
2	large eggs, lightly beaten
2	cups (200 g) coarsely grated parsnip
½	cup (90 g) currants
½	cup (75 g) flaked almonds

1. Preheat the oven to 350°F (180°C/gas 4). Lightly grease a 9-inch (23 cm) springform cake pan. Line the base with parchment paper.

2. To prepare the cake, combine the flour, ground almonds, baking powder, and cinnamon in a medium bowl. Melt the butter and sugar together in a small saucepan over low heat. Remove from the heat and set aside to cool slightly.

3. Process the orange in a food processor until finely chopped. Transfer to a medium bowl. Add the eggs, melted butter mixture, parsnip, and currants and stir to combine. Fold in the mixed dry ingredients.

4. Spoon the batter into the prepared pan and sprinkle with flaked almonds. Bake for 50–60 minutes, until a skewer comes out clean when tested. Leave to cool in the pan for 20 minutes, then turn out onto a wire rack and let cool completely.

Potato Cake

This is a very soft, moist cake. You can use leftover mashed potatoes to make it, if you have them on hand.

Serves 8–10 · Prep: 45 min. · Cooking: 35–45 min. · Level: 1

1	pound (500 g) potatoes, with peel
¼	cup (30 g) cornstarch (cornflour)
½	cup (125 g) butter, softened
¾	cup (150 g) sugar
4	large eggs, separated
1	tablespoon finely grated lemon zest
1	teaspoon freshly grated nutmeg
1	teaspoon almond extract (essence)
¾	cup (130 g) raisins
⅓	cup (60 g) pine nuts
⅓	cup (50 g) confectioners' (icing) sugar, to dust

1. Boil the potatoes in their skins in a large covered pot of lightly salted boiling water until tender when pierced with a fork. Drain and slip off the skins. Place the hot potatoes and cornflour in a bowl. Mash until smooth. Set aside to cool for 15 minutes.

2. Preheat the oven to 350°F (180°C/gas 4). Butter a 9-inch (23-cm) springform pan. Line the base with parchment paper.

3. Beat the butter and sugar in a large bowl with an electric mixer on medium speed until pale and creamy. Add the egg yolks one at a time, beating until just blended after each addition. With mixer on low speed, beat in the potatoes, lemon zest, nutmeg, and almond extract. Stir in the raisins and pine nuts.

4. With mixer at high speed, beat the egg whites in a large bowl until stiff peaks form. Use a large rubber spatula to fold them into the batter. Spoon the batter into the prepared pan.

5. Bake for 35–45 minutes, or until golden brown and a toothpick inserted into the center comes out clean. Cool the cake in the pan for 15 minutes. Turn out onto a rack. Carefully remove the paper and let cool completely. Dust with confectioners' sugar before serving.

Parsnip and Orange Cake ▷

Zucchini and Walnut Cake

Zucchini cakes have a moist texture, although this can vary depending on the moisture in the zucchini. Use fresh, in-season zucchini for best results.

Serves: 10-12 · Prep: 20 min. · Cooking: 50–60 min. · Level: 1

CAKE

2½	cups (375 g) all-purpose (plain) flour
2½	teaspoons baking powder
½	teaspoon baking soda (bicarbonate of soda)
½	teaspoon ground nutmeg
1	cup (250 g) butter
1	cup (200 g) firmly packed dark brown sugar
3	large eggs, lightly beaten
2½	cups (350 g) coarsely grated zucchini (courgettes), drained
½	cup (90 g) dates, pitted and coarsely chopped
1	cup (125 g) walnuts, coarsely chopped + extra to decorate

LEMON FROSTING

1	cup (150 g) confectioners' (icing) sugar
2	tablespoons freshly squeezed lemon juice
1	teaspoon finely grated lemon zest

1. Preheat the oven to 350°F (180°C/gas 4). Lightly grease a 9-inch (23 cm) square cake pan and line the base with parchment paper.

2. To prepare the cake, combine the flour, baking powder, baking soda, and nutmeg in a medium bowl. Melt the butter in a small saucepan over low heat. Remove from the heat and transfer to a medium bowl. Add the sugar, eggs, zucchini, dates, and walnuts and stir to combine. Stir in the mixed dry ingredients.

3. Spoon the batter into the prepared pan. Bake for 50–60 minutes, until a skewer comes out clean when inserted into the center. Leave to cool in the pan for 20 minutes, then turn out onto a wire rack and let cool completely.

4. To prepare the frosting, place the confectioners' sugar in a small bowl, add the lemon juice and zest and stir until smooth. Drizzle over the cake and top with chopped walnuts.

◁ **Zucchini and Walnut Cake**

Chocolate Zucchini Bundt Cake

This cake is moist and chocolaty, with a smooth texture.

Serves: 10-12 · Prep: 30 min. · Cooking: 55–65 min. · Level: 1

CAKE

2	cups (300 g) all-purpose (plain) flour
⅔	cup (100 g) unsweetened cocoa powder
2	teaspoons baking powder
1	teaspoon baking soda (bicarbonate of soda)
1	teaspoon ground cinnamon
¼	teaspoon salt
¾	cup (180 g) butter
2	cups (400 g) sugar
2	teaspoons vanilla extract (essence)
3	large eggs
2	cups (275 g) coarsely grated zucchini (courgettes), drained
½	cup (125 ml) milk
1	cup (100 g) walnuts, chopped

ORANGE GLAZE

2	cups (300 g) confectioners' (icing) sugar
1	tablespoon finely grated orange zest
1	teaspoon vanilla extract (essence)
2–3	tablespoons freshly squeezed orange juice

1. Preheat the oven to 350°F (180°C/gas 4). Lightly grease and flour a 10-inch (25-cm) Bundt pan.

2. To prepare the cake, combine the flour, cocoa, baking powder, baking soda, cinnamon, and salt in a large bowl. Beat the butter, sugar, and vanilla in a large bowl with an electric mixer at medium speed until creamy. Add the eggs one at a time, beating until just blended after each addition. With mixer on low, gradually beat in the mixed dry ingredients and zucchini, alternating with the milk. Spoon the batter into the prepared pan.

3. Bake until a toothpick inserted into the center comes out clean, 55–65 minutes. Cool the cake in the pan for 10 minutes. Turn out onto a wire rack to cool completely.

4. To prepare the glaze, stir the confectioners' sugar, orange zest, and vanilla in a medium bowl. Stir in enough of the orange juice to make a thick glaze. Drizzle over the cake.

Chocolate Cake with Beets

This unusual combination of ingredients make a surprisingly good, moist and chocolaty cake.

Serves: 10-12 · Prep: 30 min. · Cooking: 40–50 min. · Level: 1

- 1½ cups (225 g) all-purpose (plain) flour
- ¼ cup (30 g) unsweetened cocoa powder
- 1 teaspoon baking powder
- 1 teaspoon baking soda (bicarbonate of soda)
- 1 teaspoon pumpkin pie spice or allspice
- 3 large eggs, lightly beaten
- 1 cup (200 g) firmly packed brown sugar
- ½ cup (125 g) sour cream
- ⅓ cup (80 ml) vegetable oil
- 1 teaspoon vanilla extract (essence)
- 2 cups (300 g) coarsely grated beets (beetroot/red beet)

CHOCOLATE GLAZE
- 5 ounces (150 g) dark chocolate, coarsely chopped
- ⅓ cup (90 ml) light (single) cream
- ½ teaspoon vanilla extract (essence)

1. Preheat the oven to 325°F (170°C/gas 3). Lightly grease a 9-inch (23 cm) springform cake pan and line the base with parchment paper.

2. To prepare the cake, combine the flour, cocoa, baking powder, baking soda, and pumpkin pie spice into a medium bowl. Beat the eggs, sugar, sour cream, oil, and vanilla in a large bowl with an electric mixer on medium-low speed until smooth. With mixer on low, beat in the mixed dry ingredients. Stir the beets in by hand.

3. Spoon the batter into the prepared pan. Bake for 1 hour, or until a skewer comes out clean when inserted into the center. Leave to cool in the pan for 20 minutes, then turn out onto a wire rack and let cool completely.

4. To prepare the glaze, melt the chocolate, cream, and vanilla in a double boiler over barely simmering water, stirring occasionally until smooth. Remove from the heat and set aside to cool slightly.

5. Spread the glaze over the cake, allowing it to dribble down the sides.

Chocolate Carrot Cake

Not all dark chocolate is dairy-free, although many brands are. Read the label carefully or buy a reputable brand of clearly advertised dairy-free chocolate.

Serves: 10-12 · Prep: 30 min. · Cooking: 40–50 min. · Level: 1

CAKE
- 1½ cups (225 g) all-purpose (plain) flour
- ½ cup (60 g) walnuts, coarsely chopped
- ½ cup (50 g) raisins
- ⅓ cup (50 g) shredded (desiccated) coconut
- ⅓ cup (50 g) unsweetened cocoa powder
- 1 teaspoon ground cinnamon
- 1 teaspoon baking powder
- ½ teaspoon baking soda (bicarbonate of soda)
- ⅓ teaspoon ground ginger
- ¼ teaspoon salt
- 5 ounces (150 g) dairy-free dark chocolate
- 3 large eggs
- ¾ cup (150 g) firmly packed brown sugar
- ½ cup (125 ml) vegetable oil
- 2 cups (300 g) finely grated carrots

FROSTING
- 2 cups (300 g) confectioners' (icing)
- ¼ cup (60 g) dairy-free soy margarine, softened
- ¼ cup (60 ml) plain unsweetened almond milk or soymilk
- ⅓ cup (50 g) unsweetened cocoa powder
- ½ teaspoon vanilla extract (essence)

1. Preheat the oven to 350°F (180°C/gas 4). Lightly grease and flour a 13 x 9-inch (33 x 23-cm) baking pan.

2. To prepare the cake, stir the flour, walnuts, raisins, coconut, cocoa, baking powder, cinnamon, baking soda, ginger, and salt in a large bowl. Melt the chocolate in a double boiler over barely simmering water. Set aside to cool.

3. Beat the eggs, sugar, and oil in a large bowl with an electric mixer at medium speed until creamy. With mixer on low, beat in the dry ingredients, chocolate, and carrots. Spoon into the prepared pan.

4. Bake for 40–50 minutes, or until a toothpick inserted into the center comes out clean. Cool the cake in the pan on a rack.

5. To prepare the frosting, beat all the ingredients until smooth. Spread over the cake.

Chocolate Cake with Beets ▷

Spiced Carrot Cake

This makes a fairly dark, spicy cake that blends in well with the traditional cream-cheese frosting. See the photograph on pages 114–115.

Serves: 10–12 · Prep: 30 min. · Cooking: 75–85 min. · Level: 1

2½   cups (375 g) all-purpose (plain) flour
2   teaspoons baking soda (bicarbonate of soda)
1½   teaspoons ground cinnamon
1½   teaspoons pumpkin pie spice or allspice
½   teaspoon ground cloves
3   large eggs, lightly beaten
1⅓   cups (330 ml) vegetable oil
1   cup (200 g) firmly packed brown sugar
3   cups (300 g) coarsely grated carrots
½   cup (60 g) pecans, coarsely chopped
½   cup (90 g) raisins

CREAM CHEESE FROSTING
½   cup (125 g) cream cheese, softened
¼   cup (60 g) butter, softened
1   teaspoon vanilla extract (essence)
½   teaspoon finely grated lemon zest
1½   cups (225 g) confectioners' (icing) sugar

1. Preheat the oven to 350°F (180°C/gas 4). Lightly grease a 9-inch (23 cm) springform cake pan and line the base with parchment paper.

2. To prepare the cake, combine the flour, baking soda, cinnamon, pumpkin pie spice, and ground cloves in a medium bowl. Beat the eggs, oil, and sugar in a large bowl with an electric mixer medium speed until smooth. With mixer on low, beat in the mixed dry ingredients. Stir the carrots, pecans, and raisins in by hand.

3. Spoon the batter into the prepared pan. Bake for 75–85 minutes, or until a skewer comes out clean when inserted into the center. Leave to cool in the pan for 20 minutes, then turn out onto a wire rack and let cool completely.

4. To prepare the cream cheese frosting, beat the cream cheese, butter, vanilla, and lemon zest in a medium bowl until pale and creamy. Gradually beat in the confectioners' sugar. Spread the cake with the frosting.

Frosted Sunflower Carrot Cake

The sunflower seeds add a special flavor to this carrot cake, while the orange juice in the frosting tinges it a pretty sunflower yellow.

Serves: 10–12 · Prep: 30 min. · Cooking: 70–80 min. · Level: 1

CAKE
2½   cups (375 g) all-purpose (plain) flour
2½   teaspoons baking powder
1   teaspoon ground ginger
1   teaspoon ground nutmeg
½   teaspoon baking soda (bicarbonate of soda)
½   teaspoon salt
1   cup (250 ml) vegetable oil
1¼   cups (250 g) firmly packed brown sugar
3   large eggs
2   cups (250 g) firmly packed coarsely grated carrots
1   cup (180 g) hazelnuts, coarsely chopped
2   tablespoons sunflower seeds

ORANGE FROSTING
1   (3-ounce/90-g) package cream cheese, softened
2   tablespoons butter, softened
1   tablespoon finely grated orange zest
2   cups (300 g) confectioners' (icing) sugar

1. Preheat the oven to 350°F (180°C/gas 4). Lightly grease and flour a 10-inch (26-cm) springform pan.

2. To prepare the cake, combine the flour, baking powder, ginger, nutmeg, baking soda, and salt in a large bowl. Beat the oil, brown sugar, and eggs in a large bowl with an electric mixer on medium speed until smooth. With mixer on low, beat in the carrots, hazelnuts, sunflower seeds, and mixed dry ingredients. •Spoon the batter into the prepared pan.

3. Bake for 70–80 minutes, or until a toothpick inserted into the center comes out clean. Cool in the pan for 10 minutes. Loosen and remove the pan sides. Invert the cake onto a rack. Loosen and remove the pan bottom and let cool completely.

4. To prepare the frosting, beat the cream cheese, butter, and orange zest in a medium bowl until fluffy. Beat in the confectioners' sugar. Spread the cake with the frosting.

Frosted Sunflower Carrot Cake ▷

Carrot and Walnut Cake

This makes an attractive big cake that keeps well. Walnuts are an excellent source of omega-3 fatty acids and eating them regularly may help lower cholesterol.

Serves: 10–12 · Prep: 30 min. · Cooking: 75–85 min. · Level: 1

CAKE

2⅓	cups (350 g) all-purpose (plain) flour
2	teaspoons ground cinnamon
1	teaspoon baking powder
1	teaspoon baking soda (bicarbonate of soda)
1	teaspoon ground ginger
½	teaspoon ground nutmeg
¼	teaspoon ground cloves
¹⁄₂₄	teaspoon salt
1½	cups (375 g) butter, softened
2	cups (400 g) sugar
2	teaspoons vanilla extract (essence)
4	large eggs
2	cups (200 g) finely grated carrots
1½	cups (200 g) fairly finely chopped walnuts
⅓	cup (40 g) raisins

CREAM CHEESE FROSTING

1	(8-ounce/250-g) package cream cheese, softened
⅓	cup (90 g) butter, softened
2½	cups (375 g) confectioners' (icing) sugar
1	tablespoon finely grated lemon zest
2	teaspoons freshly squeezed lemon juice
	Walnut halves, to decorate

1. Preheat the oven to 350°F (180°C/gas 4). Lightly grease and flour a 9-inch (23-cm) springform pan.

2. To prepare the cake, combine the flour, cinnamon, baking powder, baking soda, ginger, nutmeg, cloves, and salt in a large bowl. Beat the butter, sugar, and vanilla in a large bowl with an electric mixer at medium speed until pale and creamy.

3. Add the eggs one at a time, beating until just combined after each addition. With mixer on low speed, gradually beat in the dry ingredients. Stir in the carrots, walnuts, and raisins. Spoon the batter into the prepared pan.

4. Bake for 45–55 minutes, or until a toothpick inserted into the center comes out clean. Cool the cake in the pan for 10 minutes. Loosen and remove the pan sides. Invert the cake onto a rack. Loosen and remove the pan bottom and let cool completely.

5. To prepare the frosting, beat the cream cheese, butter, confectioners' sugar, and lemon zest and juice in a large bowl until creamy and smooth. Spread the cake with the frosting. Decorate with the walnut halves.

Carrot and Walnut Cake ▷

Lumberjack Cake

Prepare this big, nutritious cake for friends and family who, even if they are not lumberjacks, have serious appetites. It keeps well and is better the day after it is baked.

Serves: 8–10 · Prep: 20 min. · Cooking: 35-40 min. · Level: 1

CAKE
- 1 cup (180 g) dried pitted dates, coarsely chopped
- 1 cup (250 ml) boiling water
- 1 teaspoon baking soda (bicarbonate of soda)
- ½ cup (125 g) butter, diced
- 1 cup (200 g) brown sugar
- 1 large egg, lightly beaten
- 1 teaspoon vanilla extract (essence)
- 1⅓ cups (200 g) all-purpose (plain) flour
- ½ teaspoon baking powder
- ¼ cup (30 g) shredded (desiccated) coconut
- 3 medium tart cooking apples, peeled, cored and coarsely chopped

CREAM CHEESE FROSTING
- ½ cup (125 g) cream cheese, softened
- ¼ cup (60 g) butter, softened
- 1 teaspoon vanilla extract (essence)
- ½ teaspoon finely grated lemon zest
- 1½ cups (225 g) confectioners' (icing) sugar
- ⅓ cup (40 g) shredded (desiccated) coconut, lightly toasted

1. Preheat the oven to 350°F (180°C/gas 4). Lightly grease an 8-inch (20 cm) round springform cake pan and line the base with parchment paper.

2. To prepare the cake, place the dates, boiling water, and baking soda in a small heatproof bowl and leave to soak for 5 minutes. Add the butter and stir until melted.

3. Beat the sugar, egg, and vanilla in a large bowl with an electric mixer on medium speed until smooth. With mixer on low, beat in the flour, baking powder, and coconut. Stir in the date mixture and apple by hand. Spoon the batter into the prepared pan.

4. Bake for 50–60 minutes. or until a skewer comes out clean when inserted into the center. Leave to cool in the pan for 20 minutes, then turn out onto a wire rack and let cool completely.

5. To prepare the frosting, beat the cream cheese, butter, vanilla, lemon zest, and confectioners' sugar until smooth. Spread over the top and sides of the cake. Cover the sides with toasted coconut.

Frosted Chocolate-Banana Cake

This is a great cake for people with allergies to dairy food. If liked, prepare it without the frosting.

Serves: 8–10 · Prep: 20 min. · Cooking: 35-40 min. · Level: 1

CAKE
- 2 cups (300 g) all-purpose (plain) flour
- ½ cup (75 g) unsweetened cocoa powder
- 1½ teaspoons baking powder
- ½ teaspoon baking soda (bicarbonate of soda)
- ¼ teaspoon salt
- 1 cup (200 g) sugar
- 2 large eggs
- ¾ cup (180 ml) hot water
- 1 cup (250 g) very ripe bananas (about 3 large bananas), mashed
- 1½ teaspoons vanilla extract (essence)

DAIRY-FREE FROSTING
- 2 cups (300 g) confectioners' (icing)
- ¼ cup (60 g) dairy-free soy margarine, softened
- ¼ cup (60 ml) plain unsweetened almond milk or soymilk
- ⅓ cup (50 g) unsweetened cocoa powder
- ½ teaspoon vanilla extract (essence)

1. Preheat the oven to 350°F (180°C/gas 4). Lightly grease a 9-inch (23-cm) square baking pan. Line with parchment paper.

2. To prepare the cake, combine the flour, cocoa, baking powder, baking soda, and salt in a large bowl. Stir in the sugar. Beat in the eggs, water, banana, and vanilla. Spoon the batter into the prepared pan.

3. Bake for 35–40 minutes, or until a toothpick inserted into the center comes out clean. Cool the cake in the pan for 10 minutes. Turn out onto a rack. Carefully remove the paper and let cool completely.

4. To prepare the frosting, beat the confectioners' sugar, soy margarine, almond or soy milk, cocoa, and vanilla in a large bowl with an electric mixer on medium-low speed until smooth. Spread the frosting over the cake.

Lumberjack Cake ▷

Pineapple Upside-Down Cake

The coconut milk in this cake adds an exotic flavor to this old favorite.

Serves: 8 · Prep: 40 min. · Cooking: 35–40 min. · Level: 2

- ½ medium pineapple, peeled, cored, quartered lengthways and cut into ¼-inch (5-mm) thick slices
- ½ cup (125 g) butter
- ½ cup (100 g) firmly packed light brown sugar
- 1 tablespoon light corn (golden) syrup
- 1½ cups (225 g) all-purpose (plain) flour
- 1½ teaspoons baking powder
- 1 teaspoon ground cinnamon
- ½ cup (100 g) sugar
- 2 large eggs
- 1 teaspoon vanilla extract (essence)
- 1 teaspoon finely grated lemon zest
- ⅔ cup (150 ml) coconut milk

1. Preheat the oven to 350°F (180°C/gas 4). Lightly grease an 8-inch (20 cm) springform cake pan. Line the base with parchment paper.

2. To prepare the topping, arrange the pineapple pieces on the base of the prepared pan. Melt 2 tablespoons of the butter, the sugar, and corn syrup in a small saucepan over medium-low heat and bring to a boil, stirring occasionally until the sugar has dissolved. Pour this caramel mixture over the pineapple and set aside.

3. To prepare the cake, combine the flour, baking powder, and cinnamon in a small bowl. Beat the remaining butter, sugar, vanilla, and lemon zest in a large bowl with an electric mixer on medium until creamy. Add the eggs in one at a time, beating until just blended after each addition. With mixer on low, beat in the mixed dry ingredients, alternating with the coconut milk. Spread the batter over the pineapple, covering evenly.

4. Bake for 35–40 minutes, until golden brown and a skewer comes out clean when inserted into the center. Leave to cool in the pan for 10 minutes. Invert onto a serving plate. Serve warm or at room temperature.

Upside-Down Apple Cake

This is a simple upside-down cake with a classic caramelized topping.

Serves: 8–10 · Prep: 25 min. · Cooking: 45–55 min. · Level: 1

- ⅓ cup (75 g) firmly packed light brown sugar
- 2 large apples, peeled and cored
- 1 tablespoon freshly squeezed lemon juice
- 2 cups (300 g) all-purpose (plain) flour
- 1½ teaspoons baking powder
- ½ teaspoon baking soda (bicarbonate of soda)
- 1 teaspoon ground cardamom
- 1 teaspoon ground cinnamon
- ¼ teaspoon salt
- ¾ cup (180 g) butter, softened
- ¾ cup (150 g) sugar
- 1 teaspoon vanilla extract (essence)
- 2 large eggs
- ½ cup (125 ml) milk

1. Preheat the oven to 350°F (180°C/gas 4). Lightly grease a 9-inch (23-cm) round cake pan.

2. To prepare the topping, sprinkle the pan with half the brown sugar. Slice one apple into thin rings and lay over the brown sugar. Sprinkle with the remaining brown sugar and drizzle with the lemon juice.

3. To prepare the cake, combine the flour, baking powder, baking soda, cardamom, cinnamon, and salt in a medium bowl. Beat the butter, sugar, and vanilla in a large bowl with an electric mixer at medium speed until pale and creamy. Add the eggs one at a time, beating until just blended after each addition. With mixer at low speed, gradually beat in the dry ingredients, alternating with the milk. Chop the remaining apple finely and stir into the batter. Spoon the batter over the sliced apple.

4. Bake for 45–55 minutes, or until a toothpick inserted into the center comes out clean. Cool the cake in the pan for 15 minutes. Turn out onto a rack. Serve warm or at room temperature.

◁ **Pineapple Upside-Down Cake**

Upside-Down Citrus Polenta Cake

Polenta is the Italian word for cornmeal. It is usually golden yellow and medium or coarse-grained. Polenta is packed with energy-giving carbohydrates and is also a good source of phosphorus, thiamin, folate, and calcium.

Serves: 8–10 · Prep: 30 min. · Cooking: 50–60 min. · Level: 2

- 1½ cups (375 ml) water
- 1¾ cups (350 g) sugar
- 3 lemons, thinly sliced
- 1 cup (150 g) all-purpose (plain) flour
- ¾ cup (120 g) polenta (yellow cornmeal)
- ½ cup (75 g) finely ground almonds
- 1 teaspoon baking powder
- ¼ teaspoon salt
- ½ cup (125 g) butter, softened
- 1 tablespoon finely grated lemon zest
- 1 teaspoon lemon extract (essence)
- 3 large eggs
- ⅓ cup (90 ml) sour cream
- ¼ cup (60 ml) freshly squeezed lemon juice

1. Preheat the oven to 350°F (180°C/gas 4). Lightly grease and flour a 9-inch (23-cm) springform pan.

2. To prepare the topping, heat 1¼ cups (310 ml) of water and ¾ cup (150 g) of sugar in a large frying pan over medium heat until the sugar has dissolved. Bring to a boil and simmer for 5 minutes, or until the syrup begins to thicken. Add the lemons and simmer for about 8 minutes, turning once, until the lemon peel is tender. Using tongs, remove the lemon slices from the syrup and press them, overlapping, onto the bottom and sides of the prepared pan.

3. Return the syrup to medium heat and stir in the remaining water. Simmer until the syrup is pale gold. Carefully spoon the syrup over the lemon slices in the pan.

4. Stir together the flour, polenta, almonds, baking powder, and salt. Beat the butter, remaining sugar, lemon zest, and lemon extract in a large bowl with an electric mixer at medium speed until pale and creamy. Add the eggs one at a time, beating until just blended after each addition. With mixer on low, beat in the dry ingredients, sour cream. and lemon juice. Spoon the batter into the prepared pan.

5. Bake for 50–60 minutes, or until a toothpick inserted into the center comes out clean. Cool the cake in the pan for 15 minutes. Invert onto a serving dish. Serve warm.

Fresh Fruit Upside-Down Cake

You can vary the fruit in this cake depending on what you have on hand.

Serves: 8–10 · Prep: 30 min. · Cooking: 45–55 min. · Level: 1

- 1⅓ cups (200 g) all-purpose (plain) flour
- 1½ teaspoons baking powder
- ¼ teaspoon salt
- ¾ cup (180 g) butter, softened
- 1½ cups (300 g) sugar
- 4 large eggs
- ¼ cup (60 ml) cold water
- 3 apricots, pitted and quartered
- 1 large apple, peeled, cored, and quartered
- 1 large pear, peeled, cored, and quartered

1. Preheat the oven to 350°F (180°C/gas 4). Butter a 9-inch (23-cm) round cake pan.

2. To prepare the cake, combine the flour, baking powder, and salt in a medium bowl. Beat ½ cup (125 g) of butter and ¾ cup (150 g) of sugar in a large bowl with an electric mixer at medium speed until creamy. Add the eggs one at a time, beating until just blended after each addition. With mixer at low speed, gradually beat in the dry ingredients.

3. Place the remaining sugar and water in a small saucepan over medium-low heat. Cook until the sugar and water are caramelized golden brown. Pour into the prepared pan, tilting it to coat the bottom evenly.

4. Melt the remaining butter and pour it into the pan with the caramel. Arrange the fruit over the caramel mixture. Spoon the batter into the pan over the fruit.

5. Bake for 35–45 minutes, or until a toothpick inserted into the center comes out clean. Cool the cake in the pan for 15 minutes. Invert the cake onto a serving plate. Serve warm or cool.

Fresh Fruit Upside-Down Cake ▷

Country Apple Bake

With the rounded apple halves poking through the top, this cake has a rustic air. Serve with ice cream or Chantilly Cream (see page 275).

Serves: 8–10 · Prep: 20 min. · Cooking: 40–50 min. · Level: 1

½	cup (125 g) butter, softened
½	cup (100 g) sugar
1½	teaspoons finely grated lemon zest
2	large eggs
1½	cups (225 g) all-purpose (plain) flour
2	teaspoons baking powder
¼	teaspoon salt
⅓	cup (90 ml) milk
4	medium apples, peeled, cored, and halved
2	tablespoons freshly squeezed lemon juice
2	tablespoons apricot preserves (jam)

1. Preheat the oven to 350°F (180°C/gas 4). Lightly grease and flour a 9-inch springform pan.

2. To prepare the cake, beat the butter, sugar, and lemon zest in a large bowl with an electric mixer at medium speed until creamy. Add the eggs one at a time, until just blended after each addition. With mixer at low speed, gradually beat in the flour, baking powder, and salt, alternating with the milk. Spoon the batter into the prepared pan. Use a sharp knife to cut a grid pattern into the rounded sides of the apples. Drizzle with the lemon juice. Arrange the apples, cut-side-down, in the batter.

3. Bake for 40–50 minutes, or a toothpick inserted into the batter comes out clean and the apples are tender.

4. Warm the apricot preserves in a small saucepan over low heat and brush over the cake. Loosen and remove the pan sides to serve. Serve warm.

Irish Apple Cake

This cake is named for the Irish whisky it contains. The frosting tastes something like a hot toddy!

Serves: 8–10 · Prep: 30 min. · Cooking: 35–45 min. · Level: 1

CAKE

2⅓	cups (375 g) all-purpose (plain) flour
2	teaspoons ground cinnamon
1½	teaspoons baking powder
1	teaspoon ground nutmeg
½	teaspoon baking soda (bicarbonate of soda)
¼	teaspoon salt
½	cup (125 g) butter, softened
¾	cup firmly packed brown sugar
1½	teaspoons vanilla extract (essence)
2	large eggs
⅓	cup (90 ml) milk
2	tablespoons Irish whisky
2	large apples, peeled, cored, and finely chopped

GLAZE

1	cup (150 g) confectioners' (icing) sugar
3	teaspoons freshly squeezed lemon juice
3	teaspoons Irish whisky

1. Preheat the oven to 350°F (180°C/gas 4). Lightly grease and flour a 9-inch tube pan.

2. To prepare the cake, combine the flour, cinnamon, baking powder, nutmeg, baking soda, and salt in a large bowl. Beat the butter, brown sugar, and vanilla in a large bowl with an electric mixer at medium speed until creamy. Add the eggs one at a time, just until blended after each addition. With mixer at low speed, gradually beat in the dry ingredients, alternating with the milk, and whisky. Stir in the apples. Spoon the batter into the prepared pan.

3. Bake for 35–45 minutes, or until a toothpick inserted into the center comes out clean. Cool the cake in the pan for 15 minutes. Turn out onto the rack to cool completely.

4. To prepare the glaze, beat the confectioners' sugar, lemon juice, and whiskey in a medium bowl. Drizzle over the cake.

Pear Cake

Replace the Marsala with the same quantity of dry sherry, if preferred.

Serves: 8–10 · Prep: 25 min. · Cooking: 30–40 min. · Level: 1

- 2 pounds (1 kg) small, ripe pears, peeled, cored, and sliced ¼ inch (5 mm) thick
- 3 tablespoons freshly squeezed lemon juice
- 1⅓ cups (200 g) all-purpose (plain) flour
- 1 tablespoon ground cinnamon
- 1½ teaspoons baking powder
- ¼ teaspoon salt
- 3 large eggs
- 1¾ cups (350 g) sugar
- ½ cup (125 g) butter, melted + 3 tablespoons cold butter, cut up
- ⅓ cup (90 ml) dry Marsala wine

1. Place the pears in a bowl and drizzle with the lemon juice. Preheat the oven to 350°F (180°C/gas 4). Lightly grease a 9-inch (23-cm) springform pan.

2. To prepare the cake, combine the flour, 2 teaspoons cinnamon, baking powder, and salt into a large bowl. Beat the eggs and ¾ cup sugar in a large bowl with an electric mixer at high speed until pale and thick. With mixer at low speed, gradually beat in the dry ingredients, alternating with the melted butter and wine.

3. Spoon half the batter into the prepared pan. Top with the pears. Dot the pears with the cold butter and sprinkle with 3 tablespoons sugar and the remaining cinnamon. Spoon the remaining batter over the top. Don't worry if the pears are not completely covered. Sprinkle with the remaining sugar.

4. Bake for 30–40 minutes, or until a toothpick inserted into the center comes out clean. Cool the cake completely in the pan on a rack. Loosen and remove the pan sides to serve.

Fresh Fruit Cake

This is a quick and easy cake to make. Vary the fruit according to the season.

Serves: 8 · Prep: 15 min. · Cooking: 25–35 min. · Level: 1

- 2 large eggs
- ¼ cup (50 g) sugar
- ½ cup (125 g) butter, melted
- ¼ cup (30 g) all-purpose (plain) flour
- 2 tablespoons water
- 1 teaspoon baking powder
- ¼ teaspoon salt
- 1 pear, peeled, cored, and finely chopped
- 1 apple, peeled, cored, and finely chopped
- 1 peach, peeled, cored, and finely chopped

1. Preheat the oven to 350°F (180°C/gas 4). Lightly grease an 8-inch (20-cm) round cake pan.

2. To prepare the cake, beat the eggs and sugar in a medium bowl with an electric mixer on medium-high speed until pale and thick. With mixer at medium-low speed, beat in the butter, flour, water, baking powder, and salt until smooth. Stir in the fruit. Spoon the batter into the prepared pan.

3. Bake for 25–35 minutes, or until a toothpick inserted into the center comes out clean. Cool the cake in the pan for 15 minutes. Turn out onto a rack to cool completely.

Cherry and Almond Cake

Bake this cake in the early summer when cherries come into season. The tastier the cherries, the better this cake will be.

Serves: 10–12 · Prep: 45 min. · Cooking: 45–50 min. · Level: 1

²/₃ cup (150 g) butter, softened
³/₄ cup (150 g) sugar
1½ teaspoons vanilla extract (essence)
2 large eggs
1¼ cups (180 g) all-purpose (plain) flour
1 teaspoon baking powder
1 teaspoon ground cinnamon
1 cup (100 g) ground almonds, lightly toasted
⅓ cup (90 ml) milk
1½ pounds (750 g) fresh ripe cherries, pitted

1. Preheat the oven to 350°F (180°C/gas 4). Lightly grease a 9-inch (23 cm) springform cake pan and line the base with parchment paper.

2. To prepare the cake, combine the flour, almonds, baking powder, and cinnamon in a medium bowl. Beat the butter, sugar, and vanilla in a large bowl with an electric mixer on medium speed until pale and creamy. Add the eggs in one at a time, beating until just blended after each addition. With mixer on low, gradually beat in the mixed dry ingredients, alternating with the milk.

3. Place the cherries in the base of the prepared pan and spoon the batter over the top.

4. Bake for 45–50 minutes, until golden brown and a skewer comes out clean when tested. Leave to cool in the pan for 10 minutes, then turn out onto a wire rack and let cool completely.

5. When ready to serve, invert the cake onto a serving plate, cherry-side up.

Pear and Hazelnut Cake

Bosc pears are a good choice for this cake. Select pears that are ripe but still firm; they should not be overripe.

Serves: 8–10 · Prep: 25 min. · Cooking: 55–65 min. · Level: 1

TOPPING
½ cup (100 g) firmly packed dark brown sugar
⅓ cup (50 g) all-purpose (plain) flour
1 teaspoon ground cinnamon
¼ cup (60 g) cold butter, cut up
¾ cup hazelnuts, coarsely chopped

1½ cups (225 g) all-purpose (plain) flour
1 teaspoon baking powder
1 teaspoon ground cinnamon
½ teaspoon baking soda (bicarbonate of soda)
¼ teaspoon salt
½ cup (125 g) butter, softened
1 cup (200 g) sugar
½ teaspoon lemon extract (essence)
2 large eggs
¾ cup (180 ml) sour cream
1½ cups (250 g) firm-ripe pears, peeled, cored, and diced

1. Preheat the oven to 350°F (180°C/gas 4). Lightly grease and flour a 13 x 9-inch (33 x 23-cm) baking pan.

2. To prepare the topping, stir the brown sugar, flour, and cinnamon in a medium bowl. Use a pastry blender to cut in the butter until the mixture resembles fine crumbs. Stir in the hazelnuts.

3. To prepare the cake, combine the flour, baking powder, baking soda, cinnamon, and salt into a medium bowl. Beat the butter, sugar, and lemon extract in a large bowl with an electric mixer at medium speed until creamy. Add the eggs one at a time, beating until just blended after each addition. With mixer on low, gradually beat in the dry ingredients, alternating with the sour cream. Stir in the pears. Spoon the batter into the prepared pan. Sprinkle with the topping.

4. Bake for 55–65 minutes, or until golden brown, the cake shrinks from the pan sides, and a toothpick inserted into the center comes out clean. Cool the cake completely in the pan on a rack.

Cherry and Almond Cake ▷

Spiced Apple Cake

This is a lovely moist cake to serve with a cup of tea or coffee or as a family dessert. Try it warm with a scoop or two of vanilla ice cream on each portion.

Serves: 8–10 · Prep: 30 min. · Cooking: 55–65 min. · Level: 1

1	cup (150 g) all-purpose (plain) flour
1	teaspoon baking powder
2	teaspoons ground cinnamon
¼	cup (60 g) butter, softened
½	cup (100 g) sugar
1	teaspoon vanilla extract (essence)
1	large egg
⅓	cup (90 ml) milk
2	tart cooking apples, such as Granny Smith, quartered, cored, and thinly sliced
1	tablespoon freshly squeezed lemon juice
2	tablespoons butter, melted
1	tablespoon superfine (caster) sugar

1. Preheat the oven to 350°F (180°C/gas 4). Lightly grease an 8-inch (20-cm) springform cake pan and line the base with parchment paper.

2. To prepare the cake, combine the flour, baking powder, and 1 teaspoon of the cinnamon in a small bowl. Beat the butter, sugar, and vanilla in a large bowl with an electric mixer on medium speed until pale and creamy. Beat in the egg until just combined. With mixer on low, gradually beat in the mixed dry ingredients, alternating with the milk. Spoon the batter into the prepared pan.

3. Place the apple slices and lemon juice in a medium bowl and toss to coat. Arrange the apple decoratively in a fan shape over the batter.

4. Bake for 25–30 minutes, or until golden brown and firm to the touch. Leave to cool in the pan for 10 minutes and then turn out onto a wire rack. Brush the top with melted butter and sprinkle with superfine sugar and the remaining cinnamon. Serve warm or at room temperature.

Glazed Apple Crumble Cake

Use tart-tasting apples such as Granny Smith in this recipe for the best results.

Serves: 8–10 · Prep: 30 min. · Cooking: 55–65 min. · Level: 1

CAKE

2	cups (300 g) all-purpose (plain) flour
2	teaspoons baking powder
¼	teaspoon salt
½	cup (125 g) butter, softened
1	cup (200 g) sugar
1	teaspoon vanilla extract (essence)
1	large egg
1	cup (250 ml) buttermilk
2	tart apples, peeled, cored, and thinly sliced

CRUMBLE

½	cup (100 g) firmly packed brown sugar
3	tablespoons butter, melted
1	teaspoon cinnamon
½	teaspoon nutmeg

GLAZE

¾	cup (200 g) apricot preserves (jam)
1	tablespoon freshly squeezed lemon juice

1. Preheat the oven to 350°F (180°C/gas 4). Lightly grease and flour a 9-inch (23-cm) square baking pan.

2. To prepare the cake, combine the flour, baking powder, and salt in a medium bowl. Beat the butter, sugar, and vanilla in a large bowl with an electric mixer at medium speed until pale and creamy. Add the egg, beating until just blended. With mixer on low, beat in the dry ingredients, alternating with the buttermilk. Spoon the batter into the prepared pan. Arrange the apples on top in layers.

3. To prepare the crumble, mix the brown sugar, butter, cinnamon, and nutmeg in a small bowl until crumbly. Sprinkle over the apples.

4. Bake for 55–65 minutes, or until the apples are tender, the crumble is brown, and a toothpick inserted into the center comes out clean. Cool the cake completely in the pan on a rack.

5. To prepare the glaze, warm the apricot preserves and lemon juice in a saucepan over low heat. Brush the cake with the glaze just before serving.

Spiced Apple Cake ▷

Hummingbird Cake

This modern classic was first recorded in the February 1978 issue of Southern Living magazine. The recipe was submitted by a Mrs. Wiggins from North Carolina. No one knows the origin of its exotic name, but it is thought to symbolize the tropics and sweetness.

Serves: 10–12 · Prep: 20 min.+ 1 hr. to stand · Cooking: 40–50 min. · Level: 1

CAKES

1½	cups (225 g) all-purpose (plain) flour
1	teaspoon baking soda (bicarbonate of soda)
1½	teaspoons ground cinnamon
1	cup (200 g) firmly packed brown sugar
½	cup (125 ml) vegetable oil
2	large eggs, lightly beaten
1	teaspoon vanilla extract (essence)
1	(15-ounce/450-g) can crushed pineapple, drained
1	cup (200 g) mashed banana
½	cup (60 g) shredded (desiccated) coconut
¾	cup (90 g) pecans, coarsely chopped

CREAM CHEESE FROSTING

¾	cup (180 g) cream cheese, softened
⅓	cup (90 g) butter, softened
1	teaspoon vanilla extract (essence)
2½	cups (375 g) confectioners' (icing) sugar

1. Preheat the oven to 325°F (170°C/gas 3). Lightly grease a 9-inch (23 cm) springform cake pan. Line the base with parchment paper.

2. To prepare the cake, combine the flour, baking soda, and cinnamon in a medium bowl. Beat the sugar, oil, eggs, and vanilla in a medium bowl with an electric mixer on low speed until smooth. Stir the pineapple, banana, coconut, and ½ cup (60 g) of the pecans in by hand. Fold in the mixed dry ingredients. Spoon the batter into the prepared pan.

3. Bake for 40–45 minutes, or until a skewer comes out clean when inserted into the center. Leave to cool in the pan for 20 minutes, then turn out onto a wire rack. Carefully remove the paper and let cool completely and let cool completely.

4. To prepare the cream cheese frosting, beat the cream cheese, butter, and vanilla in a medium bow until pale and creamy. Gradually beat in the confectioners' sugar. Spread the frosting over the top and sides of the cake. Sprinkle with the remaining chopped pecans.

Frosted Orange Coconut Cake

Use blood oranges in the frosting to obtain a lovely pink-toned frosting.

Serves: 8–10 · Prep: 20 min.+ 1 hr. to stand · Cooking: 40–50 min. · Level: 1

CAKE

1	cup (250 ml) milk
¾	cup shredded (desiccated) coconut
¼	cup (60 ml) freshly squeezed orange juice
½	cup (125 g) butter, softened
1	cup (200 g) sugar
2	tablespoons finely grated orange zest
2	large eggs
2	cups (300 g) all-purpose (plain) flour
2	teaspoons baking powder
½	teaspoon salt

ORANGE FROSTING

2	cups (300 g) confectioners' sugar
2	tablespoons butter, melted
1–2	tablespoons freshly squeezed orange juice

1. To prepare the cake, mix the milk, coconut, and orange juice in a medium bowl. Cover and let stand at room temperature for 1 hour.

2. Preheat the oven to 325°F (170°F/gas 3). Lightly grease a 9-inch (23-cm) springform pan and line the base with parchment paper.

3. Beat the butter, sugar, and orange zest in a large bowl with an electric mixer at medium speed until creamy. Add the eggs one at a time, beating until just blended after each addition. With mixer on low, gradually beat in the flour, baking powder, and salt, alternating with the coconut mixture. Spoon the batter into the prepared pan.

4. Bake for 40–50 minutes, or until a toothpick inserted into the center comes out clean. Cool the cake in the pan for 10 minutes. Turn out onto a rack. Carefully remove the paper and let cool completely.

5. To prepare the frosting, mix the confectioners' sugar and butter in a medium bowl. Add enough orange juice to make a thick, spreadable frosting. Spread over the top and sides of the cake.

Hummingbird Cake ▷

Dried Fig and Apricot Cake

This nutritious, energy-giving cake is perfect for skiers, trampers, climbers, or people engaging in other activities where sustained energy is required over long periods of time.

Serves: 10–12 · Prep: 20 min. + 10 min. to soak · Cooking: 45–55 min. · Level: 1

¾	cup (135 g) dried figs
¾	cup (135 g) dried apricots
2⅔	cup (400 g) all-purpose (plain) flour
2	teaspoons baking powder
1	teaspoon pumpkin pie spice or allspice
½	teaspoon baking soda (bicarbonate of soda)
¾	cup (150 g) sugar
⅓	cup (80 g) butter, softened
1½	teaspoons finely grated lemon zest
3	large eggs
¼	cup (60 ml) Grand Marnier or other orange liqueur
1¼	cups (300 ml) milk
	Confectioners' (icing) sugar, to dust

1. Preheat the oven to 350°F (180°C/gas 4). Lightly grease a 9-inch (23 cm) springform cake pan and line the base with parchment paper.

2. Place the figs and apricots in a medium bowl and cover with boiling water. Leave to soak for 10 minutes.

3. Combine the flour, baking powder, pumpkin pie spice, and baking soda into a medium bowl. Beat the sugar, butter, and lemon zest in a large bowl with an electric mixer on medium speed until pale and creamy. Add the eggs one at a time, beating until just blended after each addition. With mixer on low, gradually beat in the mixed dry ingredients, alternating with the milk and liqueur.

4. Drain the figs and apricots. Slice and stir into the batter by hand. Spoon the batter into the prepared pan.

5. Bake for 45–50 minutes, until a skewer comes out clean when inserted into the center. Leave to cool in the pan for 10 minutes, then turn out onto a wire rack and let cool completely. Dust with confectioners' sugar.

Polenta Cake with Candied Peel

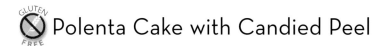

This is a traditional Italian cake from the north of Italy. Grappa is a pomace brandy made from the skins, stems, and stalks of the grapes that are leftover from making wine.

Serves: 10–12 · Prep: 20 min. + 15 min. to stand · Cooking: 75–85 min. · Level: 2

⅓	cup (60 g) coarsely chopped blanched almonds
½	cup (50 g) chopped candied peel
¼	cup (60 ml) grappa
3	tablespoons golden raisins (sultanas)
2	tablespoons chopped dried figs
1	teaspoon fennel seeds
1	quart (1 liter) milk
2½	cups (375 g) polenta (yellow cornmeal)
⅓	cup (50 g) cornstarch (cornflour)
½	cup (100 g) sugar
⅔	cup (180 g) butter
¼	teaspoon salt

1. Preheat the oven to 350°F (180°C/gas 4). Lightly grease and flour a 10-inch (25-cm) springform pan.

2. Stir the almonds, grappa, candied peel, raisins, figs, and fennel seeds in a medium bowl. Let stand for 15 minutes.

3. Bring the milk to a boil in a large saucepan over medium heat. Reduce the heat to low. Gradually add the polenta and flour, stirring constantly for 15 minutes. Stir in the sugar, butter, and salt, and cook, stirring occasionally, for 10 minutes. Remove from the heat.

4. Stir in the fruit and grappa mixture. Spoon the batter into the prepared pan.

5. Bake for 50–60 minutes, or until lightly browned. After 30 minutes cover the top of the cake loosely with a piece of aluminum foil to prevent it from drying out.

6. Cool the cake completely in the pan on a rack. Loosen and remove the pan sides to serve.

Dried Fig and Apricot Cake ▷

French Almond and Pumpkin Cake

The orange syrup and nut topping on this cake make it superb.

Serves: 8–10 · Prep: 1 hr. + 1 hr. to rest · Cooking: 25–30 min. · Level: 2

CAKE

1¼	cups (250 g) cooked pumpkin or winter squash, cut in small cubes
6	large eggs, separated
1	cup (200 g) sugar
1	teaspoon ground cinnamon
¼	teaspoon salt
2	tablespoons finely grated orange zest
2	tablespoons finely grated lemon zest
1²/₃	cups (250 g) almonds, finely ground
⅓	cup (50 g) all-purpose (plain) flour
	Scant 1 cup (100 g) candied (glacé) orange peel, finely chopped

ORANGE TOPPING

¼	cup (75 g) orange marmalade
¼	cup (60 ml) freshly squeezed orange juice
2	tablespoons freshly squeezed lemon juice
¼	cup (50 g) sugar
¾	cup (60 ml) orange liqueur
½	cup (60 g) slivered almonds

1. Preheat the oven to 400°F (200°C/gas 6). Oil and flour a 10-inch (25-cm) springform pan.

2. To prepare the cake, beat the egg yolks, ¼ cup (50 g) sugar, cinnamon, and salt with an electric mixer at high speed until frothy. Beat in the orange and lemon zest. With mixer on low, gradually beat in the almonds, flour, orange peel, and pumpkin.

3. With mixer on medium, beat the egg whites until frothy. Beat in the remaining sugar until stiff peaks form. Use a large rubber spatula to fold into the pumpkin mixture. Spoon into the prepared pan.

4. Bake for 25–30 minutes, until a toothpick inserted into the center comes out clean. Cool the cake in the pan for 10 minutes. Loosen and remove the pan sides. Invert onto a rack to cool completely.

5. Split the cake horizontally. Place a layer on a serving plate. Spread with the marmalade. Top with the other layer. Bring the citrus juices and sugar to a boil. Remove from the heat. Stir in the orange liqueur. Prick the cake with a fork and drizzle with the syrup. Sprinkle with the slivered almonds.

Crumbly Almond Cake

As its name suggests, this is a very dry, crumbly cake. Press it into the pan. When baked and cooled, cut with a large heavy knife. Don't worry if it breaks and splinters into irregular shaped pieces. It is very good served with sherry or dessert wine.

Serves: 8 · Prep: 30 min. · Cooking: 35–45 min. · Level: 1

2	cups (300 g) all-purpose (plain) flour
2	cups (300 g) finely ground almonds
1	cup (200 g) sugar
¼	teaspoon salt
¾	cup (180 g) cold butter, cut up
4–5	large eggs, lightly beaten

1. Preheat the oven to 350°F (180°C/gas 4). Lightly grease and flour a 10-inch (26-cm) springform pan.

2. Mix the flour, almonds, sugar, and salt in a large bowl. Use your fingers to rub the butter and 4 eggs into the dry ingredients until the dough resembles large crumbs. It should be quite dry and crumbly. Add the other egg if it is too dry. Transfer the dough to the prepared pan, pressing it down firmly.

3. Bake for 35–45 minutes, or until a toothpick inserted into the center comes out clean. Cool the cake in the pan for 10 minutes. Loosen the pan sides and let cool completely. Cut or break into irregular diamond shapes to serve.

French Almond and Pumpkin Cake ▷

Pumpkin Fruit Cake

This cake has a good color and texture. The orange frosting contrasts nicely with the pumpkin and fruit flavors in the cake.

Serves: 8–10 · Prep: 25 min. · Cooking: 45–55 min. · Level: 2

CAKE

2	cups (300 g) all-purpose (plain) flour
1½	teaspoons baking powder
1½	teaspoons pumpkin pie spice or allspice
¾	cup (180 g) butter
1	cup (200 g) firmly packed brown sugar
2	tablespoons light corn (golden) syrup
2	large eggs, lightly beaten
1	pound (500 g) mixed dried fruit
1	cup (200 g) cooked mashed pumpkin or winter squash
1	teaspoon finely grated orange zest

ORANGE FROSTING

1¼	cups (180 g) confectioners' (icing) sugar
½	teaspoon ground cinnamon
2½	tablespoons freshly squeezed orange juice
1	teaspoon finely grated orange zest

1. Preheat the oven to 350°F (180°C/gas 4). Lightly grease an 8-inch (20 cm) springform cake pan and line the base with parchment paper.

2. To prepare the cake, combine the flour, baking powder, and pumpkin spice in a medium bowl. Melt the butter, sugar, and corn syrup in a small saucepan over low heat, stir occasionally until dissolved. Remove from the heat and transfer to a medium bowl. Add the eggs, fruit, and pumpkin and orange zest and stir to combine. Fold in the mixed dry ingredients.

3. Spoon the batter into the prepared pan and bake for 80–90 minutes, until a skewer comes out clean when inserted into the center. Leave to cool in the pan for 20 minutes, then turn out onto a wire rack and let cool completely.

4. To prepare the frosting, combine the confectioners' sugar and cinnamon in a small bowl, add the orange juice and zest, and stir until smooth. Spread over the top of the cooled cake.

Spiced Lemon Pumpkin Cake

Steam or bake the orange pumpkin or winter squash flesh to use in the recipes on this page. Let cool, then mash until smooth with a fork. If preferred, use canned pumpkin.

Serves: 8–10 · Prep: 25 min. · Cooking: 45–55 min. · Level: 2

CAKE

1⅔	cups (250 g) all-purpose (plain) flour
1	cup (125 g) old-fashioned rolled oats
1	teaspoon baking powder
1	teaspoon ground ginger
1	teaspoon ground cinnamon
½	teaspoon baking soda (bicarbonate of soda)
½	teaspoon ground nutmeg
¼	teaspoon salt
½	cup (125 g) butter, softened
⅔	cup (150 g) honey
1	tablespoon finely grated lemon zest
1	large egg
1	cup (200 g) cooked mashed pumpkin or winter squash
¼	cup (60 ml) milk

CREAM CHEESE FROSTING

2	packages (3 ounces each) cream cheese, softened
1	cup confectioners' (icing) sugar
1	tablespoon grated lemon zest
2–3	tablespoons fresh lemon juice

1. Preheat the oven to 350°F (180°C/gas 4). Lightly grease and flour a 9-inch (23-cm) springform pan.

2. To prepare the cake, combine the flour, oats, baking powder, cinnamon, ginger, baking soda, nutmeg, and salt in a large bowl. Beat the butter, honey, and lemon zest in a large bowl with an electric mixer at medium speed until creamy. Add the egg, beating until just blended. With mixer on low, beat in the pumpkin, dry ingredients, and milk. Spoon the batter into the prepared pan.

3. Bake for 45–55 minutes, or until a toothpick inserted into the center comes out clean. Cool the cake in the pan for 15 minutes. Loosen and remove the pan sides. Invert the cake onto a rack. Loosen and remove the pan bottom and let cool completely.

4. To prepare the frosting, beat the cream cheese, confectioners' sugar, and lemon zest in a large bowl until fluffy. Add enough lemon juice to make a smooth, spreadable frosting. Spread over the cake.

Pumpkin Fruit Cake ▷

Light Fruit Cake

Serve this light tasty fruit cake with tea, coffee, or a glass of sherry.

Serves: 10-12 · Prep: 25 min. · Cooking: 50-60 min. · Level: 1

- 2   cups (300 g) all-purpose (plain) flour
- 1   teaspoon baking powder
- 1   teaspoon ground nutmeg
- 3/4 cup (180 g) butter, softened
- 1/2 cup (100 g) sugar
- 3   large eggs
- 1/2 cup (125 ml) milk
- 1   tablespoon sweet sherry
- 1   pound (500 g) candied (glacé) fruit, coarsely chopped
- 1/2 cup (90 g) blanched almonds, coarsely chopped
- 2   tablespoons apricot preserves (jam), warmed

1. Preheat the oven to 325°F (170°C/gas 3). Lightly grease an 8-inch (20-cm) square baking pan and line the base and sides with parchment paper.

2. Combine the flour, baking powder, and nutmeg into a medium bowl. Beat the butter and sugar in a large bowl with an electric mixer on medium speed until pale and creamy. Add the eggs one at a time, beating until just blended after each addition. With mixer on low speed, gradually beat in the mixed dry ingredients, alternating with the milk. Stir in the sherry, candied fruit, and almonds in by hand.

3. Spoon the mixture into the prepared pan. Bake for 1³/₄–2 hours, until a skewer comes out clean when tested. Cover the top with foil if it begins to color too much.

4. Cool the cake in the pan for 20 minutes, then turn out onto a wire rack, brush with apricot preserves, and let cool completely.

Mixed Nut Cake

Don't worry if you don't have all the different types of nuts on hand. Just use a combined total of 1 cup (120 g) of the nuts you have in your cupboards.

Serves: 8-10 · Prep: 25 min. · Cooking: 50-60 min. · Level: 1

CAKE
- 1/2 cup (125 g) butter, softened
- 1¼   cups (250 g) sugar
- 2   tablespoons finely grated lemon zest
- 3   large eggs
- 1½   cups (225 g) all-purpose (plain) flour
- 1   teaspoon baking powder
- 1/2 teaspoon baking soda (bicarbonate of soda)
- 1/4 teaspoon salt
- 1/2 cup (125 ml) milk
- 1/4 cup (30 g) walnuts, finely chopped
- 1/4 cup (30 g) almonds, finely chopped
- 1/4 cup (30 g) hazelnuts, finely chopped
- 1/4 cup (30 g) pistachios, finely chopped
- 1   tablespoon fresh lemon juice

NUT TOPPING
- 2   tablespoons walnuts, coarsely chopped
- 2   tablespoons slivered almonds
- 2   tablespoons pistachios, coarsely chopped
- 2   tablespoons hazelnuts, coarsely chopped
- 2   tablespoons sugar

1. Preheat the oven to 350°F (180°C/gas 4). Lightly grease a 9-inch (23-cm) square baking pan.

2. To prepare the cake, beat the butter, sugar, and lemon zest in a large bowl with an electric mixer at medium speed until creamy. Add the eggs one at a time, until just blended after each addition. With mixer on low, gradually beat in the flour, baking powder, baking soda, and salt, alternating with the milk. Stir in the nuts and lemon juice by hand. Spoon the batter into the prepared pan.

3. To prepare the topping, sprinkle the coarsely chopped nuts and the sugar over the batter.

4. Bake for 50-60 minutes, or until a toothpick inserted into the center comes out clean. Cool the cake completely in the pan on a rack.

Light Fruit Cake ▷

Pistachio Cake

Pistachio nuts are a lovely green color. Generally speaking, the darker the green, the higher the quality of the nut. Pistachios have a mild yet distinctive flavor.

Serves: 8 · Prep: 30 min. · Cooking: 25–35 min. · Level: 1

CAKE
1½	cups (225 g) pistachios
1	cup (200 g) sugar
3	large eggs, separated
2	tablespoons finely grated lemon zest
1	teaspoon baking powder
½	teaspoon baking soda (bicarbonate of soda)
¼	teaspoon salt

CREAM TOPPING
½	cup (125 ml) heavy (double) cream
1	tablespoon confectioners' (icing) sugar

1. Preheat the oven to 350°F (180°C/gas 4). Lightly grease a 9-inch (23-cm) springform pan.

2. To prepare the cake, plunge the pistachios into a saucepan of boiling water for 30 seconds. Drain well. Rub dry with a clean kitchen towel to remove the inner skins. Place the pistachios and sugar in a food processor and chop finely.

3. Transfer to a large bowl and stir in the egg yolks, lemon zest, baking powder, baking soda, and salt.

4. Beat the egg whites in a medium bowl with an electric mixer at high speed until stiff peaks form. Use a large rubber spatula to fold them into the batter. Spoon the batter into the prepared pan.

5. Bake for 25–35 minutes, or until a toothpick inserted into the center comes out clean. Cool the cake in the pan for 10 minutes. Loosen and remove the pan sides and let the cake cool completely on a rack.

6. To prepare the topping, beat the cream and confectioners' sugar in a medium bowl until thick. Place a dollop of cream on each slice.

PREPARING NUTS STEP-BY-STEP

Preparing nuts in your own kitchen can give a cake a whole new flavor. Freshly roasted nuts will give your cake a richness and decadence that store-prepared nuts can only imitate. Grinding and blanching nuts are simple processes that you can easily manage at home.

1 Toasting Nuts
Preheat the oven to 350°F (180°C/gas 4). Sprinkle the nuts onto a large baking sheet. Toast for 7–10 minutes, until golden brown. Rub off the inner skins in a clean kitchen towel.

2 Blanching Nuts
Bring enough water to a boil to cover the nuts. Place them in a large bowl and pour in the water. Let stand for 5 minutes. Use a slotted spoon to scoop the nuts out and place them in a clean kitchen towel. Gently rub the nuts to remove the inner skins.

3 Grinding Nuts
Place the nuts in a food processor, adding 2 tablespoons of sugar from the recipe to counteract against the oil they will produce. Grind briefly to the desired coarseness.

Streusel Nut Cake

This cake has a thick, crisp streusal topping of pecans, sugar, and spice.

Serves: 8–10 · Prep: 25 min. · Cooking: 55–60 min. · Level: 1

STREUSEL

½	cup (100 g) firmly packed brown sugar
2	tablespoons all-purpose (plain) flour
2	teaspoons ground cinnamon
1	cup (100 g) pecans, coarsely chopped
¼	cup (60 g) butter, melted

CAKE

2	cups (300 g) all-purpose (plain) flour
1	teaspoon baking powder
1	teaspoon baking soda (bicarbonate of soda)
¼	teaspoon salt
½	cup (125 g) butter, softened
1	cup (200 g) firmly packed brown sugar
1	teaspoon butterscotch or rum extract (essence)
3	large eggs
1	cup (250 ml) milk

1. Preheat the oven to 350°F (180°C/gas 4). Lightly grease and flour a 9-inch (23-cm) springform pan.

2. To prepare the streusel, stir the brown sugar, flour, and cinnamon in a small bowl. Stir in the pecans and butter.

3. To prepare the cake, combine the flour, baking powder, baking soda, and salt in a large bowl. Beat the butter, brown sugar, and butterscotch extract in a large bowl with an electric mixer at medium speed until creamy. Add the eggs one at a time, beating until just blended after each addition. With mixer on low, gradually beat in the dry ingredients, alternating with the milk. Spoon the batter into the prepared pan. Sprinkle with the streusel.

4. Bake for 55–60 minutes, or until a toothpick inserted into the center comes out clean. Cool the cake in the pan for 15 minutes. Loosen and remove the pan sides and let cool completely. Transfer the cake to the rack top-side up.

 Hungarian Hazelnut Torte

This cake has a delicious chocolate-nut flavor. Serve it as a family dessert during the cold winter months. It contains no flour and is gluten-free. If baking for someone who is allergic to gluten, check that the chocolate and vanilla extract are gluten-free.

Serves: 8–10 · Prep: 25 min. · Cooking: 45–55 min. · Level: 1

CAKE

8	ounces (250 g) dark chocolate, coarsely chopped
1¾	cups (175 g) finely ground hazelnuts
¾	cup (150 g) sugar
¾	cup (180 ml) dry white wine, such as Chablis or Chardonnay
1	tablespoon cornstarch (cornflour)
6	large eggs, separated
¼	teaspoon salt

TOPPING

1	cup (250 ml) heavy (double) cream
1	tablespoon sugar
1	teaspoon vanilla extract (essence)
	Whole hazelnuts, to decorate

1. Preheat the oven to 325°F (170°C/gas 3). Lightly grease and flour a 13 x 9-inch (33 x 23-cm) baking pan.

2. To prepare the cake, stir the chocolate, hazelnuts, sugar, wine, and cornstarch in a large saucepan over medium-low heat until the chocolate is melted. Set aside to cool.

3. Beat the egg whites and salt in a large bowl with an electric mixer at high speed until stiff peaks form. With mixer at medium speed, beat the egg yolks in a large bowl until pale. Use a large rubber spatula to fold the egg yolks into the chocolate mixture. Fold in the beaten whites. Spoon the batter into the prepared pan.

4. Bake for 45–55 minutes, or until a toothpick inserted into the center comes out clean. Cool the cake completely in the pan on a rack.

5. To prepare the Topping, beat the cream, sugar, and vanilla in a medium bowl until stiff. Spread the top of the cake with the cream and decorate with the hazelnuts.

Pine Nut Cake

Pine nuts are the small edible seeds of many species of pine trees. They are sweet with a delicious flavor and keep well. They have good nutritional properties, with many species made up of about 30 percent protein.

Serves: · Prep: 15 min. · Cooking: 35–40 min. · Level: 1

1⅓	cups (200 g) all-purpose (plain) flour
1½	teaspoons baking powder
¼	teaspoon salt
3	large eggs
¾	cup (150 g) sugar
1	teaspoon vanilla extract (essence)
⅔	cup (150 g) butter, melted
2	tablespoons brandy
1	cup (150 g) pine nuts

1. Preheat the oven to 350°F (180°C/gas 4). Lightly grease a 9-inch (23-cm) springform pan.

2. To prepare the cake, combine the flour, baking powder, and salt in a medium bowl. Beat the eggs, sugar, and vanilla in a large bowl with an electric mixer at high speed until pale and thick. With mixer at low speed, gradually beat in the dry ingredients, alternating with the butter and brandy. Stir in the pine nuts. Spoon the batter into the prepared pan.

3. Bake for 35–40 minutes, or until a toothpick inserted into the center comes out clean. Cool the cake in the pan for 10 minutes. Loosen and remove the pan sides and let cool completely.

Fruit Cake with Beer

This is a hearty, nutritious cake with plenty of body and flavor.

Serves: 10–12 · Prep: 20 min. + 12 hr. to stand · Cooking: 2 hr. 20–30 min. Level: 1

1½	cups (250 g) dark raisins
1½	cups (250 g) pitted dates, chopped
1	cup (180 g) golden raisins (sultanas)
½	cup (75 g) mixed candied (glacé) peel, chopped
½	cup (75 g) dried apricots, chopped
½	cup (75 g) halved candied (glacé) cherries
¼	cup (35 g) candied (glacé) ginger, chopped
1	(12-ounce/350-ml) can or bottle beer
¼	cup (60 ml) water
1½	cups (225 g) whole-wheat (wholemeal) flour
1½	cups (225 g) all-purpose (plain) flour
2	teaspoons baking powder
1	teaspoon ground nutmeg
1	teaspoon ground ginger
1	teaspoon ground cinnamon
½	teaspoon salt
1	cup (250 g) butter, softened
¾	cup (180 ml) honey
½	cup (125 ml) light corn (golden) syrup
3	large eggs
½	cup (50 g) slivered almonds

1. Place all the dried and candied fruits in a large bowl and pour in the beer. Cover and let stand for 12 hours.

2. Preheat the oven to 300°F (150°C/gas 2). Lightly grease a 13 x 9-inch (33 x 23-cm) baking pan. Line with parchment paper.

3. Combine both flours, baking powder, nutmeg, ginger, cinnamon, and salt in a large bowl. Beat the butter, honey, and corn syrup in a large bowl with an electric mixer at medium speed until creamy. Add the eggs one at a time, beating until just blended after each addition. With mixer on low, beat in the dry ingredients and the fruit mixture. Spoon the batter into the prepared pan. Sprinkle with the almonds.

4. Bake for 2 hours and 20–30 minutes, or until dark brown at the edges and a toothpick inserted into the center comes out clean. Cool the cake in the pan for 15 minutes. Turn out onto a rack. Carefully remove the paper and let cool completely.

Dundee Cake

Dundee Cake is a rich, buttery Scottish fruit cake from the city of Dundee where it was first recorded in the late 19th century. Before baking, the top is covered in whole blanched almonds.

Serves: 8–10 · Prep: 45 min. · Cooking: 2 hr. · Level: 1 ·

1	cup (150 g) all-purpose (plain) flour
⅓	cup (35 g) finely ground almonds
½	teaspoon baking powder
½	teaspoon baking soda (bicarbonate of soda)
¼	teaspoon salt
⅔	cup (180 g) butter, softened
¾	cup (150 g) firmly packed brown sugar
1	teaspoon vanilla extract (essence)
2	large eggs + 1 large egg white, lightly beaten
1½	cups (250 g) raisins
1½	cups (250 g) currants
½	cup chopped mixed candied lemon and orange peel
¼	cup (25 g) candied (glacé) cherries, halved
1	tablespoon finely grated lemon zest
1½	tablespoons fresh lemon juice
	About 100 whole blanched almonds

1. Preheat the oven to 350°F (180°C/gas 4). Butter a 9-inch (23-cm) springform pan.

2. To prepare the cake, combine the flour, ground almonds, baking powder, baking soda, and salt in a medium bowl. Beat the butter, brown sugar, and vanilla in a large bowl with an electric mixer at medium speed until creamy. Add the eggs one at a time, beating until just blended after each addition. With mixer on low, gradually beat in the dry ingredients. Stir in the raisins, currants, candied fruit peel, candied cherries, and lemon zest and juice by hand.

3. Spoon the batter into the prepared pan. Top with the whole almonds in a spiral pattern (see photograph right). Brush with the egg white.

4. Bake for 1 hour. Reduce the oven temperature to 300°F (150°C/gas 2) and bake for 1 hour more, or until a toothpick inserted into the center comes out clean.

5. Cool the cake in the pan for 30 minutes. Loosen and remove the pan sides. Invert the cake onto a rack. Loosen and remove the pan bottom. Turn the cake top-side up onto the rack and let cool completely.

Almond-Topped Cake

This cake is also covered in almonds, but they are flaked and combined with butter and sugar to make a lovely caramel-almond topping.

Serves: 8–10 · Prep: 30 min. · Cooking: 50-55 min. · Level: 1

CAKE

½	cup (125 g) butter, softened
1	cup (200 g) sugar
1	teaspoon vanilla extract (essence)
2	large eggs
2	cups (300 g) all-purpose (plain) flour
2	teaspoons baking powder
¼	teaspoon salt
¾	cup (180 ml) milk

ALMOND TOPPING

⅓	cup (90 g) butter, cut up
⅓	cup (75 g) sugar
¾	cup (100 g) flaked almonds
3	tablespoons milk

1. Preheat the oven to 350°F (180°C/gas 4). Lightly grease and flour a 9-inch (23-cm) springform pan.

2. To prepare the cake, beat the butter, sugar, and vanilla in a large bowl with an electric mixer at medium speed until pale and creamy. Add the eggs one at a time, beating until just blended after each addition. With mixer on low, gradually beat in the flour, baking powder, and salt, alternating with the milk. Spoon the batter into the prepared pan.

3. Bake for 40 minutes. While the cake is baking, prepare the topping: Stir the butter, sugar, and almonds in a medium saucepan over low heat until the butter has melted.

4. After the cake has baked for 40 minutes, spread with the topping. Brush with the milk. Bake for 10–15 minutes more, or until the topping is lightly browned.

5. Cool the cake in the pan for 10 minutes. Loosen and remove the pan sides. Place the cake on a rack and let cool completely.

Dundee Cake ▷

LAYER CAKES
AND ROLLS

Here you will find a selection of striking layer cakes,

sponge rolls, chiffon cakes, gateaux, angel food cakes,

tortes, and meringues. These are all cakes for special

occasions. Some are slightly more challenging to make

than simple butter cakes, but we have provided feature

panels for making the perfect génoise, which forms the

basis of many layer cakes, and for cooling an angel food

cake. Detailed instructions in the other recipes will

enable you to bake all these cakes successfully.

◀ **Strawberry and Coconut Meringue Torte (see page 182)**

Génoise

A génoise is a classic French sponge cake. It is the basis of many cakes and desserts. It is said to have been made first in the 19th century by the Parisian pastry cook, Chiboust, who also invented the delicious Saint Honoré Gateau (see page 261).

Serves: 8–10 · Prep: 25 min. · Cooking: 20–40 min. · Level: 2

- ²/₃ cup (100 g) cake flour
- ²/₃ cup (100 g) cornstarch (cornflour)
- 6 large eggs
- ³/₄ cup (150 g) superfine (caster) sugar
- ¹/₃ cup (90 g) butter, melted and cooled slightly
- 1 teaspoon vanilla extract (essence)

1. Preheat the oven to 375°F (190°C/gas 5). Butter one or two 9-inch (23-cm) springform pans. Line with parchment paper.

2. Sift the flour and cornstarch into a medium bowl.

3. Beat the eggs and superfine sugar in a large heatproof bowl. Fit the bowl into a large wide saucepan of barely simmering water over low heat; the bottom of bowl should not touch the water. Beat constantly until the sugar has dissolved, the mixture is hot to the touch, and it registers 115°F (45°C) on an instant-read thermometer. Remove from the heat. Beat the eggs with an electric mixer at high speed until cooled, pale, tripled in volume, and very thick.

4. Use a large rubber spatula to gradually fold the dry ingredients into the batter.

5. Place 2 cups of batter in a small bowl and fold in the melted butter and vanilla. Fold the butter mixture into the batter.

6. Working quickly, spoon the batter into the prepared pan(s).

7. Bake for 20–30 minutes for two pans, and 30–40 minutes for one pan, or until golden brown, the cake shrinks from the pan sides, and a toothpick inserted into the center comes out clean. Cool the cake(s) in the pan(s) for 5 minutes.

8. Loosen and remove the pan sides. Invert the cake(s) onto a rack. Loosen and remove the pan bottom(s). Carefully remove the paper. Turn the cake(s) top-side up and let cool completely.

PREPARING A GÉNOISE

Unlike a classic Sponge Cake (see page 272), or Italian Sponge Cake (see page 274), a génoise, or French sponge cake, is made with butter. It also has no baking powder and is leavened by beating whole eggs and sugar together over simmering water until they are very thick and tripled in bulk. This cake forms the basis of many layer cakes and gateaux, especially those filled with rich creams, such as Bavarian Cream (see page 275). You can bake the batter in one or two pans. The cake in the single pan can be sliced into three layers, while the others can be sliced in half to make four layers.

1 Sift the flour and cornstarch into a medium bowl.

2 Beat the eggs and sugar in a large bowl over barely simmering water until the sugar has dissolved. Remove from the heat and beat until cooled, pale, tripled in volume, and very thick.

3 Use a large rubber spatula to gradually fold the dry ingredients into the egg and sugar mixture.

4 Place 2 cups of batter in a medium bowl and fold in the melted butter and vanilla. Fold this butter mixture gently into the batter. Spoon the batter into the prepare baking pans.

Strawberry Cream Gateau

This is a great cake for a special dessert, especially if you have many other dishes to prepare. You can prepare the génoise the day before, then finish assembling the cake well ahead of time, and chill in the refrigerator until you are ready to serve.

Serves: 8–10 · Prep: 1 hr. + 7 hr. to soak and chill · Level: 2

1 Génoise, baked in one 9-inch (23-cm) pan (see page 161)

STRAWBERRY FILLING
2 pounds (1 kg) ripe strawberries, halved (reserve 12 whole to decorate)
½ cup (125 ml) orange liqueur
8 large egg yolks
1¼ cups (300 ml) dry white wine
1 cup (200 g) sugar
2 tablespoons unflavored gelatin
3 tablespoons freshly squeezed lemon juice
1 recipe Chantilly Cream (see page 275)
½ cup sliced almonds, toasted

1. Place the strawberries in a large bowl with the liqueur. Soak for 1 hour.

2. To prepare the filling, beat the egg yolks, wine, and sugar in a double boiler until well blended. Place over barely simmering water, stirring constantly with a wooden spoon, until the mixture lightly coats a metal spoon or registers 160°F (70°C) on an instant-read thermometer. Remove from the heat.

3. Sprinkle the gelatin over the lemon juice. Let stand 1 minute. Stir the gelatin into the egg yolk mixture until the gelatin has completely dissolved. Immediately plunge the pan in a bowl of ice water and stir until the egg mixture has cooled. Transfer to a large bowl, cover, and refrigerate, stirring occasionally, until well chilled.

4. Stir one-third of the Chantilly Cream into the yolk mixture. (Keep the remainder refrigerated). Drain the strawberries, reserving the juice, and stir into the yolk mixture.

5. Split the cake horizontally. Butter a 9-inch (23-cm) springform pan. Place one layer in the pan. Drizzle with enough of the reserved strawberry juice to soak it well. Spread with the strawberry mixture and top with the remaining cake layer. Drizzle with strawberry juice. Cover and refrigerate for 6 hours.

6. Loosen and remove the pan sides. Spread with the remaining cream. Decorate with the almonds and strawberries.

Orange Fruit Gateau

With its star fruit and orange topping, and almond studded sides, this is a beautiful cake.

Serves: 8–10 · Prep: 1 hr. + 6 hr. to chill · Level: 3

1 Génoise, baked in one 9-inch (23-cm) pan (see page 161)

ORANGE FILLING
4 large egg yolks
   Finely grated zest of 1 orange
½ cup (100 g) sugar
2 tablespoons unflavored gelatin
   Freshly squeezed juice of 3 oranges
1 tablespoon freshly squeezed lemon juice
¾ cup (180 ml) heavy (double) cream
2 tablespoons orange liqueur

TOPPING
3 tablespoons apricot preserves (jam)
¾ cup (75 g) flaked almonds
¼ cup (60 g) butter, softened
½ cup (100 g) sugar
3 oranges, thinly sliced
   Star fruit and candied (glacé) cherries, to decorate

1. To prepare the filling, beat the egg yolks, orange zest, and sugar in a saucepan until well blended. Simmer over low heat, stirring constantly, until the mixture lightly coats a metal spoon or registers 160°F (70°C) on an instant-read thermometer. Plunge the pan into a bowl of ice water and stir until cooled. Sprinkle the gelatin over the citrus juices in a saucepan. Let stand 1 minute. Stir over low heat until dissolved. Remove from the heat. Fold into the egg mixture.

2. Beat the cream in a large bowl until stiff. Fold into the egg mixture.

3. Split the cake horizontally. Butter a 9-inch (23-cm) springform pan. Place one layer in the pan. Sprinkle with the orange liqueur. Spread with the filling. Top with the remaining layer. Refrigerate for 6 hours.

4. To prepare the topping, warm the apricot preserves over low heat. Brush over the cake. Stick the almonds onto the sides. Melt the butter and sugar in a saucepan over low heat. Add the orange slices and cook until caramelized, about 10 minutes. Arrange the oranges on the cake. Decorate with slices of star fruit and candied cherries.

Strawberry Cream Gateau ▷

Raspberry Sour Cream Sponge

With its creamy fruit filling and spicy cinnamon frosting, this is a wonderful cake to serve as an afternoon snack with coffee or tea.

Serves: 8 · Prep: 30 min. · Cooking: 35–45 min. · Level 1

CAKE

½	cup (100 g) superfine (caster) sugar + 2 tablespoons
4	large eggs, separated
¾	cup (125 g) all-purpose (plain) flour
1	teaspoon ground cinnamon
½	cup (125 g) butter, melted and slightly cooled

RASPBERRY AND SOUR CREAM FILLING

½	cup (125 ml) heavy (double) cream
2	tablespoons confectioners' (icing) sugar
¼	cup (60 ml) sour cream
1	teaspoon finely grated lemon zest
⅛	teaspoon vanilla extract (essence)
2	cups (300 g) fresh raspberries

CINNAMON FROSTING

1⅓	cups (200 g) confectioners' (icing) sugar
1	teaspoon ground cinnamon
1–2	tablespoons boiling water

1. Preheat the oven to 350°F (180°C/gas 4). Lightly grease a 9-inch (23-cm) round cake pan and line the base with parchment paper.

2. To prepare the sponge, beat ½ cup (100 g) of sugar and the egg yolks in a large bowl with an electric mixer on medium–high speed until pale and thick. Set aside.

3. Beat the egg whites in a large bowl with an electric mixer on medium-low speed until soft peaks form. Add the remaining sugar and continue beating with mixer on medium-high speed until firm peaks form.

4. Use a large rubber spatula to fold a quarter of the egg whites into the yolk mixture.

5. Sift the flour and cinnamon into a small bowl. Sift the flour mixture again into the batter, alternating with the butter, folding until incorporated. Gently fold in the remaining egg whites. Spoon the batter into the prepared pan.

6. Bake for 35–45 minutes, or until golden brown, the sponge springs back when lightly touched, or a skewer comes out clean when inserted into the center.

7. Let cool in the pan for 10 minutes. Turn out onto a rack, and carefully peel off the parchment paper.

8. To prepare the filling, beat the cream and sugar in a medium bowl until soft peaks form. Beat in the sour cream, lemon zest, and vanilla until just combined. Add the raspberries, stirring with a wooden spoon until evenly distributed.

9. When the cake is completely cool, cut it in half horizontally. Place one cake layer on a serving plate. Spoon the filling over the top, spreading ¾ inch (2 cm) in from the edge. Place the other layer on top.

10. To prepare the cinnamon frosting, combine the confectioners' sugar and cinnamon in a small bowl. Gradually pour in the water, stirring until smooth and spreadable. Spread over the cake.

◁ **Raspberry Sour Cream Sponge**

Passion Fruit Sponge

The slightly exotic flavor of the passion fruit frosting combines beautifully with the creamy filling and light-as-air sponge cake.

Serves: 8–10 · Prep: 25 min. + 2 hr. to soak and chill · Cooking: 25–30 min. · Level: 2

CAKE

- ¾ cup (125 g) all-purpose (plain) flour
- ¼ cup (30 g) custard powder or vanilla pudding mix
- ½ teaspoon baking powder
- 4 large eggs
- ⅔ cup (150 g) superfine (caster) sugar
- 1 teaspoon finely grated lemon zest
- ½ teaspoon vanilla extract (essence)
- 2 tablespoons butter, melted and cooled

FILLING

- ¾ cup (180 ml) light (single) cream
- 1 tablespoon confectioners' (icing) sugar

PASSION FRUIT FROSTING

- 1 cup (150 g) confectioners' (icing) sugar
- ½ cup (125 g) butter, softened
- 3 large passion fruit, halved and pulp scooped out

1. Preheat the oven to 350°F (180°C/gas 4). Lightly grease an 8-inch (20 cm) springform cake pan. Line the base with parchment paper.

2. Sift the flour, custard powder, and baking powder into a small bowl.

3. Beat the eggs, sugar, and lemon zest in a large bowl with an electric mixer on medium speed until thick, creamy, and tripled in volume. Add the vanilla and beat to combine.

4. Sift the flour a second time and gently fold into the egg mixture in two batches. Fold in the melted butter. Spoon the batter into the prepared pan.

5. Bake for 25–30 minutes, until light golden and the sponge springs back when gently pressed. Let cool in the pan for 5 minutes, then turn out onto a wire rack and let cool completely. When completely cold, cut the sponge in half horizontally.

6. To prepare the filling, beat the cream and confectioners' sugar in a small bowl with an electric mixer on medium speed until soft peaks form.

7. Place one layer of cake on a serving plate. Spread with cream. Place the other cake layer on top.

8. To prepare the frosting, beat the confectioners' sugar and butter in a medium bowl and with an electric mixer until smooth and creamy. Strain the passion fruit pulp through a fine mesh sieve into the bowl, reserving some of the seeds, and stir to combine.

9. Spread the frosting over the sponge and scatter a few of the reserved seeds on top.

Passion Fruit Sponge ▷

Strawberry and Vanilla Sponge

The sponge cake in this recipe is a good basic sponge that you can use in many recipes. It has just 2 tablespoons of melted butter which should be cooled slightly before adding to the batter. Vanilla bean pasta is like a very thick vanilla extract. You can buy it at specialty baking stores. Replace with vanilla extract if you can't find it.

Serves: 8–10 · Prep: 20 min. · Cooking: 20–25 min. · Level: 2

CAKE
- ³⁄₄ cup (125 g) all-purpose (plain) flour
- ¹⁄₄ cup (30 g) cornstarch (cornflour)
- ¹⁄₂ teaspoon baking powder
- 4 large eggs
- ²⁄₃ cup (150 g) superfine (caster) sugar
- 1 teaspoon vanilla extract (essence)
- 2 tablespoons butter, melted and cooled

FILLING AND TOPPING
- 1¹⁄₄ cups (300 ml) double (heavy) cream
- 1 tablespoon confectioners' (icing) sugar
- ¹⁄₂ teaspoon vanilla bean paste
- ¹⁄₂ tablespoon Grand Mariner or other orange liqueur
- 1 pound (500 g) strawberries, sliced

1. Preheat the oven to 350°F (180°C/gas 4). Lightly grease two 8-inch (20 cm) springform cake pans. Line the bases with parchment paper.

2. Sift the flour, cornstarch, and baking powder into a small bowl. Beat the eggs and sugar in a large bowl with an electric mixer on medium speed until thick, creamy, and tripled in volume. Add the vanilla.

3. Sift the flour a second time and gently fold into the egg mixture in two batches. Fold in the melted butter. Spoon into the pans.

4. Bake for 20–25 minutes, until light golden and the sponges spring back when gently pressed. Let cool in the pan for 5 minutes, then turn out onto a wire rack and let cool completely.

5. To prepare the filling and topping, beat the cream, confectioners' sugar, and vanilla paste in a small bowl with an electric mixer on medium speed until soft peaks form. Stir in the liqueur.

6. Spread half of the cream and strawberries over one of the sponges and place the other one on top. Spread with the remaining cream and decorate with the remaining strawberries.

◁ **Strawberry and Vanilla Sponge**

Daffodil Cake

Serve this pretty cake on Mother's Day or for spring birthdays. It has a wickedly thick layer of lemon frosting.

Serves: 8–10 · Prep: 30 min. · Cooking: 40–50 min. · Level: 2

CAKE
- ²⁄₃ cup (100 g) confectioners' (icing) sugar
- ²⁄₃ cup (100 g) cake flour
- ¹⁄₄ teaspoon salt
- 8 large egg whites
- 1¹⁄₄ teaspoons vanilla extract (essence)
- 1 teaspoon cream of tartar
- ¹⁄₂ cup (100 g) sugar
- 6 large egg yolks
- 2 teaspoons finely grated lemon zest

TANGY LEMON FROSTING
- 4 cups (600 g) confectioners' (icing) sugar
- ¹⁄₂ cup (125 g) butter, softened
- 1 tablespoon finely grated lemon zest
- 4–5 tablespoons freshly squeezed lemon juice

1. Preheat the oven to 350°F (180°C/gas 4). Set out a 10-inch (25-cm) tube pan with a removable bottom.

2. Sift the confectioners' sugar, flour, and salt into a medium bowl.

3. Beat the egg whites, vanilla, and cream of tartar in a large bowl with an electric mixer on medium speed until frothy. With mixer at high speed, add the sugar, beating until stiff, glossy peaks form. Use a large rubber spatula to fold in the dry ingredients. Place half the batter in another bowl.

4. With mixer on high speed, beat the egg yolks in a large bowl until pale and thick. Add the lemon zest. Fold the beaten egg yolks into one bowl of the beaten whites. Place alternate spoonfuls of the batters into the pan.

5. Bake for 40–50 minutes, or until springy to the touch. Let cool in the pan for 5 minutes. Turn out onto a rack and let cool completely.

6. To prepare the frosting, beat the confectioners' sugar, butter, lemon zest, and lemon juice in a large bowl with an electric mixer at medium speed until smooth. Spread over the cake.

Ginger Fluff

This is a lovely light ginger sponge cake. Serve with a glass of dry champagne as a special dessert.

Serves: 8–10 · Prep: 30 min. · Cooking: 20–25 min. · Level: 2

CAKE
³/₄	cup (125 g) cornstarch (cornflour)
2	tablespoons all-purpose (plain) flour
1	teaspoon ground ginger
1	teaspoon ground cinnamon
1	teaspoon unsweetened cocoa powder
1	teaspoon baking powder
½	teaspoon cream of tartar
4	large eggs, separated
¼	teaspoon salt
³/₄	cup (150 g) superfine (caster) sugar
1	tablespoon boiling water
1	tablespoon butter
2	teaspoons light corn (golden) syrup

FILLING
³/₄	cup (180 ml) heavy (double) cream
2	tablespoons confectioners' (icing) sugar
½	teaspoon vanilla extract (essence)

CINNAMON FROSTING
1⅓	cups (200 g) confectioners' (icing) sugar
1	teaspoon ground cinnamon
1-2	tablespoons hot milk

1. Preheat the oven to 350°F (180°C/gas 4). Lightly grease an 8-inch (20-cm) springform cake pan. Line the base with parchment paper.

2. To prepare the cake, sift the cornstarch, flour, ginger, cinnamon, cocoa, baking powder, and cream of tartar into a medium bowl. Beat the egg yolks and sugar in a large bowl with an electric mixer on medium speed until pale and thick.

3. Beat the egg whites and salt in a medium bowl with an electric mixer on medium speed until soft peaks form. Fold a large spoonful of egg whites into the yolk mixture. Fold in the remaining whites.

4. Sift the flour a second time and fold into the egg mixture in two batches.

5. Stir the water, butter, and corn syrup in a small cup until melted. Fold into the batter. Spoon the batter into the prepared pan.

6. Bake for 20–25 minutes, until light golden brown and the top springs back when gently pressed.

7. Let cool in the pan for 5 minutes, then turn out onto a wire rack and let cool completely. When completely cold, cut the sponge in half horizontally.

8. To prepare the filling, beat the cream, confectioners' sugar, and vanilla in a small bowl with an electric mixer on medium speed until thickened.

9. Place one cake layer on a serving plate. Spread with the cream and cover with the remaining cake layer.

10. To prepare the frosting, combine the confectioners' sugar and cinnamon in a small bowl. Add the milk and stir until smooth. Spread the frosting over the top of the cake.

Black Forest Cake

Black Forest Cake, or Schwarzwälder Kirschtorte in German, originally comes from southern Germany. Packed with cream, chocolate, cherries, and kirschwasser (a clear cherry brandy), it is perfect for all sorts of special occasions.

Serves: 8–10 · Prep: 45 min. · Cooking · 40–45 min. Level: 3

CHOCOLATE CAKE

1⅓	cups (200 g) all-purpose (plain) flour
4	tablespoons unsweetened cocoa powder
¼	teaspoon salt
4	ounces (125 g) dark chocolate, coarsely chopped
6	large eggs, separated
1	cup (200 g) firmly packed light brown sugar
¾	cup (180 g) butter, melted and cooled
¼	cup (60 ml) kirsch (clear cherry brandy)
2	cups (500 ml) maraschino cherries, pitted + extra, to decorate

VANILLA CREAM

3½	cups (875 ml) heavy (double) cream
7	tablespoons confectioners' (icing) sugar
2	teaspoons vanilla extract (essence)

TO DECORATE

3	ounces (90 g) dark chocolate, coarsely grated
	Large piece of dark chocolate, for curls

1. Preheat the oven to 350°F (180°C/gas 4). Butter a 9-inch (23-cm) round cake pan and line with parchment paper.

2. To prepare the cake, sift the flour, cocoa, and salt into a medium bowl. Melt the chocolate in a double boiler over barely simmering water, stirring until smooth.

3. Beat the egg yolks and brown sugar in a medium bowl with an electric mixer on medium-high speed until creamy. Add the chocolate mixture, stirring with a wooden spoon or large kitchen spoon to combine.

4. Beat the egg whites in a large bowl with an electric mixer on medium speed until firm peaks form.

5. Fold a quarter of the egg whites into the chocolate mixture. Gradually fold in the mixed dry ingredients and melted butter until well mixed. Gently fold in the remaining egg whites. Spoon the batter into the prepared cake pan, smoothing well with a spoon.

6. Bake for 40–45 minutes, or until golden brown and the cake springs back when lightly touched or a skewer comes out clean when inserted into the center. Let the cake to cool in the pan for 10 minutes then turn out onto a rack. Carefully peel off the paper and let cool completely.

7. To prepare the vanilla cream, beat the cream, confectioners' sugar, and vanilla in a large bowl until stiff peaks form.

8. When the cake is cooled completely, slice into thirds horizontally and brush each round with kirsch.

9. To assemble the cake, place a layer of cake on a serving plate. Spread the cherries evenly over the top and cover with one-third of the vanilla cream. Cover with another cake layer and spread with cherries and cream. Cover with the remaining cake layer. Spread the remaining vanilla cream evenly over the top and sides of the cake using a small spatula or palette knife to create a smooth finish.

10. Coat the sides of the cake with the grated chocolate, pressing lightly with the back of a spoon to make them stick.

11. Make chocolate curls and shavings using a sharp vegetable peeler. Decorate the top of the cake with the chocolate curls and the extra cherries.

Dobos Torte

This famous Hungarian cake was created by master chef Jósef Dobos in the second half of the 19th century. He presented it officially at a national show in 1885. No one else could quite get it right until 1906, when chef Dobos finally released the recipe.

Serves: 8–10 · Prep: 1 hr. · Cooking: 25–30 min. · Level: 3

CAKE
1	cup (150 g) cake flour
¼	teaspoon salt
6	large eggs, separated
1½	cups (225 g) confectioners' (icing) sugar
1	teaspoon vanilla extract (essence)

CHOCOLATE BUTTERCREAM
5	ounces (150 g) dark chocolate, coarsely chopped
1¾	cups (430 g) butter, softened
1½	cups (225 g) confectioners' (icing) sugar
2	tablespoons unsweetened cocoa powder
1	teaspoon vanilla extract (essence)

GLAZE
1	cup (200 g) sugar
3	tablespoons water
1	tablespoon butter
2	teaspoons freshly squeezed lemon juice
10	whole, toasted and peeled hazelnuts

1. Preheat the oven to 350°F (180°C/gas 4). Butter two 9-inch (23-cm) round cake pans. Line with parchment paper.

2. To prepare the cake, sift the flour and salt into a medium bowl. Beat the egg yolks, ¾ cup (120 g) confectioners' sugar, and vanilla in a large bowl with an electric mixer at high speed until pale and thick.

3. With mixer at medium-low speed, beat the egg whites in a large bowl until frothy. With mixer at high speed, gradually add the remaining ¾ cup (120 g) of confectioners' sugar, beating until stiff, glossy peaks form.

4. Use a large rubber spatula to fold the egg whites into the batter. Fold in the dry ingredients.

5. Spoon ⅔ cup of batter into each of the prepared pans. Bake for 5–8 minutes, or until golden brown and springy to the touch. Cool the cakes in the pans for 5 minutes. Turn out onto racks. Carefully remove the paper and let cool completely.

6. Cool and clean the pans, butter and flour them, and reline with parchment paper. Repeat until all the batter is used up, making 6 or 7 layers.

7. To prepare the buttercream, melt the chocolate in a double boiler over barely simmering water. Set aside to cool.

8. With mixer at medium speed, beat the butter in a large bowl until creamy. Add the confectioners' sugar and cocoa, followed by the chocolate and vanilla.

9. To assemble the cake, place one layer on a serving plate and spread with some buttercream. Repeat with all but the top layer of cake. Place this layer on a large plate. Spread the top of the cake with the remaining buttercream.

10. To prepare the glaze, bring the sugar, water, butter, and lemon juice to a boil in a small saucepan over medium heat, stirring until the sugar has dissolved. Simmer until the mixture is caramel colored.

11. Spread the caramel over the reserved cake layer. Set aside for about 30 seconds. Use a sharp knife to cut the layer into 10 equal, wedge-shaped portions. Let cool completely.

12. Using the whole hazelnuts as props, arrange the wedges of cake on top of the cake, so that they overlap, running right around the top of the cake.

Chocolate Raspberry Sponge

This is a lovely, light chocolate sponge cake. If baking for children, replace the raspberry liqueur with a sweet raspberry cordial.

Serves: 8–10 · Prep: 1 hr. · Cooking 20–25 min. · Level: 3

CAKE
- ³⁄₄ cup (125 g) cornstarch (cornflour)
- 2 tablespoons all-purpose (plain) flour
- 3 tablespoons unsweetened cocoa powder
- 1 teaspoon baking powder
- ½ teaspoon cream of tartar
- ½ teaspoon ground cinnamon
- 4 large eggs, separated
- ¼ teaspoon salt
- ³⁄₄ cup (150 g) superfine (caster) sugar
- 2 tablespoons butter, melted and cooled

FILLING
- ³⁄₄ cup (180 ml) light (single) cream
- 2 tablespoons confectioners' (icing) sugar
- ½ teaspoon vanilla extract (essence)
- 2 tablespoons raspberry liqueur
- 2 cups (300 g) fresh raspberries

CHOCOLATE FROSTING
- 1⅓ cups (200 g) confectioners' (icing) sugar + extra, to dust
- 2 tablespoons unsweetened cocoa powder + extra, to dust
- 2 tablespoons milk

1. Preheat the oven to 350°F (180°C/gas 4). Lightly grease an 8-inch (20-cm) springform cake pan. Dust with flour. Line the base with parchment paper.

2. To prepare the cake, sift the cornstarch, flour, cocoa, baking powder, cream of tartar, and cinnamon into a small bowl.

3. Beat the egg yolks and sugar in a large bowl with an electric mixer on medium speed until pale and thick.

4. Beat the egg whites and salt in a large bowl with an electric mixer on medium speed until soft peaks form. Add a large spoonful of egg whites to the yolk mixture and fold gently to combine. Gently fold in the remaining egg whites.

5. Sift the flour a second time and gently fold into the egg mixture in two batches. Fold in the melted butter until just incorporated. Spoon the batter into the prepared pan.

6. Bake for 20–25 minutes, until light golden brown and the top springs back when gently pressed. Let cool in the pan for 5 minutes, then turn out onto a wire rack and let cool completely. When completely cold, cut the sponge in half horizontally.

7. To prepare the filling, beat the cream, confectioners' sugar, and vanilla in a small bowl with an electric mixer on high speed until soft peaks form.

8. To assemble the cake, place one layer of sponge on a serving plate and drizzle with the liqueur. Spread with the cream and cover with half the raspberries. Place the other layer of sponge on top.

9. To prepare the frosting, combine the confectioners' sugar and cocoa in a small bowl. Add the milk and stir until smooth.

10. Spread the frosting over the top of the cake and top with the remaining raspberries. Dust with the remaining cocoa powder and confectioners' sugar.

Chocolate Raspberry Sponge ▷

Cinnamon and Plum Sponge

This sponge makes an excellent dessert.

Serves: 8–10 · Prep: 30 min. · Cooking: 30–40 min. · Level: 2

CAKE
- ¾ cup (125 g) all-purpose (plain) flour
- ¼ cup (30 g) cornstarch (cornflour)
- 1½ teaspoons ground cinnamon
- ½ teaspoon baking powder
- 4 large eggs
- ⅔ cup (150 g) superfine (caster) sugar
- 1 teaspoon vanilla extract (essence)
- 2 tablespoons butter, melted and cooled

FILLING AND TOPPING
- ¾ cup (180 ml) double (heavy) cream
- 1 tablespoon confectioners' (icing) sugar
- 1½ teaspoons ground cinnamon
- ¼ cup (80 g) plum preserves (jam), warmed
- 1 (14-ounce/400-g) can whole plums, drained, pitted, and halved
  Confectioners' (icing) sugar, to dust

1. Preheat the oven to 350°F (180°C/gas 4). Lightly grease two 8-inch (20-cm) springform cake pans. Line the bases with parchment paper.

2. To prepare the cake, sift the flour, cornstarch, cinnamon, and baking powder into a small bowl. Beat the eggs and sugar in a large bowl with an electric mixer on medium speed until thick, creamy, and tripled in volume. Add the vanilla. Sift the flour into the egg mixture in two batches. Fold in the melted butter, until just incorporated. Spoon the batter into the prepared pans.

3. Bake for 20–25 minutes, until the sponges spring back when gently pressed. Let cool in the pan for 5 minutes. Turn out onto a rack and let cool completely.

4. To prepare the filling and topping, beat the cream, confectioners' sugar, and 1 teaspoon of the cinnamon until soft peaks form.

5. Spread the preserves on one of the sponges and cover with cream. Arrange plum halves over the top and top with the remaining sponge. Dust with confectioners' sugar and the remaining cinnamon.

◄ **Cinnamon and Plum Sponge**

Apricot Gateau

This is a pretty dessert cake.

Serves: 8–10 · Prep: 30 min. + 4 hr. to chill · Cooking: 30–40 min. · Level: 2

- 1 Génoise, baked in one 9-inch (23-cm) pan (see page 161)

FILLING AND TOPPING
- 1 (15-ounce/400-g) can apricots in syrup, drained (reserve the syrup)
- 2 tablespoons sugar
- ½ teaspoon almond extract (essence)
- 1½ tablespoons unflavored gelatin
- 5 tablespoons kirsch (clear cherry brandy)
- ¼ cup (60 g) apricot preserves (jam)
- ½ cup (60 g) flaked almonds, toasted
  Crème fraîche or whipped cream, to serve

1. To prepare the filling and topping, mash the apricots, sugar, and almond extract in a medium bowl with a fork until smooth.

2. Place a quarter of the reserved apricot syrup in a saucepan. Sprinkle with the gelatin. Let stand 1 minute. Stir over low heat until the gelatin has completely dissolved. Stir into the apricot mixture. Refrigerate until just beginning to set around the edges.

3. Split the cake in half horizontally. Place one layer in a 9-inch (23-cm) springform pan. Add ¼ cup (60 ml) of kirsch to the remaining syrup and drizzle over the cake in the pan. Spread with the apricot mixture and top with the remaining cake layer. Refrigerate for 4 hours.

4. Heat the preserves and remaining 1 tablespoon kirsch in a saucepan over low heat. Remove the pan sides. Brush the sides of the cake with the preserves. Sprinkle with the almonds, making them adhere to the sides of the cake.

5. Slice and serve each portion with a dollop of crème fraîche or whipped cream.

Glazed Lemon Chiffon Cake

 # Chocolate Chiffon Cake

The chiffon cake is one of the few cakes whose invention can be precisely credited and dated. It was invented in 1927 by Californian caterer Harry Baker. The cake was a great success locally and he kept the recipe secret for 20 years before selling it to General Mills. The cake became widely known in 1948 when Betty Crocker published 14 variations on the basic theme.

Chiffon cakes use vegetable oil instead of butter, which makes them ideal for people with allergies to dairy products. A good chiffon cake is light and airy, but with a rich moist crumb. To keep this cake dairy-free, be sure to choose dairy-free chocolate for the glaze. Many high-quality brands of dark chocolate do not contain milk—but always check the label.

Serves: 10–12 · Prep: 30 min. · Cooking: 55–65 min. · Level: 2

CAKE

2	cups (300 g) cake flour
1½	cups (300 g) sugar
2	teaspoons baking powder
½	teaspoon salt
½	cup (125 ml) vegetable oil
1	tablespoon finely grated lemon zest + extra, to decorate
¼	cup (60 ml) freshly squeezed lemon juice
½	cup (125 ml) water
6	large eggs, separated
½	teaspoon cream of tartar

LEMON GLAZE

2	cups (300 g) confectioners' (icing) sugar
2–3	tablespoons freshly squeezed lemon juice
1½	teaspoons finely grated lemon zest

1. Preheat the oven to 325°F (160°C/gas 3). Set out a 10-inch (25-cm) Bundt or tube pan. Do not grease the pan.

2. Combine the flour, sugar, baking powder, and salt in a large bowl. Add the oil, lemon zest and juice, water, and egg yolks and stir by hand or beat in a mixer on medium-low speed until well mixed.

3. Beat the egg whites in a large bowl with an electric mixer on low speed until foamy. Add the cream of tartar and, gradually increasing the mixer speed to medium-high, beat until very stiff, almost dry, 7–10 minutes. Use a large rubber spatula to fold into the batter.

4. Spoon the batter into the prepared pan. Bake for 55–65 minutes, or until springy to the touch and a toothpick inserted into the center of the cake comes out clean.

5. Turn the pan upside down on its feet and let the cake hang until completely cool. If you don't have a pan with little feet, hang the tube pan over a funnel or balance it on inverted coffee cups or mugs.

6. To prepare the lemon glaze, beat the confectioners' sugar with the lemon zest and juice until of drizzling consistency. Drizzle over the cake. Decorate with the lemon zest.

Serves: 10–12 · Prep: 30 min. · Cooking: 55–65 min. · Level: 2

CAKE

1½	cups (225 g) cake flour
1½	cups (300 g) sugar
½	cup (75 g) unsweetened cocoa powder
2	teaspoons baking powder
½	teaspoon salt
½	cup (125 ml) vegetable oil
¾	cup (125 ml) water
1	teaspoon vanilla extract (essence)
6	large eggs, separated
½	teaspoon cream of tartar

CHOCOLATE GLAZE

8	ounces (250 g) dairy-free dark chocolate
¼	cup (60 ml) very hot water

1. Preheat the oven to 325°F (160°C/gas 3). Set out a 10-inch (25-cm) Bundt or tube pan. Do not grease the pan.

2. Combine the flour, sugar, cocoa, baking powder, and salt in a large bowl. Add the oil, water, vanilla, and egg yolks and stir by hand or beat in a mixer on medium-low speed until well mixed.

3. Beat the egg whites in a large bowl with an electric mixer on low speed until foamy. Add the cream of tartar and, gradually increasing the mixer speed to medium-high, beat until very stiff, almost dry, 7–10 minutes. Use a large rubber spatula to fold into the batter.

4. Spoon the batter into the prepared pan. Bake for 55–65 minutes, or until springy to the touch and a toothpick inserted into the center of the cake comes out clean.

5. Turn the pan upside down on its feet and let the cake hang until completely cool. If you don't have a pan with little feet, hang the tube pan over a funnel or balance it on inverted coffee cups or mugs.

6. To prepare the chocolate glaze, melt the chocolate in a double boiler over barely simmering water. Whisk the water in all at once until smooth and satiny. Drizzle over the cake.

Glazed Lemon Chiffon Cake ▷

Lavender Rose Angel Food Cake

Angel food cakes are light, airy foam cakes made without egg yolk or fat. Food historians believe they were invented in the 19th century by the Pennsylvania Dutch community as a way to use up leftover egg whites. There are many variations on the basic recipe; this one is our favorite.

Serves: 10–12 · Prep: 15 min. · Cooking: 40–50 min. · Level: 2

1	cup (150 g) cake flour
1½	cups (225 g) confectioners' (icing) sugar
12	large egg whites
1	cup (200 g) superfine (caster) sugar
1½	teaspoons cream of tartar
¼	teaspoon salt
1	teaspoon vanilla extract (essence)
	Petals from 2 red or yellow roses, coarsely chopped + extra, to decorate
2	tablespoons dried lavender

1. Preheat the oven to 325°F (160°C/gas 3). Set out a 10-inch (25-cm) tube pan with a removable bottom.

2. Sift the flour and confectioners' sugar into a large bowl.

3. Beat the egg whites in a large bowl with an electric mixer at low speed until just broken up and beginning to froth. Add the cream of tarter and salt and beat at medium speed until soft and billowy. Keep the mixer at medium speed, and gradually add the superfine sugar, beating until glossy and smooth but not quite stiff. Add the vanilla.

4. Use a large rubber spatula to fold in the flour and confectioners' sugar, adding 2–3 tablespoons at a time. Fold in the rose petals and lavender.

5. Spoon the batter into the prepared pan. Gently rap the pan a couple of times on a work surface to release any air bubbles.

6. Bake for 40–50 minutes, or until golden brown and springy to the touch. Cool the cake following the instructions below. Decorate with the extra rose petals.

COOLING AN ANGEL FOOD CAKE

Angel food cakes are not hard to make if you follow a few simple rules. Make sure the egg whites are at warm room temperature and do not overbeat them. Beat slowly at first to develop plenty of air cells, then beat faster as the foam develops. Beat in the sugar until the whites are almost stiff, then gently fold in the dry ingredients. Do not stir the batter, or the fragile air cells will deflate. Gently pour and spoon the batter into the prepared pan as soon as it is ready; don't let it sit around before baking. Make sure the oven is heated to the right temperature ahead of time.

1 When the cake is cooked, it will be risen and golden brown and a cake tester or cocktail skewer inserted into the center will come out clean. The top will spring back when pressed gently.

2 As soon as the cake is cooked, turn the pan upside down on its feet and let the cake hang until it is completely cool. If you don't have a special pan with little feet, hang the tube pan over a funnel or balance it on inverted coffee cups or mugs.

3 To unmold, run a long knife around the edges of the pan, taking care not to separate the golden crust from the cake.

Use a serrated knife and a sawing motion to slice the cake. An ordinary knife pushed into the cake will flatten it.

Lavender Rose Angel Food Cake ▷

Raspberry Meringue Roulade

This creamy meringue roll makes a wonderful dessert. Serve with a tall glass of very cold, dry champagne.

Serves: 6–8 · Prep: 30 min. + 2 hr. to chill · Cooking: 10 min. · Level: 2

MERINGUE ROULADE

6	large egg whites
1¼	cup (250 g) superfine (caster) sugar + extra, to sprinkle
2½	tablespoons cornstarch (cornflour)
1	teaspoon white vinegar
½	teaspoon vanilla extract (essence)

FILLING

1	cup (250 ml) light (single) cream
3	tablespoons confectioners' (icing) sugar
1	teaspoon finely grated orange zest
1	teaspoon vanilla extract (essence)
1	cup (150 g) fresh raspberries

1. Preheat the oven to 400°F (200°C/gas 6). Line a 10½ x 15½-inch (38 x 25-cm) jelly-roll pan with parchment paper and lightly oil.

2. To prepare the meringue roulade, beat the egg whites in a medium bowl with an electric mixer on medium speed until soft peaks form. Gradually add the sugar, beating until dissolved and glossy. Sift in the cornstarch and fold the vinegar and vanilla in by hand. Spread the meringue evenly in the prepared pan.

3. Bake for 10 minutes. Remove from the oven and let cool for 10 minutes.

4. To prepare the filling, beat the cream, sugar, orange zest, and vanilla in a medium bowl until soft peaks form. Add the raspberries and stir gently to combine.

5. Lay a clean kitchen towel on a work surface and dust with the extra superfine sugar. Turn the meringue out onto the towel and carefully remove the paper.

6. Spread the filling over the meringue, leaving a ¾-inch (2-cm) border. Roll up in the towel, starting from the shortest side. Refrigerate, seam-side down, for 2 hours. Trim the edges and serve.

Strawberry and Coconut Meringue Torte

This is a handsome cake. See the photograph on pages 158–159. Serve for dessert on special occasions.

Serves: 6–8 · Prep: 45 min. · Cooking: 1 hr. · Level: 2

MERINGUE DISKS

6	large egg whites
1¾	cups (350 g) superfine (caster) sugar
2	cups (250 g) shredded (desiccated) coconut, lightly toasted
¼	cup (30 g) shaved coconut, lightly toasted, to decorate
½	cup (100 g) fresh whole strawberries, to decorate

STRAWBERRY CREAM

2	cups (500 ml) heavy (double) cream
4	tablespoons confectioners' (icing) sugar
1	tablespoon kirsch (clear cherry brandy)
½	teaspoon ground cinnamon
3½	ounces (100 g) white chocolate, melted and cooled
1½	cups (250 g) fresh strawberries, chopped

1. Preheat the oven to 275°F (140°C/gas 1). Line four 17 x 14-inch (43 x 35-cm) baking sheets with parchment paper and mark with 9-inch (23-cm) circles.

2. To prepare the meringue disks, beat the egg whites in a large bowl with an electric mixer on medium speed until soft peaks form. Gradually add the sugar, beating until thick and glossy. Fold in the coconut. Spoon the meringue onto 9-inch (23-cm) circles on the prepared baking sheets and spread using a spatula.

3. Bake for 1 hour, or until crisp. Remove from the oven, let cool for 10 minutes, then transfer to racks to cool completely.

4. To prepare the strawberry cream, beat the cream and sugar until soft peaks form. Fold in the kirsch, cinnamon, melted chocolate, and chopped strawberries.

5. To assemble the torte, divide the strawberry cream into quarters and spread it on top of each meringue disk. Sandwich the disks together into one tall layer cake. Arrange the whole strawberries and shaved coconut decoratively on the top layer.

Raspberry Meringue Roulade ▷

Nut and Praline Meringue Torte

*The pine nut praline will take at least an hour to cool and harden.
If liked, prepare the praline the day before.*

Serves: 8–10 · Prep: 45 min. + 1 hr. to cool · Cooking: 1 hr. · Level: 3

MERINGUE DISKS

6	large egg whites
1³/₄	cups (350 g) superfine (caster) sugar
1³/₄	cups (300 g) pine nuts, lightly toasted
1	teaspoon finely grated lemon zest

PINE NUT PRALINE CREAM

1¹/₂	cups (300 g) sugar
3	tablespoons water
1	cup (180 g) pine nuts, lightly toasted
2	cups (500 ml) heavy (double) cream
4	tablespoons confectioners' (icing) sugar
1	teaspoon finely grated lemon zest
1	teaspoon vanilla extract (essence)

1. Preheat the oven to 275°F (140°C/gas 1). Line two large baking sheets with parchment paper and mark with two 9-inch (23-cm) circles.

2. To prepare the meringue disks, beat the egg whites with an electric mixer on medium speed until soft peaks form. Gradually add the sugar, beating until thick and glossy. Fold in the pine nuts and lemon zest.

3. Spoon onto the prepared baking sheets and spread using a spatula. Bake for 1 hour, or until crisp. Remove from the oven, let cool for 10 minutes, then transfer to racks to cool completely.

4. To prepare the praline cream, line a baking sheet with parchment paper. Cook the sugar and water in a small saucepan on medium heat until a golden caramel color. Add the pine nuts, and pour onto the prepared baking sheet. Allow the praline to cool and set hard.

5. Beat the cream and confectioners' sugar until soft peaks form. Add the lemon zest and vanilla extract, beating until combined. Grind half the praline in a food processor and fold into the cream.

6. Spread each meringue disk with a quarter of the praline cream. Place the disks one on top of the other. Coarsely chop the remaining praline and sprinkle over the top layer.

Lemon and Blueberry Roulade

*This roulade can be made ahead of time and then assembled about two
hours before serving. Don't leave it more than a few hours in the
refrigerator or the meringue will melt and become watery.*

Serves: 6–8 · Prep: 30 min. + 2 hr. to chill · Cooking: 20 min. · Level: 2

ROULADE

6	large egg whites
1¹/₄	cup (250 g) superfine (caster) sugar
2	teaspoons freshly squeezed lemon juice
1	teaspoon finely grated lemon zest
	Confectioners' (icing) sugar, to dust

FILLING

³/₄	cup (180 ml) light (single) cream
3	tablespoons confectioners' (icing) sugar
1¹/₂	teaspoons finely grated lemon zest
¹/₄	cup (60 ml) storebought lemon curd
1¹/₂	cups (250 g) fresh blueberries

1. Preheat the oven to 325°F (170°C/gas 3). Line a 10¹/₂ x 15¹/₂-inch (38 x 25-cm) jelly-roll pan with parchment paper and lightly oil.

2. Beat the egg whites in a medium bowl with an electric mixer on medium speed until soft peaks form. Gradually add the sugar, beating until glossy. Fold the lemon juice and zest in by hand. Spread the batter in the prepared pan.

3. Bake for 20 minutes. Remove from the oven and let cool for 10 minutes.

4. To prepare the filling, beat the cream, sugar, and lemon zest in a medium bowl until soft peaks form. Fold in the lemon curd and blueberries.

5. Lay a clean kitchen towel on a work surface and dust with confectioners' sugar. Turn the meringue out onto the towel and carefully remove the paper.

6. Spread the filling over the meringue, leaving a ³/₄-inch (2-cm) border. Roll up in the towel, starting from the shortest side. Refrigerate, seam-side, down for 2 hours. Trim the edges and serve.

Lemon and Blueberry Roulade ▷

Chocolate and Orange Roulade

The spices in this sponge work nicely with the orange and cream filling.

Serves: 6–8 · Prep: 30 min. · Cooking: 15–20 min. · Level: 2

ROULADE
- ⅓ cup (50 g) + 1 tablespoon unsweetened cocoa powder
- 2 tablespoons all-purpose (plain) flour
- 1½ teaspoons pumpkin pie spice or allspice
- 4 large eggs
- ½ cup (100 g) superfine (caster) sugar
- 2 teaspoons finely grated orange zest
- 1 teaspoon vanilla extract (essence)
- 2 tablespoons butter, melted and cooled
- 2 tablespoons confectioners' (icing) sugar

FILLING
- ¾ cup (180 ml) light (single) cream
- ¼ cup (60 g) mascarpone cheese, softened
- 2 tablespoons confectioners' (icing) sugar
- 1 teaspoon finely grated orange zest
- ½ teaspoon ground cinnamon

1. Preheat the oven to 350°F (180°C/gas 4). Line a 10½ x 15½-inch (38 x 25-cm) jelly-roll pan with parchment paper and lightly oil.

2. To prepare the roulade, sift ⅓ cup (50 g) of cocoa powder, flour, and spice into a small bowl. Beat the eggs, sugar, and orange zest in a large bowl with an electric mixer on medium speed until thick, creamy, and tripled in volume. Add the vanilla and beat to combine.

3. Gently fold in the sifted cocoa in two batches. Fold in the melted butter until just incorporated. Spread the mixture in the pan.

4. Bake for 15–20 minutes, until it springs back when gently pressed.

5. Lay a clean kitchen towel on a work surface and dust with the remaining cocoa and confectioners' sugar. Remove the sponge from the oven and turn out onto the towel. Let to cool for 10 minutes.

6. To prepare the filling, beat the cream, mascarpone, sugar, orange zest, and cinnamon in a medium bowl until soft peaks form.

7. Peel away the paper and spread the filling over the sponge, leaving a ¾-inch (2-cm) border. Re-roll in the towel and refrigerate, seam-side down, for 2 hours. Trim the edges and serve.

Chocolate Raspberry Roll

Chocolate and raspberries are a classic combination.

Serves: 6–8 · Prep: 25 min. · Cooking: 15–20 min. · Level: 2

CHOCOLATE ROLL
- 3 ounces (90 g) dark chocolate, coarsely chopped
- ½ cup (75 g) all-purpose (plain) flour
- ½ teaspoon baking powder
- ½ teaspoon baking soda (bicarbonate of soda)
- ¼ teaspoon salt
- 4 large eggs
- ¾ cup (150 g) sugar
- 1 teaspoon vanilla extract (essence)
- 2 tablespoons cold water
- 2 tablespoons confectioners' (icing) sugar
- 1 recipe Chantilly Cream (see page 275)
  Fresh raspberries, to fill

1. Preheat the oven to 375°F (190°C/ gas 5). Butter and flour a 10½ x 15½-inch (38 x 25-cm) jelly-roll pan. Line with parchment paper.

2. To prepare the roll, melt the chocolate in a double boiler over barely simmering water. Set aside to cool.

3. Sift the flour, baking powder, baking soda, and salt into a medium bowl. Beat the eggs and sugar in a large bowl with an electric mixer at high speed until pale and thick. Add the vanilla.

4. Use a large rubber spatula to fold the dry ingredients into the egg mixture, alternating with the water. Fold in the chocolate. Spoon the batter into the prepared pan.

5. Bake for 15–20 minutes, or until springy to the touch.

6. Dust a clean kitchen towel with the confectioners' sugar. Turn the cake out onto the towel and carefully remove the parchment paper. Roll up the cake, using the towel as a guide. Let cool.

7. Unroll the cake and spread evenly with half the Chantilly Cream, leaving a 1-inch (2.5-cm) border. Sprinkle with the raspberries. Reroll the cake. Slice and serve with the remaining Chantilly Cream passed separately.

Chocolate and Orange Roulade ▷

Walnut and Coffee Roulade

This scrumptious roulade takes a little time to prepare but is well worth the effort. It's an excellent cake for a birthday.

Serves: 6–8 · Prep: 45 min. + 1 hr. to chill · Cooking: 10–12 min. · Level: 3

ROULADE
- ½ cup (75 g) all-purpose (plain) flour
- ¼ cup (30 g) cornstarch (cornflour)
- 1 teaspoon ground cinnamon
- ⅓ cup (30 g) ground walnuts
- 4 large eggs
- ½ cup (100 g) superfine (caster) sugar
- 1 teaspoon vanilla extract (essence)
- 2 tablespoons butter, melted and cooled
- 2 tablespoons confectioners' (icing) sugar

FILLING
- 1 cup (250 ml) light (single) cream
- 2 tablespoons confectioners' (icing) sugar
- 1 teaspoon vanilla extract (essence)

TOPPING
- 5 ounces (150 g) dark chocolate
- ½ cup (125 ml) heavy (double) cream
- 2 tablespoons very strong brewed coffee
- 2 tablespoons chopped walnuts, to decorate

1. Preheat the oven to 375°F (190°C/gas 5). Line a 10½ x 15½-inch (38 x 25-cm) jelly-roll pan with parchment paper and lightly oil.

2. To prepare the roulade, sift the flour, cornstarch, and cinnamon into a small bowl. Stir in the ground walnuts.

3. Beat the eggs and sugar in a large bowl with an electric mixer on medium speed until thick, creamy, and tripled in volume. Add the vanilla and beat to combine.

4. Gently fold in the sifted flour and ground walnuts in two batches. Fold in the melted butter until just incorporated. Spread the mixture into the prepared pan.

5. Bake for 10–12 minutes, until light golden and sponge springs back when gently pressed.

6. Lay a clean kitchen towel on a work surface and dust with the confectioners' sugar. Remove the sponge from the oven and turn out onto the towel. Peel away the paper and roll up the sponge in the towel, starting from the shortest side. Set aside on a wire rack, seam-side down, to cool.

7. To prepare the filling, beat the cream, sugar, and vanilla in a medium bowl until soft peaks form.

8. When the roulade is cooled, unroll it and spread with the filling, leaving a ¾-inch (2-cm) border. Re-roll in the towel and refrigerate, seam-side down, for 1 hour.

9. To prepare the topping, melt the chocolate, cream, and coffee in a double boiler over barely simmering water, stirring occasionally until smooth. Set aside to cool and thicken slightly.

10. Spread the topping over the sponge to cover. Sprinkle with chopped walnuts. Trim the edges and serve.

◁ **Walnut and Coffee Roulade**

Swiss Roll

This is a simple, light roll that goes well with a cup of tea or coffee.

Serves: 6–8 · Prep: 20 min. · Cooking: 5–8 min. · Level: 2

- ²⁄₃ cup (100 g) all-purpose (plain) flour
- ¹⁄₃ cup (50 g) cornstarch (cornflour)
- 1 teaspoon baking powder
- 3 large eggs
- ¹⁄₂ cup (100 g) superfine (caster) sugar + 2 tablespoons extra
- 1 teaspoon vanilla extract (essence)
- 2 tablespoons butter, melted and cooled
- ¹⁄₄ cup (50 g) sugar
- 1¹⁄₄ cups (300 g) raspberry preserves (jam)

1. Preheat the oven to 400 F (200 C/gas 6). Line a 10¹⁄₂ x 15¹⁄₂-inch (38 x 25-cm) jelly-roll pan with parchment paper and lightly oil.

2. Sift the flour, cornstarch, and baking powder into a small bowl.

3. Beat the eggs and sugar in a large bowl with an electric mixer on medium speed until thick, creamy, and tripled in volume. Add the vanilla and beat to combine.

4. Gently fold in the sifted flour in two batches. Fold in the melted butter until just incorporated. Spread the batter evenly in the prepared pan.

5. Bake for 5–8 minutes, until light golden and the sponge springs back when gently pressed.

6. Lay a clean kitchen towel on a work surface and dust with the extra 2 tablespoons of sugar. Remove the sponge from the oven and turn out onto the towel. Peel away the paper and roll up the sponge, starting from the shortest side, in the towel. Set aside on a wire rack, seam-side down, to cool.

7. When the sponge has cooled, unroll it and spread with the raspberry preserves. Re-roll the sponge, trim the edges, and serve.

Chocolate Hazelnut Roll

Another quick and simple roll to serve with coffee or tea.

Serves: 6–8 · Prep: 30 min. · Cooking: 10–12 min. · Level: 2

- ¹⁄₂ cup (75 g) all-purpose (plain) flour
- ¹⁄₃ cup (50 g) unsweetened cocoa powder + 2 tablespoons extra
- ¹⁄₂ teaspoon baking powder
- 5 large eggs, separated
- ³⁄₄ cup (150 g) sugar
- 2 tablespoons butter, melted
- 1 teaspoon vanilla extract (essence)
- ¹⁄₂ teaspoon salt
- 1 cup (250 g) chocolate hazelnut spread (Nutella), softened

1. Preheat the oven to 400°F (200°C/gas 6). Butter and flour a 10¹⁄₂ x 15¹⁄₂-inch (38 x 25-cm) jelly-roll pan. Line with parchment paper.

2. Sift the flour, ¹⁄₃ cup (50 g) cocoa, and baking powder into a large bowl. Beat the egg yolks, ¹⁄₄ cup (50 g) of sugar, butter, and vanilla in a large bowl with an electric mixer at high speed until pale and thick.

3. Use a large rubber spatula to fold in the mixed dry ingredients. With mixer on medium speed, beat the egg whites and salt in a large bowl until frothy. With mixer on high, gradually beat in the remaining ¹⁄₂ cup (100 g) of sugar, beating until stiff, glossy peaks form. Fold the beaten egg whites into the batter. Spoon into the prepared pan.

4. Bake for 10–12 minutes, or until springy to the touch.

5. Lay a clean kitchen towel on a work surface and dust with the extra 2 tablespoons of cocoa. Remove the sponge from the oven and turn out onto the towel. Peel away the paper and roll up the sponge, starting from the shortest side, in the towel. Set aside on a wire rack, seam-side down, to cool.

6. When the sponge has cooled, unroll it and spread with the chocolate hazelnut spread. Re-roll and place on a serving plate, seam-side down.

Swiss Roll ▷

Sponge Roll with Peach Filling

This makes a lovely dessert in the summer months when peaches are tasty and ripe.

Serves: 6–8 · Prep: 35 min. · Cooking 10–15 min. · Level: 2

PEACH FILLING
1	pound (500 g) ripe peaches, peeled, pitted, and chopped
1	cup (200 g) sugar
1½	teaspoons finely grated lemon zest

SPONGE ROLL
⅓	cup (75 g) sugar
2	large eggs
¼	teaspoon salt
½	cup (75 g) cake flour
½	teaspoon vanilla extract (essence)
3	tablespoons dark rum
1	large fresh peach, peeled and finely chopped, to decorate
¼	cup (30 g) confectioners' (icing) sugar, to dust

1. To prepare the peach filling, cook the peaches, sugar, and lemon zest in a large saucepan over medium heat, stirring frequently, until the peaches are tender and the syrup has reduced, about 20 minutes. Set aside to cool.

2. Preheat the oven to 350°F (180°C/gas 4). Butter a 13 x 9-inch (32 x 23-cm) baking pan. Line with parchment paper.

3. To prepare the roll, beat the eggs, sugar, and salt in a large bowl with an electric mixer at high speed until thick, creamy, and tripled in volume. Use a large rubber spatula to fold the flour and vanilla into the beaten eggs. Spoon the batter into the prepared pan.

4. Bake for 10–15 minutes, or until golden brown.

5. Lay a clean kitchen towel on a work surface and dust with the extra 2 tablespoons of confectioners' sugar. Turn the sponge out onto the towel. Peel away the paper and roll up, starting from the shortest side, in the towel. Set aside on a rack, seam-side down, to cool.

6. When cooled, unroll and brush with the rum. Spread with the filling, leaving a 1-inch (2.5-cm) border. Reroll the cake, wrap in plastic wrap (cling film), and refrigerate for 1 hour. Decorate with the chopped peach and dust with confectioners' sugar.

◁ **Sponge Roll with Peach Filling**

Egg-Free Macadamia Sponge

Soya cream cheese is available at health food stores.

Serves: 6–8 · Prep: 30 min. + 6 hr. to chill · Cooking 20–25 min. · Level: 2

CAKE
1	cup (150 g) cake flour
1	teaspoon baking powder
¾	cup (170 g) superfine (caster) sugar
¼	teaspoon salt
2	tablespoons grated creamed coconut
5	tablespoons melted soya fat
1	cup (250 ml) cold water
3	ounces (90 g) macadamia nuts, cut in half

TOPPING
1⅓	cups (200 g) confectioners' (icing) sugar + extra, to dust
3	ounces (100 g) soya cream cheese
	Finely grated zest and juice of 1 lime
	Fresh strawberries, to serve

1. Preheat the oven to 350°F (180°C/gas 4). Lightly grease and flour an 8-inch (20-cm) square cake pan with a little extra soya fat.

2. Sift the flour, sugar, and salt into a large bowl. Add the grated coconut and mix thoroughly.

3. Pour the melted soya fat and cold water into the mixture, and carefully fold until it is all combined. Gently fold in the macadamia nuts. Spoon the batter into the prepared pan.

4. Bake for 20–25 minutes, until golden brown. Let cool in the pan for 5 minutes before turning out onto a rack. Let cool completely.

5. To prepare the topping, beat the confectioners' sugar, soya cream cheese, and lime zest and juice until smooth.

6. When the cake is completely cooled, spread with the topping. Chill in the refrigerator for 6 hours.

7. Decorate with fresh strawberries and dust with the extra confectioners' sugar just before serving.

Pistachio Roll

Serve this roll with the Vanilla Crème Anglaise as dessert for special family dinners.

Serves: 6–8 · Prep: 30 min. + 1 hr. to chill · Cooking: 10–12 min. · Level: 2

- ½ cup (60 g) shelled and peeled pistachios
- ½ cup (100 g) sugar
- ½ teaspoon vanilla extract (essence)
- 2 large eggs, separated
- ½ cup (75 g) all-purpose (plain) flour
- ¼ teaspoon salt
- ¼ cup (30 g) confectioners' (icing) sugar
- 2 tablespoons rum
- 1 cup (300 g) raspberry or apricot preserves (jam)
- 1 recipe Vanilla Crème Anglaise (see page 278)
- ¼ cup (30 g) slivered almonds

1. Preheat the oven to 350°F (180°C/gas 4). Butter and flour a 10½ x 15½-inch (38 x 25-cm) jelly-roll pan. Line with parchment paper.

2. Process the pistachio nuts and 2 tablespoons of sugar in a food processor until finely chopped.

3. Beat the egg yolks, remaining sugar, and vanilla in a medium bowl with an electric mixer at high speed until pale and thick. With mixer at low speed, gradually beat in the flour and pistachio mixture.

4. With mixer at medium speed, beat the egg whites and salt in a medium bowl until stiff peaks form. Use a large rubber spatula to fold them into the batter. Spoon the batter into the prepared pan.

5. Bake for 10–12 minutes, or until springy to the touch. Dust a clean tea towel with the confectioners' sugar and roll up the cake. Let cool.

6. Unroll the cake and drizzle with the rum. Spread with the preserves. Reroll the cake and refrigerate for 1 hour.

7. Spread the Vanilla Crème Anglaise on serving plates and arrange slices of the roll on top. Sprinkle with the almonds.

Lemon Curd Roll

A light, lemon-flavored roll that is perfect with a cup of tea or coffee.

Serves: 6–8 · Prep: 45 min. + 2 hr. to chill · Cooking: 8–10 min. · Level: 3

ROLL
- 2 large eggs
- ⅓ cup (70 g) sugar
- ¼ teaspoon salt
- ⅔ cup (100 g) all-purpose (plain) flour
- 2 tablespoons confectioners' (icing) sugar
- ½ cup (150 g) apricot preserves (jam)
- 1 cup (250 ml) storebought lemon curd

SYRUP
- Zest of 1 lemon, cut into very thin strips
- ¼ cup (50 g) sugar
- ½ cup (125 ml) water
- ¼ cup (60 ml) rum

1. Preheat the oven to 400°F (200°C/gas 6). Butter and flour a 10½ x 15½-inch (38 x 25-cm) jelly-roll pan. Line with parchment paper.

2. To prepare the roll, beat the eggs, sugar, and salt in a medium bowl with an electric mixer at high speed until pale and very thick. Use a large rubber spatula to fold in the flour. Spoon the batter into the prepared pan.

3. Bake for 8–10 minutes, or until springy to the touch. Dust a clean kitchen towel with the confectioners' sugar. Turn the cake out onto the towel and carefully remove the parchment paper. Roll up the cake, using the towel as a guide. Let cool.

4. To prepare the syrup, cook the lemon zest, sugar, and half the water in a saucepan over medium heat. Simmer for 3–4 minutes, until slightly reduced. Strain the liquid and discard the zest. Stir the remaining water and the rum into the syrup.

5. Unroll the cake and brush with the syrup. Spread evenly with the apricot preserves and lemon curd, leaving a 1-inch (2.5-cm) border. Reroll the cake and refrigerate for 2 hours.

Pistachio Roll ▷

Almond Roll with Caramel Crunch

The caramel crunch topping contrasts deliciously with the light almond sponge and the cream.

Serves: 6–8 · Prep: 30 min. · Cooking: 15–20 min. · Level: 2

CARAMEL CRUNCH
1½	cups (300 g) sugar
¾	cup (120 g) blanched whole almonds

CAKE
5	large eggs, separated
¾	cup (150 g) sugar
⅓	cup (50 g) almonds, finely ground
1	teaspoon almond extract (essence)
¼	teaspoon salt
3	tablespoons sugar, to sprinkle
1½	cups (300 ml) heavy (double) cream

1. Preheat the oven to 350°F (180°C/gas 4). Butter a 10½ x 15½-inch (38 x 25-cm) jelly-roll pan. Line with parchment paper.

2. To prepare the toping, oil a baking sheet. Cook the sugar and almonds in a saucepan over low heat, stirring constantly, until the sugar melts. Continue cooking, stirring frequently, until deep golden brown. Pour onto the prepared sheet and set aside to cool. When cool, crush into small pieces.

3. To prepare the cake, beat the egg yolks and sugar in a large bowl with an electric mixer at high speed until pale and very thick. Add the almonds and almond extract. With mixer at high speed, beat the egg whites and salt in a large bowl until stiff peaks form. Use a large rubber spatula to fold them into the almond mixture. Spoon the batter into the prepared pan.

4. Bake for 15–20 minutes, or until a toothpick inserted into the center comes out clean.

5. Dust a clean kitchen towel with sugar. Let the cake cool for 5 minutes in the pan. Turn out onto the towel. Carefully remove the parchment paper and trim the edges. Use the towel as a guide to roll the cake up.

6. With mixer at high speed, beat the cream in a large bowl until stiff. Unroll the cake and spread evenly with the cream, leaving a 1-inch (2.5-cm) border. Reroll the cake. Press the caramel pieces into the top of the roll.

Orange Surprise

If liked, replace half the orange juice with orange liqueur.

Serves: 6–8 · Prep: 20 min. + 1 hr. to chill · Level: 1

1	cup (250 ml) heavy (double) cream
2	tablespoons sugar
1	teaspoon vanilla extract (essence)
1	Basic Sponge Cake (see page 272)
1	cup (250 ml) freshly squeezed orange juice
½	cup (150 g) + 2 tablespoons orange marmalade
	Mandarin orange segments, to decorate

1. Beat the cream, sugar, and vanilla in a medium bowl with an electric mixer at high speed until stiff.

2. Split the cake in half horizontally. Place one layer on a serving plate. Brush with half the orange juice. Spread with the cream. Top with the remaining layer and brush with the remaining orange juice.

3. Warm ½ cup (150 g) of marmalade in a small saucepan over low heat. Brush the cake with the marmalade. Cover with plastic wrap (cling film) and refrigerate for 1 hour.

4. Decorate with the orange segments. Warm the remaining marmalade and brush over the fruit.

Almond Roll with Caramel Crunch ▷

CHILLED AND FROZEN CAKES

The cakes in this chapter all make wonderful deserts.

We have included 16 superb cheesecakes, ranging from the

simple No-Bake Lime Cheesecake (see page 206) to the

very decadent Dulce de Leche Cheesecake (see page 212).

You will also find a range of frozen pies and ice cream

cakes, such as the striking Strawberry Ice Cream Cake

(see page 224) and the Black Forest Ice Cream Cake (see

page 230). To help you prepare ice cream cakes we have

included a feature panel on making ice cream.

◁ **Strawberry and Vanilla Cheesecake (see page 202)**

Raspberry Cheesecake

With its light, mousse-like filling, this cake is less rich than many cheesecakes. But it still has the pleasantly sharp flavor of cream cheese and crème fraîche—delicious!

Serves: 10–12 · Prep: 25 min. + 6 hr. 30 min. to chill · Level 1

CRUST

2	cups (250 g) graham cracker or digestive biscuit crumbs
1/2	cup (125 g) butter, melted
1	teaspoon ground cinnamon

FILLING

2	teaspoons unflavored powdered gelatin
2	tablespoons water
1	(8-ounce) package + 1 (4-ounce) package (375 g) cream cheese, softened
1/3	cup (50 g) confectioners' (icing) sugar
1	cup (250 g) crème fraîche
2	tablespoons fresh squeezed lemon juice
1²/₃	cups (250 g) fresh raspberries + extra, to decorate
	Confectioners' (icing) sugar, to dust

1. To prepare the crust, combine the crumbs, butter, and cinnamon in a small bowl. Press into the bottom of a 10-inch (25-cm) springform pan. Chill in the refrigerator for 30 minutes.

2. To prepare the filling, place the gelatin and water in a small heatproof bowl over a saucepan of barely simmering water, stirring occasionally until dissolved.

3. Beat the cream cheese and sugar in a medium bowl with an electric mixer on medium speed until smooth and creamy. Add the crème fraîche and lemon juice and beat until combined.

4. Place the raspberries in a food processor and blend until puréed. Pour the purée and gelatin into the cream cheese mixture and beat to combine.

5. Pour the filling into the prepared base and chill in the refrigerator for at least 6 hours.

6. Top with the extra raspberries just before serving.

Cranberry Cheesecake

This is a wonderful dessert to serve at Thanksgiving.

Serves: 10–12 · Prep: 30 min. + 6 hr. to chill · Cooking: 60–70 min. · Level: 1

CRUST

1³/₄	cups (200 g) graham cracker or digestive biscuit crumbs
1/4	cup (60 g) butter, melted
2	tablespoons brown sugar
1	teaspoon ground cinnamon
1/2	teaspoon ground nutmeg

FILLING

3	(8-ounce) packages (750 g) cream cheese, softened
3/4	cup (150 g) sugar
1/4	cup (30 g) all-purpose (plain) flour
2	teaspoons vanilla extract (essence)
3	large eggs
1	cup (250 ml) sour cream
1	(16-ounce/500-g) can whole berry cranberry sauce

1. Preheat the oven to 350°F (180°C/gas 4). Butter a 10-inch (25-cm) springform pan.

2. To prepare the crust, mix the crumbs, butter, sugar, cinnamon, and nutmeg in a medium bowl. Press into the bottom and partway up the sides of the prepared pan.

3. Bake for 8–10 minutes, or until lightly browned. Cool completely in the pan on a rack.

4. Reduce the oven temperature to 300°F (150°C/gas 2).

5. To prepare the filling, beat the cream cheese, sugar, flour, and vanilla in a large bowl with an electric mixer at medium speed until creamy. Add the eggs, one at a time, beating until just blended after each addition. Beat in the sour cream. Spoon the filling into the crust.

6. Bake for 50–60 minutes, or until set. Cool the cake in the pan on a rack.

7. Spread with the cranberry sauce. Chill in the refrigerator for at least 6 hours.

Raspberry Cheesecake ▷

Strawberry and Vanilla Cheesecake

This is a very attractive big cheesecake. See the photograph on pages 198-199. Vanilla bean paste is a thick, syrupy vanilla flavoring that you can buy at specialty baking stores. Substitute with vanilla extract if you can't find it.

Serves: 10–12 · Prep: 25 min. + 7 hr. to chill · Cooking: 60–70 min. · Level: 1

CRUST
- 2 cups (250 g) graham cracker or digestive biscuit crumbs
- ½ cup (125 g) butter, melted

FILLING
- 2 teaspoons unflavored powdered gelatin
- 2 tablespoons water
- 1½ cups (375 g) mascarpone cheese
- ⅓ cup (50 g) confectioners' (icing) sugar + 3 tablespoons
- 1 teaspoon vanilla bean paste
- 2 tablespoons freshly squeezed lemon juice
- 1 cup (250 ml) light (single) cream
- 2 cups (300 g) fresh strawberries, sliced
- ¼ cup (60 ml) water
- 2 tablespoons strawberry liqueur
- 1 tablespoon cornstarch (cornflour)

1. To prepare the crust, combine the crumbs and butter in a small bowl. Press into the bottom of a 10-inch (25-cm) round springform pan. Chill in the refrigerator for 30 minutes.

2. To prepare the filling, place the gelatin and water in a small heatproof bowl over a saucepan of barely simmering water, stirring occasionally until dissolved.

3. Beat the mascarpone, ⅓ cup (50 g) confectioners' sugar and vanilla until smooth and creamy. Add the lemon juice and gelatin and beat until combined. Beat the cream in a small bowl until soft peaks form. Fold into the cheese mixture.

4. Layer half the strawberries over the crust. Pour the filling over the top and chill in the refrigerator for 3 hours, until firm.

5. Place the remaining strawberries and sugar in a food processor and blend until puréed. Strain through a fine mesh into a small saucepan and pour in the water. Blend the liqueur and cornstarch in a small bowl and add to the purée. Stir over low heat until the it coats the back of a spoon. Transfer to a small bowl and chill until cooled.

6. Spread the strawberry purée over the cheesecake and chill for at least 4 hours.

Piña Colada Cheesecake

A Piña Colada is a cocktail made with a mixture of pineapple, coconut, and rum. According to cocktail lore, it was invented in 1954 at the Beachcomber Bar of the Caribe Hilton in San Juan, Puerto Rico. This delicious cheesecake mimics its flavors wonderfully.

Serves: 10–12 · Prep: 30 min. + 6 hr. 30 min. to chill · Level: 1

CRUST
- 1¾ cups (200 g) graham cracker or digestive biscuit crumbs
- ¼ cup (30 g) shredded (desiccated) coconut
- ½ cup (125 g) butter, melted
- 1 teaspoon finely grated lime zest

FILLING
- 3 teaspoons unflavored powdered gelatin
- 3 tablespoons water
- 1 (8-ounce) package + 1 (4-ounce) package (700 g) cream cheese, softened
- ⅓ cup (50 g) confectioners' (icing) sugar
- 1 teaspoon finely grated lime zest
- ⅓ cup (90 ml) pineapple juice
- 2 tablespoons white rum, such as Malibu
- 1 cup (250 ml) light (single) cream
- ½ cup (125 g) fresh or canned pineapple, chopped, to decorate
- ¼ cup (30 g) shredded (desiccated) coconut, lightly toasted

1. To prepare the crust, combine the crumbs, coconut, butter, and lime zest in a small bowl. Press into the bottom of a 10-inch (25-cm) springform pan. Chill in the refrigerator for 30 minutes.

2. To prepare the filling, place the gelatin and water in a small heatproof bowl over a saucepan of barely simmering water, stirring occasionally until dissolved.

3. Beat the cream cheese, sugar, and lime zest in a medium bowl, with an electric mixer on medium until smooth and creamy. Add the pineapple juice, rum, and gelatin and beat until combined.

4. Beat the cream in a small bowl until soft peaks form. Fold into the cream cheese mixture.

5. Pour the filling over the prepared base. Chill in the refrigerator for at least 6 hours. Decorate with pineapple and toasted coconut.

Piña Colada Cheesecake ▷

Orange and Ricotta Cheesecake

The gingersnap cookies give the crust on this cheesecake a lovely spicy flavor. You can also make it with graham cracker or digestive biscuit crumbs.

Serves: 10–12 · Prep: 30 min. + 6 hr. 30 min. to chill · Level: 1

CRUST

1¼   cups (150 g) gingersnap (gingernut) cookie crumbs
¼   cup (40 g) ground almonds
½   cup (125 g) butter, melted

FILLING

3   teaspoons unflavored powdered gelatin
3   tablespoons water
1   (8-ounce) package (250 g) cream cheese, softened
1½   cups (375 g) ricotta cheese, drained
½   cup (75 g) confectioners' (icing) sugar
2   tablespoons finely grated orange zest
2   tablespoons orange liqueur, such as Grand Mariner
1   tablespoon freshly squeezed lemon juice
1   cup (250 ml) light (single) cream
2   oranges, peeled and segmented, to decorate

1. To prepare the crust, combine the crumbs, almonds, and butter in a small bowl. Press into the bottom of a 10-inch (25-cm) springform pan. Refrigerate for 30 minutes.

2. To prepare the filling, place the gelatin and water in a small heatproof bowl over a saucepan of barely simmering water, stirring occasionally until dissolved.

3. Beat the cream cheese, ricotta, sugar, and orange zest in a medium bowl with an electric mixer on medium until smooth. Add the orange liqueur, lemon juice, and gelatin and beat until combined.

4. Beat the cream in a small bowl until soft peaks form. Fold into the cheese mixture.

5. Pour the filling over the prepared base and refrigerate for at least 6 hours, until set.

6. Decorate with orange segments.

◁ **Orange and Ricotta Cheesecake**

Key Lime Cheesecake

Key Lime cheesecake is as delicious as the pie it is named after.

Serves: 10–12 · Prep: 30 min. + 4 hr. 45 min. to chill · Level: 2

CRUST

1¾   cups (200 g) graham cracker or digestive biscuit crumbs
¾   cup (150 g) sugar
⅔   cup (150 g) butter, melted

FILLING

2   tablespoons unflavored gelatin
1   cup (250 ml) freshly squeezed lime juice
¼   cup (60 ml) water
1½   cups (300 g) sugar
5   large eggs
2   teaspoons finely grated lime zest
½   cup (125 g) butter, softened
2   (8-ounce) packages (500 g) cream cheese, softened
½   cup (125 ml) heavy (double) cream
    Fresh lime slices, to decorate

1. To prepare the crust, combine the crumbs, sugar, and butter in a medium bowl. Press into the bottom and partway up the sides of a 9-inch (23-cm) springform pan.

2. To prepare the filling, sprinkle the gelatin over the lime juice and water in a saucepan. Let stand 1 minute. Beat the sugar, eggs, and lime zest into the lime juice. Cook over low heat, stirring constantly with a wooden spoon, until the mixture lightly coats a metal spoon or registers 160°F (70°C) on an instant-read thermometer. Plunge the pan into a bowl of ice water and stir until the egg mixture has cooled.

3. Beat the butter and cream cheese in a large bowl with an electric mixer at medium speed until creamy. With mixer on low, add the lime mixture. Refrigerate for 45 minutes.

4. With mixer on high, beat the cream in a large bowl until stiff. Use a large rubber spatula to fold into the lime mixture. Spoon the filling into the crust.

5. Refrigerate for at least 4 hours before serving. Decorate with the slices of lime.

Lemon and Lime Cheesecake

A nice citrus cheesecake with great flavor and texture.

Serves: 10–12 · Prep: 45 min. + 7 hr. to chill · Cooking: 60–75 min. · Level: 1

CRUST

1⅓	cups (200 g) all-purpose (plain) flour
½	cup (100 g) sugar
1	tablespoon finely grated lemon zest
¼	cup (60 g) butter, melted
1	large egg, lightly beaten with 1 tablespoon water

FILLING

2	(8-ounce) packages (500 g) cream cheese, softened
1	cup (200 g) sugar
½	cup (125 ml) honey
2	tablespoons cornstarch (cornflour)
1	tablespoon each freshly grated lemon and lime zest
2	teaspoons lemon extract (essence)
1	teaspoon vanilla extract (essence)
3	large eggs
1	cup (250 ml) sour cream

TOPPING

¾	cup (250 g) lemon preserves or fine-cut lemon marmalade
1	tablespoon freshly squeezed lime juice

1. Preheat the oven to 400°F (200°C/gas 6). Butter a 10-inch (25-cm) springform pan.

2. To prepare the crust, mix the flour, sugar, and lemon zest in a medium bowl. Stir in the butter, egg, and water until the mixture resembles coarse crumbs. Press into the bottom of the pan. Bake for 10–15 minutes, until golden brown. Cool in the pan on a rack.

3. To prepare the filling, reduce the oven temperature to 350°F (180°C/gas 4). Beat the cream cheese, sugar, honey, cornstarch, lemon and lime zest, lemon extract, and vanilla until creamy. Add the eggs one at a time, beating until just blended after each addition. Beat in the sour cream. Spoon the filling into the crust.

4. Bake for 50–60 minutes, until set. Cool in the pan on a rack. Refrigerate for at least 6 hours.

5. To prepare the topping, bring the lemon preserves and lime juice to a boil in a saucepan over medium heat. Let cool for 15 minutes. Spread with the preserves. Refrigerate for 1 hour.

No-Bake Lime Cheesecake

This cheesecake is equally good if made using lemons.

Serves: 8–10 · Prep: 35 min. + 5 hr. to chill · Level: 1

CRUST

2	cups (250 g) graham cracker or digestive biscuit crumbs
2	tablespoons brown sugar
¼	cup (60 g) butter, melted

LIME FILLING

1	(14-ounce/400-g) can sweetened condensed milk
1	(8-ounce) package (250 g) reduced-fat cream cheese, softened
½	cup (125 ml) light (single) cream
2	tablespoons finely grated lime zest
¼	cup (60 ml) freshly squeezed lime juice

TOPPING

¾	cup (180 ml) heavy (double) cream
	Sliced ripe fresh fruit, to decorate

1. To prepare the crust, mix the crumbs, sugar, and butter in a small bowl. Press into the bottom of a 9-inch (23-cm) springform pan. Refrigerate for 1 hour.

2. To prepare the filling, beat the condensed milk, cream cheese, cream, and lime zest in a large bowl with an electric mixer at low speed until creamy. Beat in the lime juice.

3. Spoon the filling into the crust. Refrigerate for at least 4 hours.

4. With mixer at high speed, beat the cream in a medium bowl until stiff. Spread the top of the cheesecake with the cream. Decorate with the fruit.

Lemon and Lime Cheesecake ▷

Caramel Cheesecake

Butterscotch extract can be found at specialty baking stores and from online suppliers.

Serves: 10–12 · Prep: 25 min. + 6 hr. to chill · Cooking: 55–65 min. · Level: 1

CRUST
- 1 cup (150 g) graham cracker (digestive biscuit) crumbs
- ¼ cup (50 g) firmly packed brown sugar
- ¼ cup (60 g) butter, melted
- 1 teaspoon vanilla extract (essence)

FILLING
- 3 (8-ounce) packages (700 g) cream cheese, softened
- 1 cup (200 g) firmly packed brown sugar
- 1 teaspoon vanilla extract (essence)
- 1 teaspoon butterscotch extract (optional)
- 3 large eggs
- ½ cup (125 ml) sour cream
- ½ cup (60 g) toasted macadamia nuts, coarsely chopped

TOPPING
- 1½ cups (300 ml) sour cream
- ¼ cup (50 g) firmly packed brown sugar
- 1 teaspoon butterscotch or vanilla extract (essence)

1. Preheat the oven to 350°F (180°C/gas 4). Butter a 9-inch (23-cm) springform pan.

2. To prepare the crust, mix the crumbs, brown sugar, butter, and vanilla in a large bowl. Press into the bottom and partway up the sides of the prepared pan. Bake for 8–10 minutes, or until lightly browned. Cool completely in the pan on a rack.

3. To prepare the filling, beat the cream cheese, brown sugar, vanilla and butterscotch extracts in a large bowl with an electric mixer at medium speed until creamy. Add the eggs one at a time, beating until just blended after each addition. With mixer at low speed, add the sour cream. Add the nuts. Spoon into the crust.

4. Bake for 35–45 minutes, or until set.

5. To prepare the topping, beat the sour cream, sugar, and butterscotch extract in a medium bowl. Spread over the cheesecake. Bake for 10 minutes, or until set. Cool the cake in the pan on a rack. Refrigerate for 6 hours.

Tiramisù Cheesecake

This cake is made with ladyfingers, coffee, and chocolate, like its Italian namesake.

Serves: 10–12 · Prep: 20 min. + 6 hr. to chill · Cooking: 35–40 min. · Level: 1

- 2 (8-ounce) packages (500 g) cream cheese, softened
- ½ cup (100 g) sugar
- 2 teaspoons vanilla extract (essence)
- 2 large eggs
- 12 ladyfingers, each cut in half lengthwise
- ⅓ cup (90 ml) strong cold coffee
- ¼ cup (60 ml) kirsch (clear cherry brandy)
- 1 cup (250 ml) heavy (double) cream
- 2 ounces (60 g) dark chocolate, grated

1. Preheat the oven to 350°F (180°C/gas 4). Butter a 9-inch (23-cm) springform pan.

2. Beat the cream cheese, sugar, and vanilla in a large bowl with an electric mixer on medium speed until creamy. Add the eggs one at a time, beating until just blended after each addition.

3. Arrange the ladyfingers in the base of the prepared pan, fitting them together tightly, and using small pieces to fill in any gaps. Cut the remaining ladyfingers in half crosswise. Arrange with the rounded sides against the pan sides.

4. Mix the coffee and kirsch and drizzle over the ladyfingers. Spoon the cheese mixture carefully into the pan.

5. Bake for 35–40 minutes, or until set. Cool the cake completely in the pan on a rack. Refrigerate for 6 hours.

6. With mixer at high speed, beat the cream in a medium bowl until stiff . Spread the cream over the cheesecake. Sprinkle with the chocolate.

Passion Fruit Cheesecake

Serves: 10–12 · Prep: 35 min. + 6 hr. to chill · Cooking 60–70 min. · Level: 1

BASIC CRUST
1½	cups (225 g) graham cracker or digestive biscuit crumbs
⅓	cup (90 g) butter, melted
¼	cup (50 g) sugar

FILLING
2	(8-ounce) packages (500 g) cream cheese, softened
½	cup (100 g) sugar
3	large eggs, separated
⅓	cup (50 g) all-purpose (plain) flour
1	teaspoon finely grated lemon zest
1	tablespoon freshly squeezed lemon juice
1	teaspoon vanilla extract (essence)
½	cup (125 ml) heavy (double) cream
¼	cup (60 ml) strained fresh passion fruit pulp

1. Preheat the oven to 350°F (180°C/gas 4). Butter a 9-inch (23-cm) springform pan.

2. To prepare the crust, mix the crumbs, butter, and sugar in a medium bowl. Press into the bottom and up the sides of the pan.

3. Bake for 8–10 minutes, or until lightly browned. Cool completely in the pan on a rack.

4. To prepare the filling, lower the oven temperature to 300°F (160/gas 2). Beat the cream cheese and sugar in a large bowl with an electric mixer at low speed until smooth Add the egg yolks one at a time, beating until just blended after each addition. Add the flour, lemon zest and juice, and vanilla.

5. With mixer on high, beat the cream in a small bowl until stiff. With mixer at high speed, beat the egg whites in a medium bowl until stiff peaks form. Stir the passion fruit pulp into the cream cheese mixture. Use a large rubber spatula to fold the cream and whites into the batter. Spoon the filling into the crust.

6. Bake for 50–60 minutes, or until set. Cool in the pan on a rack. Refrigerate for at least 6 hours.

Apple Streusel Cheesecake

Serves: 10–12 · Prep: 35 min. + 6 hr. to chill · Cooking 80–90 min. · Level: 1

CRUST
1	Basic Crust (see recipe, left)

TOPPING
⅓	cup (50 g) all-purpose (plain) flour
¼	cup (50 g) firmly packed brown sugar
1	teaspoon ground cinnamon
½	teaspoon ground nutmeg
¼	cup (60 g) cold butter, cut up
½	cup (60 g) walnuts, hazelnuts, almonds, or pecans, chopped

FILLING
3	(8-ounce) packages (700 g) cream cheese, softened
1	cup (200 g) sugar
¾	cup (180 ml) sour cream
2	teaspoons vanilla extract (essence)
1	teaspoon ground cinnamon
1	teaspoon ground nutmeg
1	teaspoon ground ginger
4	large eggs
2	cups peeled, cored, and diced apples

1. To prepare the topping, mix the flour, sugar, cinnamon, and nutmeg in a large bowl. Use a pastry blender to cut in the butter until the mixture resembles fine crumbs. Stir in the nuts.

2. To prepare the filling, beat the cream cheese and sugar in a large bowl with an electric mixer at medium speed until creamy. Beat in the sour cream, vanilla, cinnamon, nutmeg, and ginger. Add the eggs one at a time, beating until just blended after each addition. Stir in the apples. Spoon the filling into the crust. Sprinkle the topping over the filling.

3. Bake for 80–90 minutes, or until set. Cool in the pan on a rack. Refrigerate for at least 6 hours.

Passion Fruit Cheesecake ▷

Dulce de Leche Cheesecake

Dulce de leche is a thick, caramel-flavored sauce. It is available in specialty baking stores and many supermarkets.

Serves: 10–12 · Prep: 30 min. + 8 hr. to chill · Cooking: 50–60 min. · Level: 1

BASIC CHOCOLATE CRUST
- 2 cups (250 g) plain chocolate wafer (biscuit) crumbs
- ½ cup (125 g) butter, melted

FILLING
- 2 teaspoons unflavored powdered gelatin
- 2 tablespoons water
- 1 (8-ounce) package + 1 package (4-ounce) (375 g) cream cheese, softened
- ⅓ cup (50 g) confectioners' (icing) sugar
- 1 cup (250 ml) light (single) cream
- 1 teaspoon vanilla extract (essence)
- 1 cup (250 g) dulce de leche (thick caramel sauce)

1. To prepare the crust, combine the crumbs and butter in a small bowl. Press into the bottom of a 10-inch (25 cm) springform pan. Refrigerate for 1 hour.

2. To prepare the filling, place the gelatin and water in a small heatproof bowl over a saucepan of barely simmering water, stirring occasionally until dissolved.

3. Beat the cream cheese and sugar in a medium bowl with an electric mixer on medium speed until smooth and creamy. Add the vanilla and gelatin and beat until combined.

4. Beat the cream in a small bowl until soft peaks form. Fold into the cheese mixture.

5. Pour half of the filling over the prepared base. Scatter small spoonfuls of dulce de leche over the top and pour the remaining filling over the top. Refrigerate for 3 hours, until firm.

6. Place the remaining dulce de leche in a small saucepan and heat over low heat, stirring, until runny. Set aside to cool slightly, about 10 minutes. Pour the sauce over the cheesecake and create a swirl pattern using a skewer or end of a small knife. Refrigerate for at least 4 more hours, until set.

Amaretto Chocolate Chip Cheesecake

Deliciously rich and sweet, children will especially love this cheesecake.

Serves: 10–12 · Prep: 30 min. + 6 hr. to chill · Cooking: 50–60 min. · Level: 1

CRUST
- 2 cups (250 g) crushed amaretti cookies
- ½ cup (60 g) almonds, finely chopped
- ½ cup (125 g) butter, melted

FILLING
- 3 (8-ounce) packages (700 g) cream cheese, softened
- 1 cup (200 g) sugar
- 2 tablespoons cornstarch (cornflour)
- 3 large eggs
- 3 tablespoons amaretto liqueur
- 1 tablespoon vanilla extract (essence)
- ¾ cup (135 g) dark chocolate chips

1. Preheat the oven to 400°F (200°C/gas 6). Butter a 10-inch (25-cm) springform pan.

2. To prepare the crust, mix the crumbs, almonds, and butter in a medium bowl. Press into the bottom and partway up the sides of the prepared pan. Bake for 8–10 minutes, or until lightly browned. Cool the crust completely in the pan on a rack.

3. To prepare the filling, beat the cream cheese, sugar, and cornstarch in a large bowl with an electric mixer on medium speed until smooth. Add the eggs one at a time, beating until just blended after each addition. With mixer on low, beat in the amaretto and vanilla. Stir in the chocolate chips. Spoon the filling into the crust.

4. Bake for 50–60 minutes, until set. Cool the cake in the pan on a rack. Refrigerate for at least 6 hours.

Dulce de Leche Cheesecake ▷

Marbled Chocolate Cheesecake

This is a great cheesecake, with a rich, smooth texture and a pretty marbled pattern.

Serves: 10–12 · Prep: 30 min. + 6 hr. 30 min. to chill · Level: 1

CRUST

1²/₃ cups (220 g) plain chocolate wafer (biscuit) crumbs
¹/₃ cup (30 g) ground hazelnuts
½ cup (125 g) butter, melted

FILLING

2 teaspoons unflavored powdered gelatin
2 tablespoons water
5 ounces (150 g) dark chocolate
2 (8-ounce) packages (500 g) cream cheese, softened
¹/₃ cup (50 g) confectioners' (icing) sugar
2 tablespoons hazelnuts, lightly toasted and finely chopped
2 tablespoons hazelnut liqueur, such as Frangelico
1 cup (250 ml) light (single) cream

1. To Prepare the crust, combine the crumbs, ground hazelnuts, and butter in a small bowl. Press into the bottom of a 10-inch (25 cm) springform pan. Refrigerate for 30 minutes.

2. To prepare the filling, place the gelatin and water in a small heatproof bowl over a saucepan of barely simmering water, stirring occasionally until dissolved.

3. Melt the chocolate in a double boiler over barely simmering water, stirring occasionally, until smooth. Set aside to cool.

4. Beat the cream cheese and sugar together in a medium bowl, using an electric mixer, until smooth and creamy. Add the gelatin and beat until combined.

5. Divide the mixture evenly between two bowls. Add the melted chocolate to one bowl and stir to combine. Add the hazelnuts and frangelico to the other and stir to combine.

6. Whip the cream in a small bowl, using an electric mixer, until soft peaks form. Divide in half and fold through the chocolate and hazelnut mixtures.

7. Pour the fillings alternately into the prepared base and create a swirl pattern, using a skewer or the end of a small knife. Refrigerate for at least 6 hours, or until set.

Rum and Raisin Cheesecake

Serves: 10–12 · Prep: 45 min. + 6 hr. to chill · Cooking: 40–50 min. · Level: 2

CRUST

2 cups (250 g) old-fashioned rolled oats
½ cup (100 g) firmly packed dark brown sugar
¼ cup (60 g) butter, melted

FILLING

1 pound (500 g) cream cheese, softened
½ cup (100 g) sugar
2 tablespoons all-purpose (plain) flour
2 large eggs
½ cup (125 ml) sour cream
3 tablespoons dark rum

TOPPING

3 tablespoons cold butter, cut up
2 tablespoons all-purpose (plain) flour
½ cup (100 g) firmly packed brown sugar
½ cup (60 g) raisins
½ cup (60 g) chopped nuts
2 tablespoons old-fashioned rolled oats

1. Preheat the oven to 350°F (180°C/gas 4). Butter a 9-inch (23-cm) springform pan.

2. To prepare the crust, mix the oats, brown sugar, and butter in a medium bowl. Press into the bottom of the prepared pan. Bake for 15 minutes. Cool completely in the pan on a rack.

3. To prepare the filling, beat the cream cheese, sugar, and flour in a large bowl with an electric mixer at medium speed. Add the eggs one at a time, beating until just blended after each addition. With mixer at low speed, beat in the sour cream and rum. Spoon the filling into the crust.

4. To prepare the topping, use a pastry blender to cut the butter into the flour and brown sugar until the mixture resembles coarse crumbs. Stir in the raisins, nuts, and oats. Sprinkle the cake with the topping. Bake for 40–50 minutes, until set. Cool the cake in the pan on a rack. Refrigerate for 6 hours.

Marbled Chocolate Cheesecake ▷

Frozen Mississippi Mud Pie

This is the frozen version of the famous Mississippi Mud Pie which is believed to have been invented in the state of Mississippi.

Serves: 10–12 · Prep: 35 min. + 10 hr. to freeze · Cooking: 25 min. · Level 2

BASE

1½	cups (185 g) plain chocolate wafer (biscuit) crumbs
3½	ounces (100 g) butter, melted
2	tablespoons light brown sugar

FILLING

8	large egg yolks
½	cup (100 g) superfine (caster) sugar
1¾	cups (430 ml) heavy (double) cream
1½	cup (375 ml) milk
8	ounces (250 g) dark chocolate, coarsely chopped

TOPPING

1	cup (250 ml) heavy (double) cream
1	tablespoon confectioners' (icing) sugar
2	ounces (60 g) dark chocolate, grated, to decorate

1. Preheat the oven to 350°F (180°C/gas 4).

2. To prepare the base, place the crumbs, butter, and sugar in a small bowl and stir to combine. Press into the base and up the sides of a 9-inch (23-cm) pie pan. Bake for 10–12 minutes, until lightly toasted. Remove from the oven and set aside to cool.

3. To prepare the filling, beat the egg yolks and sugar in a medium bowl with an electric mixer on medium-high speed until pale and thick.

4. Place the cream and milk in a large saucepan over medium heat and bring to a boil. Gradually pour half of the cream into the yolk mixture, stirring to combine.

5. Place the chocolate in a small heatproof bowl and pour in the remaining hot cream, stirring until melted. Add to the egg mixture and stir to combine.

6. Return the chocolate mixture to the pan and swimmer over low heat, stirring constantly, until thickened enough to coat the back of the spoon. Do not allow the mixture to boil. Remove from the heat, transfer to a medium bowl and refrigerate until cooled.

7. Pour the cooled chocolate custard into an ice-cream machine and churn according to manufacturer's instructions until almost frozen. Spoon the ice-cream into the prepared pan.

8. Cover with plastic wrap (cling film) and freeze for 2 hours.

9. To prepare the topping, beat the cream and sugar in a medium bowl with an electric mixer until soft peaks form.

10. Place the cream in a pastry bag fitted with a star-shaped nozzle. Pipe cream around the border of the pie and decorate with grated chocolate.

11. Cover and return to the freezer for at least 8 hours.

Frozen Mississippi Mud Pie ▷

Chocolate Orange Cake

This intense, deeply chocolate-flavored cake makes a perfect dessert at the end of a dinner party. We have suggested you flavor it with Grand Marnier, but you may vary the flavoring by replacing that liqueur with the same quantity of strong espresso coffee or coffee or liqueur. Use bittersweet or semisweet, not unsweetened chocolate.

Serves: 10–12 · Prep: 35 min. + 8 hr. to chill · Cooking: 25 min. · Level 2

8	large eggs, chilled (straight from the refrigerator)
1	pound (500 g) dark chocolate, 70 percent pure cocoa
1	cup (250 g) butter
¼	cup (60 ml) Grand Marnier
	Unsweetened cocoa powder, to dust
	Fresh mandarin segments, to serve
1	recipe Chantilly Cream, to serve (see page 275)

1. Preheat the oven to 325°F (170°C/gas 3). Line an 8-inch (20-cm) springform pan with parchment paper. Butter the sides of the pan. Wrap the outsides of the pan in aluminum foil; it needs to be waterproof.

2. Beat the eggs in a large bowl with an electric mixer on medium-high speed until doubled in volume, about 5 minutes.

3. Melt the chocolate and butter in a double boiler over barely simmering water. Remove from the heat and stir in the Grand Marnier.

4. Fold one-third of the egg mixture into the chocolate mixture, folding until no streaks of egg remain. Fold in half the remaining egg mixture in the same way. Repeat with the remaining egg mixture.

5. Pour the batter into the prepared pan, smoothing the top. Place the pan in a roasting dish. Fill the roasting dish with enough boiling water to come halfway up the sides of the springform pan.

6. Bake for 45–50 minutes, until the cake has risen slightly and a thin glazed crust is just beginning to form on the surface. The center of the cake should still jiggle slightly. Remove from the water bath and place on a rack. Let cool to room temperature in the pan.

7. Refrigerate for at least 8 hours.

8. About 30 minutes before serving, remove from the refrigerator and invert onto a serving plate. remove the paper and dust with cocoa. Serve each portion with a few segments of mandarin and a dollop of Chantilly Cream.

Sicilian Cassata

This is a classic Sicilian cake. Orange flower water may be found at specialty food stores or at pharmacies.

Serves: 8–10 · Prep: 45 min. + 2 hr. to chill · Level: 3

1	Italian Sponge Cake (see page 274), thinly sliced
1¼	cups (250 g) sugar
½	cup (125 ml) water
1	whole vanilla bean
1	(15-ounce) container (450 g) ricotta cheese, drained and pressed through a strainer
5	ounces (150 g) dark chocolate, finely chopped
1½	cups (250 g) mixed candied fruit, chopped
2	tablespoons pistachios
2	tablespoons kirsch
6	tablespoons apricot preserves or jam, warmed
2	tablespoons orange-flower water
1	tablespoon confectioners' sugar
1	recipe Fondant (see page 257), colored with green food coloring
1	cup (150 g) confectioners' (icing) sugar
1–2	tablespoons lukewarm water

1. Bring the sugar, water, and vanilla bean to a boil in a saucepan over medium heat. Simmer, stirring frequently, until the sugar has completely dissolved. Set aside to cool; discard the vanilla bean.

2. Beat the ricotta in a large bowl with an electric mixer at high speed until smooth. Gradually stir in the syrup. Stir in the chocolate, candied fruit, pistachios, and kirsch.

3. Line a 9-inch (23-cm) springform pan with half the cake slices. Warm 2 tablespoons of apricot preserves and brush over the cake slices. Spread with a layer of the ricotta mixture. Top with the remaining cake slices. Refrigerate for 2 hours.

4. Loosen and remove the pan sides. Invert onto a serving plate and remove the pan bottom. Warm the apricot preserves, orange flower water, and confectioners' sugar in a saucepan over low heat until syrupy. Drizzle over the cake.

5. Roll our the fondant and spread over the cake. Mix the confectioners' sugar and enough water in a small bowl to form a light frosting. Spoon into en envelope. Cut off the end to create a tiny opening. Pipe over the cake in swirling patterns.

Chocolate Orange Cake ▷

Frozen Lemon Meringue Pie

This is the frozen, ice-cream cake version of the famous pie.

Serves: 8–10 · Prep: 1 hr. + 8 hr. to chill · Cooking: 10–12 min. · Level: 2

BASE
1½	cups (185 g)	graham cracker or digestive biscuit crumbs
3½	ounces (100 g)	butter, melted
2	tablespoons	superfine (caster) sugar

FILLING
6	large egg yolks	
½	cup (100 g)	superfine (caster) sugar
1½	cups (375 ml)	heavy (double) cream
1¼	cups (300 ml)	milk
2	tablespoons	finely grated lemon zest
1	cup (250 g)	storebought lemon curd

TOPPING
1½	cups (375 ml)	heavy (double) cream
2	tablespoons	confectioners' (icing) sugar

1. Preheat the oven to 350°F (180°C/gas 4).

2. To prepare the base, place the crumbs, butter, and sugar in a small bowl and stir to combine. Press into the base and up the sides of a 9-inch (23-cm) pie pan. Bake for 10–12 minutes, until lightly toasted. Set aside to cool.

3. Beat the egg yolks and sugar in a medium bowl with an electric mixer on medium-high speed until pale and thick.

4. Place the cream, milk, and lemon zest in a large saucepan over medium heat and bring to a boil. Gradually pour into the yolk mixture, stirring to combine. Return mixture to the pan and simmer over low heat, stirring until thickened enough to coat the back of a spoon. Do not allow the mixture to boil. Remove from the heat and transfer to a medium bowl. Stir in the lemon curd and refrigerate until cooled.

5. Pour the custard into an ice-cream machine and churn according to manufacturer's instructions until almost frozen. Spoon the ice-cream into the prepared pan.

6. Beat the cream and sugar in a medium bowl until soft peaks form. Spoon onto the pie and create peaks using a spatula. Cover and return to the freezer for 8 hours.

◁ **Frozen Lemon Meringue Pie**

Mascarpone Mold

This is an Italian cake. Alchermes is a bright red, rather sweet liqueur traditionally made by the monks of San Marco, in Florence. Substitute with sweet Marsala wine or sherry.

Serves: 6–8 · Prep: 25 min. + 4 hr. to chill · Cooking: 15 min. · Level: 1

MASCARPONE MOLD
14	ounces (400 g)	ladyfingers
½	cup (125 ml)	Alchermes liqueur, sweet Marsala wine or sherry
1	cup (250 ml)	heavy (double) cream
1	cup (150 g)	confectioners' (icing) sugar
½	teaspoon	ground cinnamon
2	cups (500 g)	mascarpone cheese, softened

ZABAGLIONE
4	large egg yolks	
¼	cup (50 g)	sugar
½	cup (125 ml)	dry Marsala wine or dry sherry

1. To prepare the mascarpone mold, line an 8-cup (2-liter) mold with plastic wrap (cling film). Dip the ladyfingers in the liqueur or wine. Line the sides of the mold with ladyfingers.

2. Beat the cream, confectioners' sugar, and cinnamon until thick.

3. Use a large rubber spatula to mix the mascarpone and cream mixture in a large bowl.

4. Spread the mold with half the mascarpone mixture. Layer with ladyfingers. Alternate ladyfingers and mascarpone mixture until the mold is packed, finishing with ladyfingers.

5. Refrigerate for 4 hours.

6. To prepare the zabaglione, beat the egg yolks and sugar in the top pan of a double boiler with an electric mixer at high speed until pale and very thick. Gradually add the Marsala. Place over barely simmering water and simmer, beating constantly, until very thick, about 15 minutes.

7. Dip the mold into a cold water. Invert onto a serving plate with the zabaglione passed separately.

White Chocolate Mousse Cake

You will only need half the Basic Butter Cake. Wrap the other half in plastic wrap (cling film) and freeze for later use.

Serves: 8–10 · Prep: 1 hr. + 12 hr. to chill · Level: 2

- 1   Basic Butter Cake, baked in one 9-inch (23-cm) pan (see page 80)

MOUSSE
- 6   ounces (180 g) white chocolate, coarsely chopped
- 2   (3-ounce) packages (180 g) cream cheese, softened
- ¼   cup (50 g) sugar
- 4   teaspoons unflavored gelatin
- ⅓   cup (90 ml) freshly squeezed orange juice
- 1½   cups (375 ml) heavy (double) cream

LEMON TOPPING
- ½   cup (125 ml) freshly squeezed lemon juice
- ¼   cup (50 g) sugar
- 1   teaspoon unflavored gelatin
- 3–4   medium kiwifruit, peeled and sliced, to decorate

1. To prepare the mousse, melt the white chocolate in a double boiler over barely simmering water. Set aside to cool.

2. Beat the cream cheese and sugar in a large bowl with an electric mixer at medium speed until smooth. Add the white chocolate. Sprinkle the gelatin over the orange juice in a saucepan. Let stand 1 minute. Stir over low heat until the gelatin has completely dissolved. Set aside to cool for 30 minutes.

3. Beat the cooled orange juice into the cream cheese mixture. With mixer at high speed, beat the cream in a medium bowl until stiff. Use a rubber spatula to fold the cream into the cream cheese mixture.

4. Trim the rounded top off the cake. Place the cake in a 9-inch (23-cm) springform pan. Spoon the mousse over the cake and refrigerate for 6 hours.

5. To prepare the topping, stir the lemon juice and sugar in a saucepan over low heat until the sugar has dissolved. Remove from the heat and stir in the gelatin until dissolved. Set aside to cool.

6. Pour the topping over the cake and refrigerate for 6 hours. Decorate with the kiwi fruit before serving.

◁ **White chocolate mousse cake with lemon and kiwi**

Strawberry Charlotte

You will only need half the Basic Pound Cake. Wrap the other half in plastic wrap (cling film) and freeze for later use.

Serves: 8–10 · Prep: 30 min. + 1 hr. to freeze · Level: 1

- ½   cup (125 ml) dry white wine
- ¼   cup (60 ml) kirsch
- ½   Basic Pound Cake (see page 85), cut into ½-inch (1-cm) thick slices
- 3   packed cups (750 g) vanilla ice cream, softened
- 1   pound (500 g) strawberries, halved (reserve 10 whole to decorate)
- 1   recipe Chantilly Cream (see page 275), to serve

1. Mix the wine and kirsch in a small bowl and drizzle a little on each cake slice.

2. Use the cale slices to line an 8-cup (2-liter) straight-sided soufflé dish. Spoon one-third of the ice cream over the cake. Top with one-third of the strawberries. Cover with cake slices. Repeat the layers of ice cream, strawberries, and cake slices until they have all been used, finishing with a layer of ice cream. Freeze for 1 hour.

3. Soak the mold in hot water for 10 seconds. Turn out onto a serving dish. Decorate with the whole strawberries.

Strawberry Ice Cream Cake

If you are pressed for time, this striking cake can be made with storebought ice cream and sponge cake. But for best results we suggest you use homemade butter cake and ice cream. We have provided the recipes for both.

Serves: 8–10 · Prep: 15 min. + 12 hr. to chill · Level: 2

- 1 recipe Basic Butter Cake, baked in two 8-inch (20-cm) pans (see page 80)

STRAWBERRY ICE CREAM
1½ pounds (750 g) fresh strawberries
1½ cups (300 g) sugar
2 tablespoons water
2 cups (500 ml) milk
1 cup (250 ml) heavy (double) cream

TO DECORATE
1 cup (150 g) fresh strawberries
Confectioners' (icing) sugar, to dust

1. To prepare the strawberry ice cream, purée 1 pound (500 g) of the strawberries in a blender with ¼ cup (50 g) of the sugar and the water until smooth. Press the purée through a fine mesh strainer to remove the seeds.

2. Place the milk, cream, and remaining sugar in a saucepan over medium-low heat. Stir until the sugar has completely dissolved and bring to a boil.

3. Remove from the heat and let cool completely. Add the strawberry purée and mix well. Transfer to your ice cream machine and freeze following the manufacturer's instructions.

4. Leave the ice cream out to soften to a spreadable consistency.

5. Slice the top off one of the butter cakes to make a flat surface. Cut each cake in half horizontally. Reserve the only remaining rounded layer for the top of the cake. Set aside. Place one cake layer on a serving plate and spread evenly with one-third of the ice cream. Top with another layer of cake and repeat with the softened ice cream. Repeat with the third layer of cake and top with the remaining ice cream. Top with the domed layer of cake. Decorate with the whole strawberries and dust with confectioners' sugar.

6. Place in the freezer overnight. Remove 15 minutes prior to serving.

PREPARING VANILLA ICE CREAM STEP-BY-STEP

Making ice cream at home is simple, especially if you own an ice cream machine. The method is the same for all flavors; first you make a milk- or cream-based custard, then flavoring is added, before being tipped into the machine to churn.

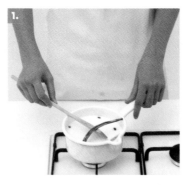

1 Simmer 3½ cups (875 ml) of milk with the coffee, cinnamon, lemon zest, vanilla, and salt over medium-low heat.

2 Beat the egg yolks, sugar, and cornstarch in a bowl with an electric mixer on high speed until pale and creamy.

3 Add the remaining cold milk to the egg mixture then the hot milk mixture. Return to the pan and simmer over low heat, stirring constantly, for 2 minutes. Do not let the mixture boil.

4 Remove from the heat and filter into a chilled bowl. Let cool, stirring often. Refrigerate for 30 minutes.

5 Beat 2 egg whites until stiff peaks form. Fold into the mixture. Transfer to an ice cream machine and churn.

Neapolitan Ice Cream Cake

This is an attractive cake that will delight your guests.

Serves: 10–12 · Prep: 1 hr. + 10 hr. to freeze · Cooking: 25–30 min. · Level 2

CAKE BASE

⅓	cup (90 g) butter, softened
¾	cup (150 g) superfine (caster) sugar
½	teaspoon vanilla extract (essence)
1	large egg
¾	cup (125 g) all-purpose (plain) flour
⅓	cup (50 g) unsweetened cocoa powder
1	teaspoon baking powder
½	cup (125 ml) sour cream

ICE CREAM

3	ounces (90 g) dark chocolate, coarsely chopped
¾	cup (180 g) strawberries
8	large egg yolks
½	cup (100 g) superfine (caster) sugar
1¾	cups (430 ml) heavy (double) cream
1½	cup (375 ml) milk
1	vanilla bean, split lengthwise and seeds scraped

TOPPING

1	cup (250 ml) heavy (double) cream
1	tablespoon confectioners' (icing) sugar
	Colored sprinkles (100's and 1000's)

1. Preheat the oven to 350°F (180°C/gas 4). Lightly grease a 9-inch (23-cm) springform pan and line the base with parchment paper.

2. To prepare the cake base, beat the butter, sugar, and vanilla in a medium bowl with an electric mixer on medium speed until pale and creamy. Beat in the egg until just blended.

3. Sift the flour, cocoa, and baking powder into a small bowl. With mixer on low, add the flour and sour cream alternately to the batter, beating until incorporated. Spoon the batter into the prepared pan

4. Bake for 25–30 minutes, until a skewer comes out clean when inserted into the center. Let cool in the pan for 10 minutes, then turn out onto a wire rack and let cool completely.

◁ **Neapolitan Ice Cream Cake**

5. To prepare the ice cream, place the chocolate in a double boiler over barely simmering water, stirring occasionally, until smooth. Remove from the heat and set aside to cool.

6. Place the strawberries in a food processor and blend until puréed. Simmer in a small saucepan over medium-low heat until thick and syrupy, about 5 minutes. Strain through a fine mesh sieve into a small bowl and set aside to cool.

7. Beat the egg yolks and sugar in a medium bowl with an electric mixer on medium-high speed until pale and thick.

8. Place the cream, milk, and vanilla bean and seeds in a large saucepan over medium heat and bring to a boil. Gradually pour into the yolk mixture, stirring to combine. Return the mixture to the pan and cook over low heat, stirring, until thickened slightly. Do not boil. Remove from the heat and divide among three bowls. Pour the melted chocolate into one bowl and stir to combine. Add the strawberry purée to another bowl and stir to combine. Leave the remaining bowl plain. Refrigerate until cooled.

9. Line the sides of a clean 9-inch (23-cm) springform pan with parchment paper. Place the cake back in the pan..

10. Pour the cooled chocolate custard into an ice-cream machine and churn according to manufacturer's instructions until almost frozen. Spoon the ice-cream over the sponge base and place in the freezer for 2 hours, until firm. Churn the strawberry custard until almost frozen and spread over the chocolate layer. Return to the freezer for 2 hours, until firm. Churn the vanilla custard, spread over the strawberry layer, and return to the freezer for 2 hours, until firm.

11. Whip the cream and sugar in a medium bowl until soft peaks form. Spread most of the cream over the top of the cake. Place the remaining cream in a pastry bag fitted with a star-shaped nozzle.

12. Pipe cream around the border of the pie and decorate with colored sprinkles. Cover and return to the freezer for at least 4 hours, until frozen.

Strawberry Cream Pie

This striking pie makes a wonderful birthday or celebration cake for someone special who loves ice cream.

Serves: 8–10 · Prep: 45 min. + 12 hr. to freeze · Cooking: 10–12 min. · Level 3

CRUST

1½	cups (185 g) graham cracker or digestive biscuit crumbs
3½	ounces (100 g) butter, melted
2	tablespoons light brown sugar

TOPPING

9	large egg yolks
½	cup (100 g) sugar
1¾	cups (450 ml) heavy (double) cream
1½	cups (375 ml) milk
1	vanilla bean, split lengthwise, seeds scraped
3	cups (450 g) strawberries
3½	ounces (100 g) white chocolate, melted, to decorate

1. To prepare the crust, preheat the oven to 350°F (180°C/gas 4). Place the crumbs, butter, and brown sugar in a small bowl and stir to combine. Press into the base of a 9-inch (23-cm) springform pan. Bake for 10–12 minutes, until lightly toasted. Set aside to cool.

2. To prepare the topping, beat the egg yolks and sugar in a medium bowl with an electric mixer until pale and creamy. Bring the cream, milk, and vanilla bean and seeds in a large saucepan to a boil over medium heat. Gradually stir into the yolk mixture. Return the mixture to the pan and simmer over low heat, stirring until thickened slightly. Do not allow the mixture to boil. Remove from the heat, transfer to a medium bowl and refrigerate until cooled, about 30 minutes.

3. Place the strawberries in a food processor and blend until puréed. Cook in a small saucepan over medium-low heat until thick and syrupy, 5–10 minutes. Transfer to a small bowl and refrigerate until cooled, about 30 minutes.

4. Pour the cooled custard into an ice cream machine and churn according to manufacturer's instructions until almost frozen. Pour in half of the strawberry purée and finish churning.

5. Spread the base of the pie with half of the remaining strawberry purée. Spoon the ice cream in over the top. Cover with plastic wrap (cling film) and freeze overnight. Drizzle the pie with the remaining strawberry purée and the melted chocolate.

Strawberries and Cream Zuccotto

There are step-by-step instructions for making Zuccotto on page 234.

Serves: 6 · Prep: 1 hr. + 12 hr. to freeze · Level 2

½	Italian Sponge Cake (see page 274), thinly sliced
⅓	cup (90 ml) rum
2	cups (500 ml) heavy (double) cream
2	tablespoons confectioners' (icing) sugar
1	teaspoon vanilla extract (essence)
3	cups (450 g) fresh strawberries, sliced

1. Line a 6-cup (1.5-liter) domed pudding mold or a stainless steel domed bowl with plastic wrap (cling film).

2. Dip the cake in the rum until moist. Line the prepared mold with the cake slices.

3. Beat 1½ cups (375 ml) of the cream with the confectioners' sugar, and vanilla in a large bowl until stiff. Gently fold in the strawberries. Spoon the mixture into the mold, smoothing the top. Cover with a layer of cake. Cover with a sheet of parchment paper and freeze for 12 hours, or overnight.

4. Invert and turn out onto a serving plate. Beat the remaining cream in a medium bowl until stiff. Spread the cream over the top.

Frozen Raspberry Cake

For a slightly different cake, replace the raspberries with the same quantity of sliced fresh strawberries and use strawberry preserves instead of raspberry.

Serves: 6–8 · Prep: 30 min. + 6 hr. to freeze · Level 2

1	Italian Sponge Cake (see page 274), thinly sliced
1	large egg + 3 large egg yolks
3/4	cup (150 g) sugar
1/2	cup (75 g) all-purpose (plain) flour
1	teaspoon vanilla extract (essence)
1/4	teaspoon salt
1²/₃	cups (400 ml) milk
1	tablespoon unflavored gelatin
1/4	cup (60 ml) water
2/3	cup (160 ml) raspberry liqueur
1/2	cup (150 g) raspberry preserves (jam)
1	cup (250 ml) heavy (double) cream
2	tablespoons confectioners' (icing) sugar
1/2	cup (75 g) fresh raspberries, to decorate
1/4	cup (30 g) slivered almonds, to decorate

1. Beat the egg and egg yolks, sugar, flour, vanilla, and salt in a large bowl with an electric mixer on high speed until well blended. With the mixer on low speed, gradually beat in the milk.

2. Transfer the mixture to a large saucepan. Cook over low heat, stirring constantly with a wooden spoon, until the mixture lightly coats a metal spoon or registers 160°F (80°C) on an instant-read thermometer.

3. Sprinkle the gelatin over the water in a saucepan. Let soften 1 minute. Stir the gelatin over low heat until completely dissolved. Stir the gelatin mixture into the egg mixture.

4. Brush the sides of an 8-cup (2-liter) domed pudding bowl with liqueur. Moisten slices of sponge cake with liqueur and spread with preserves. Stick the slices, preserve-side facing inward, onto the sides of the bowl. Spread with cream. Moisten the remaining cake with liqueur and spread with preserves and layer it into the pudding bowl, alternating with the cream. Finish with a layer of cake slices, preserves-side facing inward. Press down lightly.

5. Freeze for at least 6 hours. Beat the cream and confectioners' sugar until stiff. Turn the cake out onto a serving dish. Spread with cream and decorate with raspberries and almonds.

Coffee Gelato Cake

This recipe makes a pretty ring cake.

Serves: 6–8 · Prep: 30 min. + 6 hr. to freeze · Level 2

GELATO

2	cups (500 ml) milk
1/2	cup (125 ml) heavy (double) cream
4	large egg yolks
1/3	cup (75 g) granulated sugar
2	teaspoons vanilla extract (essence)
1/4	cup (30 g) confectioners' (icing) sugar
4	ounces (125 g) dark chocolate, coarsely chopped
1/2	cup (125 ml) strong black coffee, cold

TOPPING

1	cup (250 ml) heavy (double) cream
2	tablespoons brandy
2	tablespoons confectioners' (icing) sugar
1	tablespoon whole coffee beans

1. To prepare the gelato, place the milk and cream in a heavy-based saucepan over medium heat and bring to a boil.

2. Beat the egg yolks and sugar with an electric mixer on high speed until pale and creamy. Pour the hot milk mixture over the egg mixture, beating constantly with a wooden spoon. Return to the saucepan. Simmer over very low heat, stirring constantly, until it just coats the back of the spoon. Do not let the mixture boil.

3. Stir in the vanilla. Chill in the refrigerator for 30 minutes. Transfer the mixture to your ice cream machine and freeze following the manufacturer's instructions.

4. Divide the gelato equally between two bowls and let soften a little. Stir the chocolate into one bowl and the coffee into the other. Place alternate spoonfuls of the mixture into an oiled 9-inch (23-cm) ring mold, pressing down with the back of the spoon to eliminate air pockets. Freeze for 1 hour.

5. To prepare the topping, beat the cream, brandy, and confectioners' sugar in a medium bowl with an electric mixer until thick.

6. Unmold the gelato cake onto a serving plate. Top with the cream and decorate with the coffee beans.

Black Forest Ice Cream Cake

This handsome ice cream cake is the frozen version of the famous Black Forest Cake (see page 172).

Serves: 10–12 · Prep: 30 min. + 6 hr. to freeze · Cooking: 25–30 min. · Level 2

CAKE BASE
- ⅓ cup (90 g) butter, softened
- ¾ cup (150 g) superfine (caster) sugar
- ½ teaspoon vanilla extract (essence)
- 1 large egg
- ¾ cup (125 g) all-purpose (plain) flour
- ⅓ cup (50 g) unsweetened cocoa powder
- 1 teaspoon baking powder
- ½ cup (125 ml) sour cream

ICE CREAM
- 8 large egg yolks
- ½ cup (100 g) superfine (caster) sugar
- 1¾ cups (430 ml) heavy (double) cream
- 1½ cup (375 ml) milk
- 1 vanilla bean, split lengthwise and seeds scraped
- 8 ounces (250 g) dark chocolate, coarsely chopped
- 2 tablespoons kirsch, or cherry liqueur
- 1 (14-ounce/400-g) can pitted black cherries, drained

TOPPING
- 1½ cups (375 ml) heavy (double) cream
- 2 tablespoon confectioners' (icing) sugar
- 3 ounces (90 g) dark chocolate, shaved, to decorate

1. Preheat the oven to 350°F (180°C/gas 4).

2. Lightly grease a 9-inch (23 cm) round springform pan and line the base with parchment paper.

3. To prepare the cake base, beat the butter, sugar, and vanilla in a medium bowl with an electric mixer on medium speed until pale and creamy. Beat in the egg until just blended. Combine the flour, cocoa, and baking powder in a small bowl. With mixer on low, add the flour and sour cream alternately to the batter.

4. Spoon the batter into the prepared pan and bake for 25–30 minutes, until a skewer comes out clean when inserted into the center. Let cool in the pan for 10 minutes, then turn out onto a wire rack and let cool completely.

5. To prepare the ice cream, beat the egg yolks and sugar in a medium bowl with an electric mixer on medium speed until pale and thick.

6. Place the cream and milk in a medium saucepan over medium heat and bring to a boil. Gradually pour half of the cream mixture into the yolk mixture, stirring to combine.

7. Place the chocolate in a small heatproof bowl and pour in the remaining hot cream, stirring until melted. Add to the egg mixture with the kirsch, stirring to combine.

8. Return the chocolate mixture to the pan and simmer over low heat, stirring until thickened enough to coat the back of a spoon. Do not allow the mixture to boil. Remove from the heat, transfer to a medium bowl, and refrigerate until cooled.

9. Line the sides of a clean 9-inch (23-cm) springform pan with parchment paper and tighten the sides. Place the cooled sponge base back in the pan. Sprinkle with the cherries.

10. Pour the cooled chocolate custard into an ice-cream machine and churn according to manufacturer's instructions until almost frozen. Spoon the ice-cream over the cherries and smooth the top.

11. Cover with plastic wrap (cling film) and freeze for 4 hours.

12. To prewpare the topping, beat the cream and confectioners' sugar in a medium bowl with an electric mixer until soft peaks form. Remove the cake from the pan and spread the cream over the top and sides. Decorate with the chocolate shavings and freeze for at least 4 more hours, until frozen.

Birthday Gelato Cake

This is an Italian recipe for a birthday ice cream cake. It requires half an Italian Sponge Cake. Freeze the other half and use to make Zuccotto (see page 234).

Serves: 6–8 · Prep: 30 min. + 6 hr. to freeze · Level 2

½ Italian Sponge Cake (see page 274)

GELATO
2 cups (500 ml) milk
1 vanilla pod
   Zest of 1 lemon, in 1 long piece
4 large egg yolks
¾ cup (150 g) sugar
2 tablespoons Cointreau
⅓ cup (90 g) heavy (double) cream
2 ounce (60 g) dark chocolate, finely grated

MERINGUE
2 large egg whites
1 cup (150 g) confectioners' (icing) sugar

FILLING AND DECORATION
5 ounces (150 g) dark chocolate
2 tablespoons Cointreau
¾ cup (200 ml) heavy (double) cream

1. To prepare the gelato, heat the milk with the vanilla pod and lemon zest in a heavy-based saucepan over medium heat and bring to a boil. Remove from the heat and discard the vanilla pod.

2. Beat the egg yolks and sugar in a medium bowl with an electric mixer on high speed until very pale and creamy.

3. Pour the hot milk mixture into the egg yolk mixture, beating constantly with a wooden spoon. Return the mixture to the saucepan. Simmer over low heat, beating constantly, until it coats the back of the spoon. Do not let the mixture boil.

4. Divide the mixture evenly among two bowls. Let cool completely.

5. Stir the Cointreau into one of the bowls. Transfer to your ice cream machine and freeze following the manufacturers' instructions.

6. Beat the cream in a small bowl with an electric mixer on high speed until stiff. Fold it into the second bowl together with the chocolate. Transfer to your ice cream machine and freeze following the manufacturers' instructions.

7. To prepare the meringue, preheat the oven to 225°F (110°C/gas ½). Line a baking sheet with parchment paper. Lightly butter the parchment paper and dust with flour.

8. Place a 9-inch (23-cm) springform pan on the parchment paper and use a pencil to draw a line around the pan.

9. Beat the egg whites and confectioners' sugar in a medium bowl with an electric mixer on high speed until stiff. Use a spatula to spread the meringue within the pencil disk on the baking sheet. Bake until crisp and dry, about 90 minutes. Remove from the oven and let cool completely.

10. To prepare the filling and decoration, line the 9-inch (23-cm) springform pan with parchment paper and place in the refrigerator.

11. When the Cointreau gelato is frozen, spread it in an even layer on the bottom of the prepared springform pan.

12. Placed the cooled meringue over the layer of Cointreau gelato (trim the edges if the meringue has spread during cooking). Cut the sponge cake in half horizontally. Cover the meringue with a layer of sponge cake. Drizzle with the Cointreau. Top with an even layer of the chocolate gelato, leveling well and pressing down to eliminate pockets of air. Cover with plastic wrap (cling film) and freeze for at least 2 hours.

13. Melt the chocolate in a double boiler over barely simmering water. Let cool. Place most of the cooled chocolate into a piping bag with a plain nozzle and pipe out 8–12 small disks. Place in the refrigerator to set.

14. Beat the cream with an electric mixer until stiff. Fold into the remaining chocolate. Carefully unmold the cake and decorate with the chocolate cream and disks of chocolate.

Zuccotto

Zuccotto is an Italian ice cream cake from Florence. This recipe uses half an Italian sponge cake. You can freeze the rest for the next time you make Zuccotto. If short of time, use storebought sponge cake.

Serves: 6–8 · Prep: 30 min. + 12 hr. to freeze · Cooking: 2–3 min. · Level 2

½	Italian Sponge Cake (see page 274)
¾	cup (150 g) sugar
1	cup (200 ml) water
3	tablespoons brandy
3	tablespoons rum
2	cups (500 ml) heavy (double) cream
⅓	cup (50 g) confectioners' (icing) sugar
⅓	cup (30 g) almonds, toasted and chopped
⅓	cup (30 g) hazelnuts, toasted and chopped
4	tablespoons candied (glacé) fruit, chopped
5	ounces (150 g) dark chocolate, chopped

1. Cut the sponge cake into thin slices.

2. Place the sugar and water in a saucepan over medium heat and simmer until the sugar is dissolved, 2–3 minutes. Remove from heat, add the brandy and rum, and let cool.

3. Moisten the sides of a domed 6-cup (1.5-liter) pudding mold with a little sugar syrup.

4. Line the mold with three-quarters of the sliced sponge cake. Make sure there are no gaps between the pieces of sponge cake. Brush with the remaining syrup.

5. Beat the cream in a large bowl with an electric mixer on high speed until thick. Mix the confectioners' sugar, nuts, candied fruit, and chocolate into the whipped cream.

6. Spoon the cream mixture into the mold and cover with the remaining sponge slices. Freeze for 12 hours or overnight. Turn out onto a serving dish and serve in slices.

PREPARING ZUCCOTTO

1 Cut the sponge cake into thin slices.

2 Simmer the sugar and water over medium heat until dissolved, 2–3 minutes. Remove from heat, add the brandy and rum. Let cool.

3 Moisten the sides of a domed 6-cup (1.5-liter) pudding mold with a little sugar syrup.

4 Line the mold with three-quarters of the cake. Make sure there are no gaps between the pieces of sponge cake.

5 Beat the cream until thick. Mix in the confectioners' sugar, nuts, candied fruit, and chocolate.

6 Spoon the cream mixture into the mold and cover with the remaining sponge slices.

FESTIVE CAKES

The recipes in this chapter are all for classic cakes that are either associated with special days or celebrations, such as Christmas, Passover, or Valentine's Day, or are famous in themselves, like Sacher Torte (see page 264) or Saint Honoré Gateau (see page 261). Here you will find a wonderful selection of cakes, nearly all with rich and fascinating histories. Some of these cakes are fairly challenging to bake, but we have provided in-depth instructions to ensure success every time.

◁ Simnel Cake (see page 256)

Glazed Christmas Cake

Many countries have a traditional cake to celebrate a very special time in the Christian calendar—the birth of Christ. In Great Britain the traditional Christmas cake is a rich fruit cake, usually covered in marzipan and a heavy butter frosting. Our version is a moist, dark cake with a lavish fruit and nut glaze.

Serves: 8–10 · Prep: 30 min. + 12 hr. to steep · Cooking: 3 hr. 30 min. Level 1

CAKE
- 1 cup (180 g) raisins
- 1 cup (180 g) currants
- 1 cup (180 g) golden raisins (sultanas)
- 2/3 cup (120 g) candied (glacé) green and red cherries, coarsely chopped
- 1/3 cup (60 g) dried apricots, coarsely chopped
- 1/3 cup (30 g) chopped mixed peel
- 1 1/2 teaspoons finely grated orange zest
- 1/2 cup (125 ml) brandy
- 3/4 cup (180 g) butter, softened
- 1 cup (200 g) firmly packed dark brown sugar
- 4 large eggs
- 1 1/2 cups (225 g) all-purpose (plain) flour
- 1 teaspoon pumpkin pie spice or allspice
- 1 teaspoon ground cinnamon
- 1/2 teaspoon ground ginger
- 1/3 cup (50 g) blanched almonds, coarsely chopped
- 1/3 cup (50 g) Brazil nuts, coarsely chopped

FRUIT GLAZE
- 1/2 cup (90 g) candied (glacé) green and red cherries
- 1/2 cup (90 g) candied (glacé) pineapple, coarsely chopped
- 1/4 cup (40 g) blanched almonds
- 1/4 cup (40 g) Brazil nuts
- 1/4 cup (30 g) walnut halves
- 1/2 cup (160 ml) apricot preserves (jam), warmed

1. To prepare the cake, combine the raisins, currants, golden raisins, cherries, apricots, mixed peel, zest, and 1/3 cup (90 ml) of the brandy in a medium bowl. Cover and set aside overnight to steep.

2. Preheat the oven to 300°F (150°C/gas 2).

3. Lightly grease a deep 8-inch (20-cm) round cake pan. Line the base and sides with a triple layer of parchment paper, extending 5 inches (13 cm) above the rim.

4. Beat the butter and sugar in a large bowl with an electric mixer on medium-high until creamy. Add the eggs one at a time, beating until just blended after each addition.

5. Combine the flour, pumpkin pie spice, cinnamon, and ginger in a small bowl. Add the flour, soaked fruits, and nuts alternately to the egg mixture, stirring with a large metal spoon to combine. Spoon the batter into the prepared pan.

6. Bake for 3 1/2 hours, or until a skewer comes out clean when inserted into the center. Remove the cake from the oven and prick the top several times with a skewer. Drizzle with the remaining brandy and leave to cool in the pan.

7. To prepare the fruit glaze, combine the cherries, pineapple, almonds, Brazil nuts, and walnuts in a medium bowl. Brush the top of the cake with apricot preserves and decorate with the candied fruit and nut mixture. Glaze with the remaining preserves.

Glazed Christmas Cake ▷

Yule Log

Yule is a winter festival that was celebrated by pagan Germanic peoples in pre-Christian Europe. The festival was later absorbed into Christianity and has become equated with Christmas. A Yule log is a large wooden log that is burnt during Christmas celebrations and also this traditional cake.

Serves: 8 · Prep: 45 min. · Cooking: 15–20 min. · Level 2

CAKE
- ½ cup (75 g) all-purpose (plain) flour
- 2 tablespoons unsweetened cocoa powder
- 1 teaspoon ground cinnamon
- 4 large eggs
- ½ cup (100 g) superfine (caster) sugar + extra, to sprinkle
- 1 teaspoon vanilla extract (essence)
- 2 tablespoons butter, melted and cooled

FILLING
- ½ cup (125 ml) heavy (double) cream
- 1 (8-ounce/250-g) can sweetened chestnut purée
- ¼ cup (40 g) hazelnuts, lightly toasted and finely chopped

CHOCOLATE BUTTERCREAM
- 3 ounces (90 g) dark chocolate
- 1 cup (250 g) butter, softened
- ½ teaspoon vanilla extract (essence)
- 2 cups (300 g) confectioners' (icing) sugar + extra, to dust (optional)

1. Preheat the oven to 350°F (180°C/gas 4). Line a jelly-roll pan with parchment paper and lightly oil.

2. To prepare the cake, sift the flour, cocoa, and cinnamon into a small bowl.

3. Beat the eggs and ½ cup (100 g) of sugar in a large bowl with an electric mixer on medium speed until thick, creamy, and tripled in volume. Add the vanilla and beat to combine. Gently fold in the flour mixture in two batches. Fold in the melted butter until just incorporated. Spoon the batter into the prepared pan.

4. Bake for 15–20 minutes, until the sponge springs back when gently pressed.

5. Lay a clean kitchen towel on a work surface and dust with the extra superfine sugar. Remove the sponge from the oven and turn out onto the towel. Roll up lengthwise and place on a wire rack, seam-side down, to cool.

6. To prepare the filling, beat the cream in a small bowl until soft peaks form. Add the chestnut purée and stir to combine.

7. Unroll the sponge, peel away the paper, and spread the filling over the top, leaving a ¾-inch (2-cm) border. Sprinkle the hazelnuts over the top, re-roll the cake, and trim the ends.

8. Place the cake on a large serving plate. Diagonally cut 4 inches (10 cm) off the end of the end and place it along the log to resemble a branch. Place in the refrigerator.

9. To prepare the chocolate buttercream, melt the chocolate in a double boiler over barely simmering water, stirring until smooth. Remove from the heat and let cool.

10. Beat the butter and vanilla in a large bowl with an electric mixer on medium-high speed until pale and creamy. Pour in the cooled chocolate, beating until blended. With mixer on low, gradually add the confectioners' sugar, beating until blended.

11. Spread the buttercream over the Yule log. Using the prongs of a fork, create a bark pattern. If liked, dust with confectioners' sugar to resemble snow, and decorate with holly leaves.

◁ **Yule Log**

Individual Christmas Cakes

This is a fun way to serve Christmas cake. Children will especially enjoy them.

Serves: 12 · Prep: 1 hr. + 8 hr. to soak · Cooking: 75–80 min. · Level: 2

CAKES

4	cups (200 g) chopped mixed candied fruit
1½	cups (375 ml) white grape juice
¾	cup (150 g) firmly packed dark brown sugar
2½	cups (375 g) all-purpose (plain) flour
1½	teaspoons baking powder
1	teaspoon baking soda (bicarbonate of soda)
1	teaspoon ground cinnamon
1	teaspoon ground nutmeg
½	teaspoon salt
2	large egg whites, lightly beaten
¼	cup (60 ml) vegetable oil
⅓	cup (90 ml) milk or reduced fat milk
¼	cup (60 ml) brandy

HOLLY DECORATIONS

2	ounces (60 g) marzipan
¼	teaspoon green food coloring

WHITE FROSTING

⅓	cup (100 g) apricot preserves (jam)
2	recipes Fondant (see page 257)
1	tablespoon confectioners' (icing) sugar
1	teaspoon water
	Red currants, to decorate

1. To prepare the cakes, stir the candied fruit, grape juice, and brown sugar in a large bowl. Cover and set aside for 8 hours.

2. Preheat the oven to 300°F (150°C/gas 2). Butter a 12-cup muffin pan and line with paper baking cups.

3. Combine the flour, baking powder, baking soda, cinnamon, nutmeg, and salt in a large bowl. Use a large rubber spatula to stir the egg whites, oil, milk, and 2 tablespoons brandy into the fruit mixture. Stir in the dry ingredients. Spoon the batter evenly into the cups.

4. Bake for 75–80 minutes, or until a toothpick inserted into the center comes out clean. Drizzle the hot cakes with the remaining brandy. Cool the cakes completely in the pan. Turn out onto racks to decorate.

5. To prepare the decorations, dust a work surface lightly with confectioners' sugar. Knead the marzipan until malleable. Roll out to ⅛ inch (3 mm) thick. Use a leaf-shaped cutter to stamp out 24 small holly shapes. Lightly brush green coloring over each leaf. Dry the leaves on waxed paper.

6. To prepare the frosting, warm the preserves in a saucepan over low heat. Brush each cake with a thin layer of preserves. Knead the fondant until malleable. Divide into 12 equal pieces. Roll out one piece at a time to ⅛ inch (3 mm) thick. Fit the fondant over each cake, trimming the edges if needed.

7. Mix the confectioners' sugar and water to make a smooth paste. Dot the leaves and 2 red currants with a little frosting and arrange on each cake in a decorative manner.

Twelfth Night Cake

The Twelfth Night, or Epiphany Eve, falls on 5 January and marks the end of the twelve days of Christmas. It is a time of merrymaking and eating. According to English custom a Twelfth Night Cake should contain a dried bean and a dried pea. Those who receive the slices with these in them become the king and the queen of the evening's celebrations.

Serves: 12–14 · Prep: 30 min. + 75 min. to rise · Cooking: 30–35 min. · Level 2

½	cup (90 g) raisins
½	cup (90 g) currants
1	teaspoon finely grated lemon zest
1	tablespoon rum
1	(¼-ounce/7-g) package active dry yeast or ½ ounce (15 g) compressed fresh yeast
1¼	cups (300 ml) milk, warmed
⅓	cup (70 g) (caster) superfine sugar + 1 teaspoon extra
3⅓	cups (500 g) all-purpose (plain) flour
½	teaspoon salt
1	teaspoon ground nutmeg
2	large eggs + 1 large egg yolk, lightly beaten
½	cup (125 g) butter, softened
1	dried black bean
1	dried pea
15	candied (glacé) cherries, to decorate
¼	cup (40 g) slivered almonds, to decorate

1. Combine the raisins, currants, zest, and rum in a medium bowl and set aside to plump. Lightly grease a baking sheet.

2. Combine the yeast, ¼ cup (60 ml) of milk, and 1 teaspoon of the sugar in a large bowl. Set aside until foamy, about 10 minutes. Add the remaining milk and 1⅔ cups (250 g) of the flour, stirring to combine. Set aside until doubled in bulk, about 45 minutes.

3. Beat the remaining sugar, eggs, and butter in a medium bowl until just combined. Stir in the remaining flour, salt, and nutmeg. Stir into the yeast mixture to form a dough. Turn out onto a floured work surface. Knead, working in the dried fruit mixture, until smooth and elastic.

4. Shape into seven 2½-ounce (70-g) balls and hide the bean and pea separately inside. Use the remaining dough to shape a larger ball. Place the large ball in the center of the baking sheet and arrange the smaller ones around the outside. Cover and set aside until doubled in bulk, about 30 minutes.

5. Preheat the oven to 400°F (200°C/gas 6). Brush the cake with the remaining egg yolk and decorate with the cherries and almonds. Bake for 30–35 minutes, until golden brown. Let cool on a wire rack.

Tuscan Grape Harvest Cake

This recipe for sweet focaccia cake comes from Tuscany, where it is made every year throughout the grape harvest with the small black grapes used to make the local Chianti wines.

Serves: 10–12 · Prep: 30 min. + 3 hr. to rise · Cooking: 40–50 min. · Level: 2

SWEET FOCACCIA

2	(¼-ounce/7-g) packages active dry yeast or 1 ounce (30 g) compressed fresh yeast
⅔	cup (150 ml) lukewarm water + extra, as required
3	cups (450 g) all-purpose (plain) flour
¼	cup (50 g) sugar
¼	teaspoon salt

TOPPING

1	pound (500 g) black grapes (preferably seedless), lightly crushed
¾	cup (150 g) sugar

1. Lightly grease a large baking sheet. Line with parchment paper.

2. Stir the yeast and water in a small bowl. Set aside until foamy, about 10 minutes. Combine the flour, sugar, and salt in a large bowl and make a well in the center. Stir in the yeast mixture until the flour has all been absorbed, adding enough extra water to obtain a smooth dough.

3. Transfer to a lightly floured work surface and knead by hand until smooth and elastic, about 10 minutes, or beat with a dough hook until smooth and elastic, 5 minutes. Shape into a ball. Cover with a clean kitchen towel and set aside to rise in a warm place until doubled in bulk, about 1 hour.

4. Divide the dough in two. Roll out the dough into two sheets about 1 inch (2.5 cm) thick. Place a dough sheet on the prepared baking sheet. Cover with half the grapes and sprinkle with half the sugar. Top with the remaining dough sheet and seal the edges. Spread the remaining grapes over the top, pressing them down into the dough. Sprinkle with the remaining sugar and set aside to rise for 1 hour.

5. Preheat the oven to 350°F (180°C/gas 4). Bake for 40–50 minutes, or until lightly browned. Serve warm or at room temperature.

Twelfth Night Cake ▷

Panettone

Panettone is just one of many Christmas cakes that are baked in Italy. It is sweet and much lighter than a traditional English Christmas cake. In Italy, during the days after Christmas, when the panettones begin to grow stale, they are sliced open and filled with Chantilly Cream (see page 275), Zabaglione (see page 221), or Vanilla Pastry Cream (see page 262).

Serves: 10–12 · Prep: 30 min. + 3 hr. to rise · Cooking: 40–50 min. · Level: 2

³⁄₄	cup (135 g) raisins
¹⁄₂	cup (50 g) mixed chopped peel
1	teaspoon finely grated orange zest
1	teaspoon finely grated lemon zest
1	tablespoon brandy
2	(¹⁄₄-ounce/7-g) packages active dry yeast or 1 ounce (30 g) compressed fresh yeast
²⁄₃	cup (150 ml) lukewarm milk
¹⁄₃	cup (70 g) superfine (caster) sugar + 1 teaspoon extra
3¹⁄₃	cups (500 g) all-purpose (plain) flour
1	large egg + 4 large egg yolks
³⁄₄	cup (180 g) butter, softened
¹⁄₂	teaspoon salt

1. Lightly grease a deep 6-inch (15-cm) round cake pan. Line the base and sides with a double layer of parchment paper, extending 5 inches (13 cm) above the rim.

2. Combine the raisins, mixed peel, zest, and brandy in a small bowl and set aside to plump.

3. Combine the yeast, ¹⁄₄ cup (60 ml) of milk, and 1 teaspoon of the sugar in a large bowl. Cover and set aside in a warm place until foamy, about 10 minutes. Add the remaining milk and ³⁄₄ cup (125 g) of the flour, stirring to combine. Cover and set aside in a warm place to rise for 30 minutes.

4. Beat the remaining sugar, the egg, egg yolks, and butter in a medium bowl until combined. Sift in the remaining flour and the salt. Add to the yeast mixture and mix until a soft dough begins to form.

5. Turn out onto a lightly floured work surface and knead until smooth and elastic, about 10 minutes, or beat with a dough hook until smooth and elastic, 5 minutes.

6. Return to the bowl, cover and set aside to rise until doubled in bulk, about 2 hours.

7. Knock the dough down and work in the raisin and peel mixture. Shape the dough into a ball and place in the prepared pan. Cover and set aside to rise in a warm place, until the dough is about 1-inch (1.5 cm) about the rim.

8. Preheat the oven to 400°F (200°C/gas 6). Bake for 15 minutes, then decrease the oven temperature to 350°F (180°C/gas 4) and bake for a 35–40 more minutes, until golden brown and well risen.

9. Let cool in the pan for 10 minutes. Turn out onto a wire rack and let cool completely.

Panettone ▷

Galette Des Rois

The Galette de Rois is a traditional French cake baked or bought from bakeries around Epiphany (6 January). Like the English Twelfth Night Cake (see page 244), this cake also has a hidden dried bean. The person who receives the bean in their slice of cake becomes king for the day and must offer the next cake.

Serves: 10–12 · Prep: 30 min. + 3 hr. to rise · Cooking: 40–50 min. · Level: 2

- 1 pound (500 g) ready made puff pastry, thawed if frozen
- ½ cup (125 g) butter, softened
- ⅓ cup (70 g) superfine (caster) sugar
- ¾ cup (75 g) ground almonds
- 3 large egg yolks, lightly beaten + 1 large egg, lightly beaten, to glaze
- 1 tablespoon kirsch (clear cherry brandy) or other brandy
- ½ teaspoon almond extract (essence)
- 1 dried bean

1. Preheat the oven to 400°F (200°C/ gas 6). Lightly grease a baking sheet.

2. Roll out half of the pastry and cut out a 10-inch (25-cm) circle and place on the prepared baking sheet.

3. Beat the butter and sugar in a medium bowl with an electric mixer on medium-high speed until pale and creamy. Add the ground almonds, egg yolks, brandy, and almond extract, beating until just blended. Hide the bean in the filling and spread on the pastry round leaving a ¾-inch (1-cm) border. Lightly brush the border with some of the remaining egg.

4. Roll out the remaining pastry, cut out an 11-inch (28-cm) circle and place on top of the other round. Press to seal and trim to size. Using a sharp knife, score the pastry in a swirl pattern, starting from the center and working outward. Do not cut through to the filling.

5. Glaze the top of the pastry with the remaining egg, taking care not to brush the edges as this will stop the pastry from rising.

6. Bake for 30–35 minutes, until well puffed and golden brown. Serve warm or at room temperature.

April Fool's Day Fish

Bake this cake for friends and family on April 1st.

Serves: 6–8 · Prep: 20 min. · Cooking: 25–30 min. · Level: 1

- 1 cup (150 g) all-purpose (plain) flour
- 1 teaspoon baking powder
- ⅛ teaspoon salt
- 2 large eggs
- 1 cup (200 g) sugar
- ½ teaspoon vanilla extract (essence)
- ¼ cup (60 g) butter, melted and cooled
- ½ cup (60 g) flaked almonds
- 2 tablespoons confectioners' (icing) sugar, to dust

1. Preheat the oven to 350°F (180°C/gas 4). Butter and flour a 10-inch (25-cm) fish-shaped baking pan.

2. Combine the flour, baking powder, and salt in a medium bowl. Beat the eggs, sugar, and vanilla in a large bowl with an electric mixer at high speed until pale and very thick. Use a large rubber spatula to fold in the butter, followed by the mixed dry ingredients. Fold in the half the almonds. Spoon the batter into the prepared pan.

3. Bake for 25–30 minutes, or until a toothpick inserted into the center comes out clean. Cool the cake in the pan for 10 minutes. Turn out onto a rack to cool completely. Transfer to a serving plate.

4. Decorate with the remaining almonds and dust with the confectioners' sugar.

Galette De Rois ▷

Stollen

A Stollen is a sweet yeast cake traditionally baked in Germany at Christmas time. This recipe makes two loaves, so you can keep one and give one away.

Serves: 15–20 · Prep: 45 min. + 1 hr. 45 min. to rise · Cooking: 15 min. · Level: 2

- ½ cup (90 g) raisins
- ½ cup (90 g) currants
- ½ cup (80 g) slivered almonds
- ½ cup (50 g) chopped mixed peel
- 2 tablespoons rum
- 1 (¼-ounce/7-g) package active dry yeast or ½ ounce (15 g) compressed fresh yeast
- 1¼ cups (300 ml) milk, warmed
- ⅓ cup (70 g) superfine (caster) sugar + 1 teaspoon
- 4¼ cups (630 g) all-purpose (plain) flour
- 2 large eggs
- 1 cup (250 g) butter, softened + ¼ cup (60 g) butter, melted
- 1 teaspoon finely grated lemon zest
- ½ teaspoon salt
- ½ teaspoon ground cinnamon
- Confectioners' (icing) sugar, to dust

1. Combine the raisins, currants, almonds, mixed peel, and rum in a medium bowl and set aside to plump. Lightly grease a baking sheet.

2. Combine the yeast, ¼ cup (60 ml) of milk, and 1 teaspoon of sugar in a large bowl. Cover and set aside until foamy, about 10 minutes. Add the remaining milk and 1⅔ cups (250 g) of flour, stirring to combine. Cover and set aside in a warm place to rise until doubled in bulk, about 45 minutes.

3. Beat the remaining sugar, eggs, softened butter, and lemon zest in a medium bowl to combine. Add to the yeast mixture with the remaining flour, salt, and cinnamon, stirring to form a dough. Turn out onto a lightly floured work surface. Work in the dried fruit and nut mixture and knead until smooth and elastic. Set aside to rise for 30 minutes.

4. Gently knead the dough on a lightly floured surface and shape into two balls. Roll out into two 12 x 8-inch (30 x 20-cm) ovals. Fold the dough over lengthwise, almost in half, to create a stollen shape. Place on the prepared baking sheet, and let rise for 30 minutes.

6. Preheat the oven to 400°F (200°C/gas 6). Bake for 40–45 minutes, until golden brown. Brush with melted butter. When cool, dust generously with confectioners' sugar.

Cappuccino Sweetheart

This is the perfect cake for Valentine's Day.

Serves: 6–8 · Prep: 30 min. + 1 hr. to chill · Cooking: 15 min. · Level: 2

- 1 Basic Butter Cake, (see page 80), baked in a 9-inch (23-cm) heart-shaped cake pan

COFFEE LIQUEUR TRUFFLES
- 4 ounces (125 g) dark chocolate, coarsely chopped
- 3 tablespoons heavy (double) cream
- 2 teaspoons freeze-dried coffee granules
- ½ tablespoon coffee liqueur

COFFEE BUTTERCREAM
- 10 ounces (300 g) white chocolate, coarsely chopped
- ⅔ cup (150 ml) heavy (double) cream
- 1¾ cups (430 g) butter, softened
- 1 cup (150 g) confectioners' (icing) sugar
- 1 tablespoon freeze-dried coffee granules dissolved in 1 tablespoon boiling water, cooled
- 1 cup (120 g) hazelnuts, toasted and coarsely chopped
- ¼ cup (30 g) unsweetened cocoa powder, to dust

1. To prepare the truffles, melt the chocolate with the cream in a double boiler over barely simmering water. Let cool a little. Dissolve the coffee in the liqueur and stir into the chocolate mixture. Refrigerate for 1 hour, or until thick and malleable.

2. Roll teaspoonfuls of the truffle mixture into rounds and place on a dish lined with parchment paper. This should yield about 12 truffles. Cover and refrigerate until firm.

3. To prepare the buttercream, melt the white chocolate with the cream in a double boiler over barely simmering water. Let cool.

4. Beat the butter in a large bowl with an electric mixer at high speed until creamy. Gradually beat in the confectioners' sugar. Beat in the chocolate mixture and dissolved coffee.

5. Split the cake horizontally. Place one layer on a serving plate and spread with a quarter of the buttercream. Place the remaining layer on top. Spread the top and sides with buttercream. Press the hazelnuts into the sides of the cake and arrange the truffles on top. Dust with the cocoa.

Stollen ▷

Passover Fruit Cake

Passover is the Jewish festival that celebrates the ancient Hebrews' escape from slavery in Egypt. At this time observant Jewish people do not eat leavened bread and many other grain products.

Serves: 8–10 · Prep: 20 min. · Cooking: 80–90 min. · Level: 1

- ³/₄ cup (135 g) raisins
- ³/₄ cup (135 g) currants
- ³/₄ cup (135 g) golden raisins (sultanas)
- ¹/₄ cup (45 g) candied (glacé) red and green cherries, coarsely chopped
- ¹/₄ cup (25 g) chopped mixed peel
- ¹/₃ cup (80 ml) sweet sherry
- 1 cup (250 g) butter, softened
- 1 cup (200 g) firmly packed brown sugar
- 4 large eggs, lightly beaten
- 1½ cups (150 g) ground almonds
- 1 teaspoon ground cinnamon
- ½ teaspoon ground nutmeg
- ½ teaspoon ground ginger
- ¹/₃ cup (50 g) slivered almonds

1. Combine the raisins, currants, golden raisins, cherries, mixed, peel and sherry in a medium bowl. Cover and let steep overnight.

2. Preheat the oven to 350°F (180°C/gas 4). Lightly grease a deep 8-inch (20-cm) round cake pan. Line the base and sides with a triple layer of parchment paper.

3. Beat the butter and sugar in a large bowl with an electric mixer on high speed until pale and creamy. Add the eggs one at a time, beating until just blended after each addition.

4. Combine the ground almonds, cinnamon, nutmeg, and ginger in a small bowl. Add the ground almond mixture and soaked fruits alternately to the egg mixture, stirring with a large metal spoon to combine. Spoon the mixture into the prepared pan and sprinkle the slivered almonds on top.

5. Bake for 80–90 minutes, or until a skewer comes out clean when inserted into the center. Let the cake cool in the pan on a wire rack.

Passover Banana Cake

This is a delicious banana cake that can be enjoyed at Passover but also at other times of the year.

Serves: 6–8 · Prep: 20 min. · Cooking: 25–30 min. · Level: 1

- Matzo meal, to dust
- 7 large eggs, separated
- 1 cup (200 g) sugar
- ¹/₄ teaspoon salt
- 1 cup (150 g) very ripe mashed bananas
- ³/₄ cup (120 g) potato starch
- 1 cup (120 g) walnuts, coarsely chopped
- 1 cup (250 ml) heavy (double) cream
- 1 banana, peeled and finely sliced

1. Preheat the oven to 350°F (180°C/gas 4). Butter two 9-inch (23-cm) round cake pans. Dust with matzo meal.

2. Beat the egg yolks, sugar, and salt in a large bowl with an electric mixer on high speed until pale and thick. Use a large rubber spatula to fold in the banana, potato starch, and walnuts.

3. With mixer on medium, beat the egg whites in a large bowl until stiff peaks form. Fold them into the batter. Spoon half the batter into each of the prepared pans.

4. Bake for 25–30 minutes, or until a toothpick inserted into the center comes out clean. Cool the cakes completely in the pans on racks. Turn out onto racks.

5. With mixer at high speed, beat the cream in a large bowl until stiff. Place one cake on a serving plate. Spread with the cream and the banana slices. Top with the remaining layer.

◁ **Passover Fruit Cake**

Childrens' Party Cake

This is a good choice for a children's birthday party.

Serves: 8–10 · Prep: 30 min. + 1 hr. to chill · Cooking: 25–30 min.· Level: 2

CAKE

- 2 cups (300 g) cake flour
- 2 teaspoons baking powder
- ¼ teaspoon salt
- 4 large eggs
- 2 cups (400 g) sugar
- 1 cup (250 ml) boiling milk
- 2 teaspoons vanilla extract (essence)
- ½ cup M & M's

SEVEN-MINUTE FROSTING

- 1½ cups (300 g) sugar
- 2 large egg whites
- ⅓ cup (90 ml) water
- ¼ teaspoon salt
- ¼ teaspoon cream of tartar
- 1 teaspoon vanilla extract (essence)

1. Preheat the oven to 350°F (180°C/gas 4). Lightly grease three 8-inch (20-cm) round cake pans. Line with parchment paper.

2. To prepare the cake, combine the flour, baking powder, and salt in a large bowl. Beat the eggs and sugar in a medium bowl with an electric mixer on medium speed until pale and thick. With mixer on low, beat in the dry ingredients, milk, and vanilla. Spoon into the pans.

3. Bake for 25–30 minutes, or until a toothpick inserted into the center comes out clean. Cool the cakes in the pans for 10 minutes. Turn out onto racks. Remove the paper and let cool completely.

4. To prepare the frosting, stir the sugar, egg whites, water, salt, and cream of tartar in a saucepan. Cook over low heat, beating constantly with mixer on low until the whites register 160°F (70°C) on an instant-read thermometer. Transfer to a bowl and beat at high speed until the egg whites form stiff peaks. Remove from the heat and stir in the vanilla. Beat until smooth and spreadable.

5. Place a cake on a plate and spread with frosting. Top with another cake and spread with frosting. Place the remaining cake on top. Spread with the remaining frosting and sprinkle with the M & M's, pressing them into the frosting. Refrigerate for 1 hour before serving.

Bishops' Cake

This is a very old English recipe for a fruit cake that is traditionally baked at Christmas. It is said to be named Bishops' Cake because the fruit and nut topping looks like a stained glass window.

Serves: 6–8 · Prep: 30 min. + 6 hr. to freeze · Level 2

- ½ cup (125 g) mixed candied (glacé) fruit, such as pineapple, pears, apricots, coarsely chopped
- ¾ cup (120 g) cashew nuts
- ¾ cup (120 g) Brazil nuts
- ¾ cup (90 g) walnut halves
- ½ cup (90 g) raisins
- ⅓ cup (60 g) red and green candied (glacé) cherries
- ¼ cup (45 g) dried pitted dates
- 2 tablespoons chopped mixed peel
- ½ cup (75 g) all-purpose (plain) flour
- ½ teaspoon baking powder
- ½ cup (100 g) sugar
- 2 large eggs, lightly beaten
- ¼ cup (60 ml) brandy or rum
- 1 teaspoon vanilla extract (essence)

1. Preheat the oven to 275°F (140°C/gas 1). Lightly grease a 9 x 3-inch (23 x 8-cm) loaf pan and line with parchment paper.

2. Combine the fruit and nuts in a large bowl. Add in the flour and baking powder and stir to coat.

3. Beat the sugar, eggs, brandy, and vanilla in a medium bowl with an electric mixer on low speed until combined. Add to the fruit mixture and mix well. Spoon the batter into the prepared pan.

4. Bake for 2½ hours, or until a skewer comes out clean when inserted into the center. Cover the top with aluminum foil if it begins to brown too much.

5. Leave to cool in the pan for 10 minutes, then turn out onto a wire rack and let cool completely.

Bishops' Cake ▷

Simnel Cake

According to tradition, this rich British fruit and marzipan cake was given by servant girls to their mothers on the fourth Sunday of Lent. On that day, the girls were allowed a day off to visit their families. It is now usually prepared at Easter.

Serves: 12–14 · Prep: 30 min. + 12 hr. to steep · Cooking: 1 hr 45 min. · Level 2

CAKE

³⁄₄	cup (135 g) raisins
³⁄₄	cup (135 g) currants
¹⁄₂	cup (90 g) pitted prunes, coarsely chopped
¹⁄₂	cup (90 g) red and green candied (glacé) cherries, coarsely chopped
¹⁄₂	cup (50 g) chopped mixed peel
¹⁄₃	cup (80 ml) sweet sherry, brandy, or whisky
1	cup (200 g) firmly packed light Muscovado sugar
³⁄₄	cup (180 g) butter, softened
1	teaspoon finely grated orange zest
3	large eggs
2	cups (300 g) all-purpose (plain) flour
2	teaspoons baking powder
1	teaspoon ground cinnamon
¹⁄₂	teaspoon ground nutmeg
¹⁄₄	teaspoon salt
2	tablespoons apricot preserves (jam), warmed

MARZIPAN

3	cups (300 g) ground almonds
1¹⁄₄	cups (200 g) confectioners' (icing) sugar + extra, to dust
³⁄₄	cup (150 g) superfine (caster) sugar
1	large egg white, lightly beaten
	Water, to bind

1. Combine the raisins, currants, prunes, cherries, mixed peel and sherry in a medium bowl. Cover and set aside overnight, to steep.

2. To prepare the marzipan, combine the ground almonds, confectioners' and superfine sugar in a medium bowl. Add the egg white and enough water to form a firm, moist ball of paste. Shape into three different sized balls weighing approximately 12 ounces (350 g), 8 ounces (250 g), and 5 ounces (150 g). Wrap the balls in plastic wrap (cling film) and refrigerate for 1 hour until firm.

3. Lightly dust a clean work surface with confectioners' sugar. Roll the medium sized ball of marzipan out and cut into an 8-inch (20-cm) disk. Put on a plate and refrigerate until required.

4. Preheat the oven to 300°F (150°C/gas 2).

5. Lightly grease a deep 8-inch (20-cm) round cake pan. Line the base and sides with a triple layer of parchment paper.

6. Beat the sugar, butter, and orange zest in a large bowl with an electric mixer on medium-high speed until pale and creamy. Add the eggs one at a time, beating until just blended after each addition.

7. Combine the flour, baking powder, cinnamon, nutmeg, and salt in a small bowl. Add the flour and soaked fruits alternately to the egg mixture, stirring with a large metal spoon to combine. Pour half of the mixture into the prepared pan. Place the disk of marzipan on top and then spoon in the remaining cake batter.

8. Bake for 1 hour and 45 minutes, or until a skewer comes out clean when inserted into the center. Remove the cake from the oven and leave in the pan to cool for 20 minutes. Place on a wire rack, discard the paper and leave to cool completely. Brush the top of the cake with the warmed preserves.

9. Remove the remaining balls of marzipan from the refrigerator. Lightly dust a clean work surface with confectioners' sugar. Roll the larger ball out and cut a 10-inch (25-cm) disk. Place on top of the cake, gently pressing to secure.

10. Shape twelve small balls with the remaining marzipan and arrange decoratively on top of the cake.

Easter Egg Cake

This recipe requires an egg-shaped mold, which can be located in a specialty cake store.

Serves: 8–10 · Prep: 45 min. + 4 hr. to chill · Level: 3

CAKE

1	Italian Sponge Cake (see page 274), cut into ½-inch (1-cm) slices
⅓	cup (90 ml) rum or fruit liqueur
¼	cup (60 ml) water
2	cups (500 ml) heavy (double) cream
1	teaspoon almond extract (essence)
2	ounces (60 g) dark chocolate, coarsely chopped
⅔	cup (90 g) candied (glacé) fruit, chopped

FONDANT

2	cups (400 g) sugar
¾	cup (200 ml) cold water
¼	teaspoon cream of tartar
¼	cup (30 g) confectioners' (icing) sugar, to dust
1	teaspoon purple or pink food coloring

1. Cut the cake slices in half diagonally to make long triangular pieces. Brush a 10-inch (25-cm) egg-shaped mold with 2 tablespoons of rum. Line with cake, pointed ends facing inward to the center of the mold. Mix the remaining rum and water and drizzle over the cake.

2. Beat the cream and almond in a large bowl with an electric mixer at high speed until stiff. Fold in the chocolate and candied fruit. Spoon the filling into the mold and top with a layer of cake slices. Drizzle with the remaining rum mixture. Refrigerate for 4 hours.

3. Prepare the fondant following the step-by-step instructions below.

4. Place the fondant on a work surface dusted with confectioners' sugar and knead in the food coloring. Roll out thinly and cut into strips. Place the strips in a crisscross pattern over the cake.

PREPARING FONDANT STEP-BY-STEP

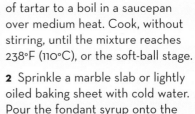
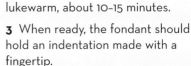

1 Bring the sugar, water, and cream of tartar to a boil in a saucepan over medium heat. Cook, without stirring, until the mixture reaches 238°F (110°C), or the soft-ball stage.

2 Sprinkle a marble slab or lightly oiled baking sheet with cold water. Pour the fondant syrup onto the slab or sheet and let cool until lukewarm, about 10–15 minutes.

3 When ready, the fondant should hold an indentation made with a fingertip.

4 Use a large spatula to work the fondant, lifting from the edges toward the center, folding it until it begins to thicken, lose its gloss, and turn pure white.

5 Dust your hands with confectioners' sugar and knead the fondant until smooth and creamy.

6 Cover with a clean cloth. Let stand overnight before using.

When cooking the sugar and water mixture wash down the sides of the pan with a pastry brush dipped in cold water to prevent sugar crystals from forming. This recipe will make about 1 cup. The fondant should rest for 12 hours before use.

Honey Cake

Traditionally served on the first night of Rosh Hashanah, this cake expresses the hope that the year to come will be sweet. The flavor improves over time, so make it ahead and store it in an airtight container.

Serves: 12–15 · Prep: 30 min. · Cooking: 70–80 min. · Level: 1

3	cups (450 g) all purpose (plain) flour
3	teaspoons baking powder
1½	teaspoons ground ginger
1	teaspoon ground cinnamon
1	teaspoon baking soda (bicarbonate of soda)
½	teaspoon ground cloves
1	cup (200 g) firmly packed brown sugar
2	large eggs, lightly beaten
1	teaspoon vanilla extract
1	cup (250 ml) honey
1	cup (250 ml) water
1	cup (250 ml) rice bran oil
	Confectioners' (icing) sugar, to dust

1. Preheat the oven to 350°F (180°C/gas 4). Lightly grease a 9 x 4-inch (24 x 10-cm) loaf pan and line the base with parchment paper.

2. Sift the flour, baking powder, ginger, cinnamon, baking soda, and cloves into a medium bowl.

3. Place the honey, water, and oil in a small saucepan over low heat and bring to a boil. Remove from the heat and set aside.

4. Beat the sugar, eggs, and vanilla in a medium bowl with an electric mixer on medium-high speed until pale and thick. With mixer on low speed, add the sifted flour and honey mixture. Spoon the batter into the prepared pan.

5. Bake for 1¼ hours, until a skewer comes out clean when tested. Leave to cool in the pan for 10 minutes, then turn out onto a wire rack and let cool completely.

6. Dust with confectioners' sugar.

Orange and Nut Passover Cake

Another delicious Passover cake.

Serves: 6–8 · Prep: 15 min. · Cooking: 80–90 min. · Level: 1

	Matzo meal, to dust
6	large eggs, separated
1½	cups (300 g) sugar
¾	cup (100 g) finely ground almonds
	Finely grated zest and juice of 1 orange
1½	cups (180 g) walnuts, coarsely chopped

1. Preheat the oven to 325°F (170°C/gas 5). Lightly grease a 9-inch (23-cm) springform pan. Dust with matzo meal.

2. Beat the egg yolks and sugar in a large bowl with an electric mixer at high speed until pale and thick. With mixer at low speed, beat in the almonds, orange zest and juice, and walnuts.

3. With mixer on high, beat the egg whites in a large bowl until stiff peaks form. Use a large rubber spatula to fold them into the nut mixture. Pour the batter into the prepared pan.

4. Bake for 80–90 minutes, or until a toothpick inserted into the center comes out clean. Cool the cake completely in the pan on a rack.

Honey Cake ▷

Saint Honoré Gateau

This stunning cake is named for Saint Honoré, or Honoratus, Bishop of Amiens in early medieval times, who is the patron saint of bakers and pastry chefs. The cake is thought to have been created by the famous pastry chef Chiboust in 1846.

Serves: 10–12 · Prep: 1 hr. 45 min. · Cooking: 35–45 min. · Level: 3

BASE

- 1⅓ cups (200 g) all-purpose flour
- 1 tablespoon sugar
- ⅓ cup (90 g) cold butter + 1 tablespoon
- 1 large egg yolk + 1 large egg, lightly beaten
- 1 recipe Choux Pastry (see page 274)
- 1 large egg, lightly beaten

FILLING

- 2 cups (500 ml) milk
- 4 large egg yolks
- ¾ cup (150 g) sugar
- ½ cup (75 g) all-purpose (plain) flour
- 1 tablespoon dark rum
- 1 teaspoon vanilla extract (essence)

CARAMEL GLAZE

- 1 cup (200 g) sugar
- 2 tablespoons water

FROSTING

- 1 cup (150 g) confectioners' (icing) sugar
- 2 tablespoons water
- 1 tablespoon unsweetened cocoa powder

1. Preheat the oven to 400°F (200°C/gas 6).

To prepare the base, combine the flour and sugar in a medium bowl. Use a pastry blender to cut in the butter until the mixture resembles coarse crumbs. Stir in the egg yolk until a smooth dough is formed. Roll the dough out on a lightly floured surface to form a 10-inch (25-cm) round. Prick all over with a fork and place on a baking sheet. Brush a little beaten egg around the edge.

2. Prepare the Choux Pastry. Fit a pastry bag with a plain ¾-inch (2-cm) tip and fill half-full with pastry. Pipe the pastry around the edge of the pastry round. Set aside the remaining pastry. Brush some beaten egg over the top.

3. Bake for 20–25 minutes, or until golden. Cool the pastry completely on a rack.

4. Line a baking sheet with parchment paper. Fill a pastry bag with the remaining choux pastry. Pipe heaps the size of small nuts on the prepared sheet. Brush with the remaining beaten egg.

5. Bake for 15–20 minutes, or until golden. Cool the pastry puffs completely on racks.

6. To prepare the filling, warm the milk in a saucepan over low heat. Beat the egg yolks and sugar in a large bowl with an electric mixer at high speed until pale and thick. Use a large rubber spatula to fold in the flour. Gradually stir in the hot milk.

7. Transfer the mixture to a medium saucepan. Bring to a boil, stirring constantly. Remove from the heat and stir in the rum and vanilla. Set aside to cool completely.

8. To prepare the caramel glaze, warm the sugar and water in a saucepan over medium heat until the sugar has dissolved. Continue cooking, without stirring, until pale gold in color. Remove from the heat.

9. Spread the cooled filling into the pastry base. Dip the tops of the choux puffs in the caramel to glaze. Dip the bases of the puffs in the caramel and stick on the crown, pressing down lightly.

10. To prepare the frosting, mix the confectioners' sugar and enough water to make a smooth frosting. Spoon half the frosting over the filling. Trace crossing diagonal lines on the frosting with a small knife. Stir the cocoa into the remaining frosting. Spoon the frosting into a pastry bag. Use the lines as a guide to pipe thin lines over the cake.

◁ **Saint Honoré Gateau**

Sénateur

This is a classic French cake. Be sure to assemble the cake just before serving so that the puff pastry doesn't get soggy.

Serves: 8–10 · Prep: 45 min. · Cooking: 15 min. · Level: 2

1½	pounds (750 g) frozen puff pastry, thawed
1	tablespoon kirsch (clear cherry brandy) or other fruit brandy
1	recipe Vanilla Pastry Cream (see recipe below)
1	cup (300 g) red currant jelly
1	cup (120 g) toasted flaked almonds

1. Preheat the oven to 450°F (225°C/gas 7). Line 3 baking sheets with parchment paper. Unroll or unfold the pastry on a lightly floured surface. Roll out to measure ⅛ inch (3 mm) thick. Cut into three rounds, each measuring 10 inches (25 cm) across. Prick all over with a fork. Place the pastry on the prepared baking sheets. Bake for 10–15 minutes, or until golden brown. Cool the pastry on racks.

2. Stir the kirsch into the pastry cream. Place one pastry round on a serving plate and spread with half the pastry cream. Cover with another layer of pastry and cream. Top with the remaining pastry.

3. Heat the jelly in a small saucepan over low heat until liquid. Pour onto the cake. Spread over the top and sides of the cake. Press the almonds into the sides and sprinkle over the top.

PREPARING VANILLA PASTRY CREAM

Makes: About 3 cups (750 ml) · Prep: 10 min. · Cooking: 10–15 min. · Level: 1

5	large egg yolks
¾	cup (150 g) sugar
2–4	tablespoons cornstarch (cornflour)
	Pinch of salt
2	cups (500 ml) milk
2	teaspoons vanilla extract (essence)

Vanilla Pastry Cream is not a pouring custard but is used as a filling for millefeuille (napoleons), pastry squares, and many cakes. Add more or less cornstarch depending on how thick you want the pastry cream to be.

You may flavor the custard in the following ways:

CHOCOLATE PASTRY CREAM: Add 5 ounces (150 g) of coarsely chopped or grated dark chocolate to the milk. Stir until dissolved as the milk heats.

COFFEE PASTRY CREAM: Dissolve 1 tablespoon of instant coffee granules in the milk while heating.

LEMON PASTRY CREAM: Boil the finely grated zest of 1 lemon in the milk, omitting the vanilla extract. You may also add 2–3 teaspoons freshly squeezed juice to the finished custard.

FLAVORING PASTRY CREAM WITH LIQUEURS: add 1–2 tablespoons of the desired liqueur to the custard after it is cooked. Grand Marnier produces a lovely orange-flavored custard.

1 Beat the egg yolks and sugar until pale and creamy. Beat in the cornstarch and salt. Add more or less cornstarch depending on how thick you want the pastry cream to be.

2 Bring the milk to a boil, then stir into the egg and sugar mixture.

3 Simmer over low heat until thickened, about 10 minutes. During the first 5 minutes, stir often with a wooden spoon. Then stir constantly with a whisk, breaking up any lumps.

4 Remove from the heat and stir in the vanilla (or other flavoring). If not using immediately, pour into a bowl and place a piece of plastic wrap (cling film) on the surface to stop a skin forming.

Sacher Torte

This famous Austrian chocolate cake was invented by Franz Sacher for Metternich in Vienna, in 1832.

Serves: 8–10 · Prep: 45 min. + 2 hr. 30 min. to chill · Cooking: 30–40 min. · Level: 3

CAKE
- ¼ cup (60 g) butter
- ¾ cup (120 g) all-purpose (plain) flour
- ¼ cup (30 g) unsweetened cocoa powder
- ½ teaspoon salt
- 6 large eggs
- 1 cup (200 g) sugar
- 1 teaspoon vanilla extract (essence)

FILLING
- 1¼ cups (350 g) apricot preserves (jam)

CHOCOLATE FROSTING
- ½ cup (125 ml) heavy (double) cream
- 2 tablespoons light corn (golden) syrup
- 5 ounces (150 g) dark chocolate, coarsely grated
- ½ teaspoon vanilla extract (essence)

- 1 cup (250 ml) heavy (double) cream

1. Preheat the oven to 350°F (180°C/gas 4). Line a 9-inch (23-cm) springform pan with parchment paper. Lightly grease the sides of the pan.

2. To prepare the cake, melt the butter in a small saucepan over low heat. Set aside. Sift the flour, cocoa, and salt into a medium bowl.

3. Beat the eggs and sugar with an electric mixer on medium speed until well combined. Place the bowl over a pan of barely simmering water, making sure that the base of the bowl does not touch the water. Heat the mixture, beating constantly, until warm to the touch. Remove from the heat and beat at medium-high speed until the mixture is pale, thick, and tripled in volume. Beat in the vanilla.

4. Place about 1 cupful of the egg mixture in a small bowl and stir in the melted butter.

5. Fold in the mixed dry ingredients by hand. Fold in the butter mixture, taking care not to deflate the batter. Spoon the batter into the prepared pan.

6. Bake until springy to the touch, 30–40 minutes. Cool the cake in the pan on a wire rack. Run a knife around the edge of the pan then carefully remove the pan sides. Turn the cake upside-down onto a plate and remove the pan bottom and paper. Set right side up and cut in half horizontally.

7. To prepare the filling, place the apricot preserves in a small saucepan over medium heat and bring to a gentle simmer, stirring constantly.

8. To prepare the frosting, place the cream and corn syrup in a medium saucepan over medium heat and bring to a gentle boil. Remove from the heat and stir in the chocolate. Cover with a clean kitchen towel and let sit until the chocolate is melted, about 5 minutes. Stir in the vanilla extract. Let cool until tepid and almost setting.

9. To assemble the torte, place one layer of cake cut-side up on a plate. Spread with one-third of the apricot preserves. Cover with the remaining cake layer and spread the top and sides with the remaining apricot preserves. Chill in the refrigerator until the apricot preserves are set, about 30 minutes.

10. Pour the almost set chocolate frosting over the cake. Spread evenly over the top and sides. Chill for at least 2 hours before serving.

11. Just before serving, beat the cream in a medium bowl on high speed until thick. Serve pieces of cake with a dollop of cream.

Bee-Sting Cake

This German cake is traditionally filled with custard and topped with honey-glazed chopped almonds. According to the folklore surrounding the cake, it is named by a baker who was stung by a bee while baking it.

Serves: 10–12 · Prep 1 hr. + 2–3 hr. to rise · Cooking: 15–20 min. · Level: 3

DOUGH
- 1 (¼-ounce/7-g) package active dry yeast or ½ ounce (15 g) compressed fresh yeast
- ¾ cup (180 ml) lukewarm milk
- 2⅔ cups (400 g) all-purpose (plain) flour
- ¼ cup (60 g) superfine (caster) sugar
- ¼ teaspoon salt
- 2 tablespoons vanilla sugar
- 1 teaspoon finely grated lemon zest
- 2 eggs, lightly beaten
- ⅓ cup (90 g) butter, melted

TOPPING
- ⅔ cup (150 g) butter
- ⅓ cup (70 g) sugar
- 1 packet vanilla sugar or 1 teaspoon vanilla extract (essence)
- 1 tablespoon honey
- 3 tablespoons light (single) cream
- 1 cup (150 g) blanched almonds, coarsely chopped

FILLING
- 1 recipe Vanilla Pastry Cream (see page 262)

1. Mix the yeast with the milk in a small bowl. Set aside until foamy, about 10 minutes. Combine the flour, salt, both sugars, and zest in a large bow. Add the yeast mixture, eggs, and butter. Stir with a spatula or your hands to form a medium-soft dough, adding a little more flour if needed. Transfer to a lightly floured work surface and knead until smooth and elastic, about 10 minutes, or beat with a dough hook until smooth and elastic, 5 minutes.

2. Place in an oiled bowl. Cover the bowl with a clean kitchen towel and leave to rise in a warm place until doubled in bulk, 60–80 minutes.

3. To prepare the topping, melt the butter in a small saucepan over low heat. Stir in the sugar, vanilla sugar or extract, honey, and cream. Bring to a boil, stirring all the time. Take the pan off the heat and mix in the almonds. Stir the mixture every now and then while it is cooling.

4. To prepare the filling, prepare the pastry cream. Cover the surface with plastic wrap (cling film) to stop a film from forming, and chill in the refrigerator until needed.

5. Butter and line a 10½ x 15½-inch (39 x 29 cm) jellyroll pan with parchment paper.

6. Dust your hands with flour, punch the risen dough down, and take it out of the bowl. Briefly knead on a lightly floured work surface then roll out. Place the dough in the prepared jellyroll pan, stretching and spreading with your fingers so that it covers the bottom of the pan evenly. Spread the topping over the top evenly. Leave to rise again in a warm place until visibly puffed up, 15–30 minutes.

7. Preheat the oven to 375°F (190°C/gas 5). Bake for 15–20 minutes, or until golden brown. Leave to cool in the pan on a rack.

8. When completely cooled, cut into squares or 6-inch (15-cm) wide strips and then cut the strips in half horizontally. Spread the pastry cream on the bottom half and sandwich together with the almond top half. Cut into smaller squares for serving.

Lemon and Rum Savarin

This is a great way to serve Savarin. Vary the fruit according to the season. In winter, you may like to serve it with warm stewed apples.

Serves: 10–12 · Prep: 30 min. · Level: 2

1	recipe Basic Savarin (see recipe, right)
1½	cups (300 g) sugar
2	cups (500 ml) cold water
2	tablespoons finely grated lemon zest
1	cinnamon stick
2	cups (500 ml) rum
½	cup (125 ml) apricot preserves (jam)
1½	cups (375 ml) heavy (double) cream
⅓	cup (50 g) confectioners' (icing) sugar
	Fresh berry fruit and slivered almonds, to serve

1. Bring the sugar, water, lemon zest, and cinnamon stick to a boil in a saucepan.

2. Place the savarin (still on a wire rack) on a large plate. Remove the cinnamon stick from the syrup. Drizzle the hot syrup over the cake. Scoop up any excess syrup with a spoon and drizzle over the cake. Drizzle with the rum.

3. Heat the apricot preserves in a saucepan until liquid. Pour over the cake and set aside to cool.

4. Beat the cream and confectioners' sugar in a medium bowl with an electric mixer at high speed until stiff. Fill the center of the savarin with the fruit and serve with the cream passed separately.

Basic Savarin

Jean Anthelme Brillat-Savarin (1755–1826) was a French lawyer and politician but he is best known as an epicure and food writer. His famous work, Physiologie du goût (The Physiology of Taste), was published in December 1825, two months before his death. This yeast cake is named in his honor.

Serves: 10–12 · Prep: 30 min. + 1 hr. 40 min. to rise · Cooking: 35–40 min. · Level: 2

1	(¼-ounce/7-g) package active dry yeast or ½ ounce (15 g) compressed fresh yeast
¼	cup (50 g) sugar
¼	cup (60 ml) lukewarm water
1⅔	cups (250 g) all-purpose (plain) flour
1	teaspoon salt
3	large eggs
½	cup (125 g) butter, softened
¼	cup (60 ml) dark rum

1. Butter a 10-inch (25-cm) savarin mold. Stir the yeast, sugar, and water in a small bowl. Set aside until foamy, about 10 minutes.

2. Sift the flour and salt into a large bowl. Beat the eggs, butter, and rum in a large bowl with an electric mixer at high speed until creamy. Stir in the yeast mixture. Use a large rubber spatula to gradually fold in the dry ingredients. Knead until a smooth dough is formed. Cover with plastic wrap (cling film) and let rise in a warm place until doubled in bulk, about 1 hour.

3. Punch down the dough, transfer to the prepared pan, and let rise until doubled in bulk, about 40 minutes.

4. Preheat the oven to 375°F (190°C/gas 5). Bake for 35–40 minutes, or until golden. Cool the savarin in the pan for 15 minutes. Turn out onto a rack to cool completely.

Lemon and Rum Savarin

BASIC RECIPES

Here you will find a series of basic recipes that you will

need to complete some of the cakes in this book.

We have included three basic sponge cakes (Plain,

Chocolate, and Italian), as well as Choux Pastry, Vanilla

Crème Anglaise (with several variations), and some

other basic creams and frostings. You will also find other

basic recipes throughout the book, such as Vanilla

Pastry Cream (see page 262) and Basic Butter Cake

(see page 80). They are all listed in the index.

◁ **Italian Sponge Cake (see page 274)**

Basic Chocolate Sponge Cake

It is very important that the eggs be at a warm room temperature. Take them out of the refrigerator several hours before you begin baking the sponge.

Serves: 8–10 · Prep: 15 min. · Cooking: 15–20 min. · Level: 1

- ³/₄ cup (120 g) cornstarch (cornflour)
- 2 tablespoons all-purpose (plain) flour
- ¼ cup (30 g) unsweetened cocoa powder
- 1 teaspoon cream of tartar
- ½ teaspoon baking soda (bicarbonate of soda)
- 4 large eggs, separated
- ³/₄ cup (150 g) sugar

1. Preheat the oven to 350°F (180°C/gas 4). Butter two 9- or 10-inch (23- or 25- cm) round cake pans. Line with parchment paper.

2. Sift the cornstarch, flour, cocoa, cream of tartar, and baking soda into a large bowl.

3. Beat the egg whites in a large bowl with an electric mixer at medium speed until stiff peaks form. Add the egg yolks and sugar and beat until pale and thick. Use a large rubber spatula to fold in the dry ingredients. Spoon the batter into the prepared pans.

4. Bake for 15–20 minutes, or until a toothpick inserted into the center comes out clean. Cool the cakes in the pans for 15 minutes. Turn out onto racks and carefully remove the paper. Let cool completely.

Basic Sponge Cake

When making a butter or pound cake there is normally no need to sift the flour. However, for sponges, where every drop of air is vital, it pays to sift the dry ingredients before use.

Serves: 8–10 · Prep: 15 min. · Cooking: 15–20 min. · Level: 2

- 4 large eggs, separated
- ³/₄ cup (150 g) sugar
- ³/₄ cup (120 g) cornstarch (cornflour)
- 2 tablespoons all-purpose (plain) flour
- 1 teaspoon cream of tartar
- ½ teaspoon baking soda (bicarbonate of soda)

1. Preheat the oven to 350°F (180°C/gas 4). Butter two 9-inch (23-cm) round cake pans. Line with parchment paper.

2. Beat the egg yolks in a large bowl with an electric mixer on medium speed until pale yellow in color. Gradually add ½ cup (100 g) of sugar, beating constantly on medium speed. Beat until the mixture is thick and pale.

3. Beat the egg whites in a large bowl with an electric mixer on medium-low speed until frothy. Gradually add the remaining ¼ cup (50 g) of sugar, beating on medium-high speed, until stiff but not dry.

4. Use a large rubber spatula to fold in half the egg whites. Sprinkle a little of the mixed dry ingredients into the batter and gently fold them in. Gradually fold in all the mixed dry ingredients then fold in the remaining egg whites.

5. Spoon the batter into the prepared pans. Bake for 15–20 minutes, until the edges are golden and shrinking away from the sides of the pan, and a toothpick comes out clean when inserted into the center.

6. Turn the cakes out onto a rack. Carefully remove the paper and let cool completely.

Basic Chocolate Sponge Cake ▷

Choux Pastry

Choux pastry is made by melting butter into hot water, adding flour, and then cooking the mixture until it is smooth and not sticky. The eggs are then added one by one. The raw pastry is soft and usually piped in a pastry bag. Choux pastry rises well and is very versatile. It is used to make cream puffs and éclairs and many other cakes and desserts.

Serves: 8–10 · Prep: 20 min. · Level: 3

2	cups (500 ml) water
²/₃	cup (180 g) butter, cut up
1	tablespoon sugar
¼	teaspoon salt
1²/₃	cups (250 g) all-purpose (plain) flour
5–6	large eggs

1. Line a baking sheet with parchment paper.

2. Place the water, butter, sugar, and salt in a large pan over medium-low heat. When the mixture boils, remove from the heat and add the flour all at once. Use a wooden spoon to stir vigorously until a smooth paste forms.

3. Return to medium heat and stir constantly until the mixture pulls away from the pan sides. Remove from the heat and let cool for 5 minutes.

4. Add the eggs, one at a time, beating until just blended after each addition. The batter should be shiny and stiff enough to hold its shape if dropped onto a baking sheet. Add another egg if required. Bake the pastry as explained in the recipes.

Italian Sponge Cake

This classic Italian sponge cake contains no butter or oil, and the leavening comes entirely from the beaten egg whites. It is used as the basis for many different layer cakes and desserts.

Serves: 8–10 · Prep: 20 min. · Cooking: 35–45 · Level: 3

1	cup (150 g) cake flour
¼	teaspoon salt
6	large eggs, separated
1¼	cups (250 g) sugar
½	tablespoon finely grated lemon zest

1. Preheat the oven to 350°F (180°C/gas 4). Butter a 10-inch (25-cm) springform pan. Line with parchment paper.

2. Sift the flour and salt into a medium bowl. Beat the egg yolks, sugar, and lemon zest in a large bowl with an electric mixer at high speed until pale and very thick.

3. Beat the egg whites in a large bowl until stiff peaks form. Use a large rubber spatula to fold the dry ingredients into the egg yolk mixture. Carefully fold in the beaten whites. Working quickly, spoon the batter into the prepared pan.

4. Bake for 35–45 minutes, or until springy to the touch and the cake shrinks from the pan sides. Cool the cake in the pan for 5 minutes. Loosen and remove the pan sides. Invert the cake onto a rack. Loosen and remove the pan bottom. Carefully remove the paper. Turn the cake top-side up and let cool completely.

Chantilly Cream

These quantities will make 2 cups (500 ml) of Chantilly Cream. If you need more, double the recipe. For a light, white Chantilly Cream, make sure that the cream is well chilled before you start. Place the mixing bowl in the freezer for 10 minutes before you begin beating the cream.

Makes: 2 cups (500 ml) · Prep: 15 min. · Level: 1

- 1 cup (250 ml) heavy (double) cream
- 2 tablespoons sugar
- 1 teaspoon vanilla extract (essence)

1. Beat the cream, sugar, and vanilla in a medium bowl with an electric beater or whisk on medium speed until thick and creamy.

Bavarian Cream

Bavarian cream has an egg custard base which is usually mixed with a flavoring and whipped cream and then set with gelatin in a mold. Food historians are not sure if it was actually invented in Bavaria in southern Germany, or if this is just a name given to it by the French chefs who made it famous in the 19th century.

Makes: 4 cups (1 liter) · Prep: 30 min. + 4 hr. to chill · Level: 2

- 1 tablespoon unflavored gelatin
- ¼ cup (60 ml) cold water
- 5 large egg yolks
- ½ cup (100 g) sugar
- ⅛ teaspoon salt
- 1½ cups (375 ml) milk
- 1½ teaspoons vanilla extract (essence)
- 1 cup (250 ml) heavy (double) cream, chilled

1. Sprinkle the gelatin over the cold water in a saucepan. Let stand 1 minute. Stir over low heat until the gelatin has completely dissolved.

2. Beat the egg yolks, sugar, and salt in a saucepan until well blended.

3. Bring the milk and vanilla to a boil in a saucepan. Remove from the heat and stir about ¼ cup (60 ml) hot milk into the yolk mixture. Cook over low heat, stirring constantly with a wooden spoon, until the mixture lightly coats a metal spoon or registers 160°F (70°C) on an instant-read thermometer. Gradually pour in the remaining milk, stirring constantly.

4. Pour through a strainer into a large bowl and add the gelatin mixture. Immediately plunge the bowl into a bowl of ice water until the mixture has cooled, stirring occasionally.

5. Beat the cream in a medium bowl with an electric mixer at high speed until stiff. When the custard has cooled, but not set, fold in the cream. Refrigerate for 4 hours.

White Chocolate Ganache

Use the same quantities and method to make dark chocolate ganache.

Makes: About 1½ cups · Prep: 15 min. + 30 min. to chill · Level: 1

½	cup (125 ml) heavy (double) cream
14	ounces (400 g) white chocolate, coarsely chopped

1. Heat the cream almost to a boil in a small saucepan over low heat. Place the chocolate in a large bowl. Pour the cream over the chocolate and stir until the chocolate is melted and smooth.

2. Refrigerate until thickened and spreadable, about 30 minutes, stirring occasionally

Chocolate Buttercream

This makes a lovely smooth cream, perfect for sandwiching cakes together.

Makes: About 1 cup (250 ml) · Prep: 15 min. · Level: 1

3	ounces (90 g) dark chocolate
½	cup (125 g) butter, softened
¼	teaspoon vanilla extract (essence)
½	tablespoon milk
1	cup (150 g) confectioners' (icing) sugar

1. Melt the chocolate in a double boiler over barely simmering water, stirring until smooth. Remove from the heat and let cool.

2. Beat the butter and vanilla in a small bowl with an electric mixer on medium-high speed until pale and creamy.

3. Pour in the milk and cooled chocolate, beating until blended. Gradually add the sugar, beating until well blended.

White Chocolate Ganache ▷

Rich Chocolate Frosting

This is a delicious chocolate frosting. It is very versatile and can be used on many cakes.

Makes: About 2 cups (500 ml) · Prep: 15 min. · Cooking: 10–15 min. Level: 2

- 2 cups (400 g) sugar
- 1 cup (250 ml) heavy (double) cream + 1–2 tablespoons as needed
- 8 ounces (250 g) dark chocolate, coarsely chopped
- 2 tablespoons butter
- 1 teaspoon vanilla extract (essence)

1. Bring the sugar and 1 cup (250 ml) of cream to a boil in a saucepan over medium heat. Boil for 1 minute, then remove from the heat. Stir in the chocolate. Return the saucepan to medium heat and cook, without stirring, until the mixture reaches 238°F (112°C), or the soft-ball stage. Remove from the heat.

2. Add the butter and vanilla, without stirring, and place the saucepan in a larger pan of cold water for 5 minutes before stirring. Beat with a wooden spoon until the frosting begins to lose its sheen, 5–10 minutes. Immediately stir in 1 tablespoon cream. Do not let the frosting harden too much before adding the cream.

3. Let stand for 3–4 minutes, then stir until it is smooth and spreadable. Add more cream, 1 teaspoon at a time, if it is too stiff.

Vanilla Crème Anglaise

Vanilla is the classic aroma used to flavor Crème Anglaise, but you can also create other flavors. See our suggestions below the recipe.

Makes: About 1½ cups (375 ml) · Prep: 10 min. · Cooking: 10 min. Level: 1

- 1 cup (250 ml) milk
- ½ vanilla bean, split lengthwise
- 3 large egg yolks
- ¼ cup (50 g) sugar

1. Heat the milk and vanilla bean in a small saucepan over medium-low heat to simmering point. Remove from the heat.

2. Whisk the egg yolks and sugar in a medium bowl until pale and creamy. Slowly pour in one-third of the hot milk, whisking continuously. Then pour in the rest and whisk until fully combined.

3. Pour the mixture into a clean small saucepan and cook over low heat, stirring continuously with a wooden spoon, until it has thickened enough to coat the back of the spoon.

4. Strain the custard through a fine-mesh sieve into a small pitcher (jug) for serving.

Cinnamon Crème Anglaise: Add a stick of cinnamon to the milk as it gently heats. Remove before adding to the egg mixture.

Coffee Crème Anglaise: Dissolve 2 teaspoons of freeze-dried instant coffee granules in the milk while heating.

Chocolate Crème Anglaise: Add 2 ounces (60 g) of coarsely chopped or grated dark chocolate to the milk. Stir until dissolved as the milk heats.

Flavoring Crème Anglaise with Liqueurs: Add 1 tablespoon of the desired liqueur to the custard after it is cooked. Grand Marnier produces a lovely orange-flavored custard.

Rich Chocolate Frosting ▷

Index in alphabetical order

Index by chapter

Notes